Christian's Fleet

A Dorset Shipping Tragedy

Chesil Beach, Dorset, scene of the tragedy, from an Ordnance Survey map, 1811.

Christian's Fleet

A Dorset Shipping Tragedy

Edwina Boult

TEMPUS

To

Selwyn, Les and Julie
Sea Dogs of the Twentieth Century

First published 2003

PUBLISHED IN THE UNITED KINGDOM BY:
Tempus Publishing Ltd
The Mill, Brimscombe Port
Stroud, Gloucestershire GL5 2QG

PUBLISHED IN THE UNITED STATES OF AMERICA BY:
Tempus Publishing Inc.
2 Cumberland Street
Charleston, SC 29401

British Library Cataloguing in Publication Data.
A catalogue record for this book is available from the British Library.

ISBN 0 7524 2783 0

Typesetting and origination by Tempus Publishing.
Printed in Great Britain by Midway Colour Print, Wiltshire.

Contents

Acknowledgements

I would like to thank the following institutions for their assistance:

Archives of the Manchesters Museum,
Stalybridge, Cheshire

Archivist, Berkeley Castle Muniments,
Glos

Bristol Museum and Art Gallery

Bristol University Library

Clevedon Salerooms, Bristol

Dorchester Reference Library

Dorset Library Services

Dorset Record Office

Fullwood Barracks Museum, Preston,
Lancs

Gloucester Family History Society

Gloucester Record Office

Hampshire County Council (Victoria
Park, Netley)

Hampshire Record Office

Lancashire Record Office

Library and Archive, the Met. Office,
Bracknell, Berks

National Army Museum, Chelsea

National Maritime Museum Library,
Greenwich

Naval Library, Plymouth Library

Netley Library, Hampshire

Pendle Heritage Centre, Barrowford,
Lancashire

Portsmouth Museum, Local Studies

Preston County Museum

Public Record Office, Kew and, in
particular, the Reprographics Office

Royal Armouries, Leeds and Fort
Nelson, Fareham, Hants

Royal Army Medical Corps Museum,
Ash Vale, Aldershot

Royal Historic Dockyard Library,
Portsmouth

Royal Hospital Museum, Chelsea

Royal Logistics Corps Museum and
Archive, Deepcut, Camberley, Surrey

Royal Signals Museum, Blandford
Forum, Dorset

Soldiers of Gloucestershire Museum
and Archive, Gloucester

Southampton Library, Local Studies

Southampton Record Office

St Mary's Church office, Berkeley, Glos
and Mr Peter Yardley

The British Library, London

The Guildhall Library, London

The Jenner Museum, Berkeley, Glos

The Museum of the Manchesters,
Ashton-under-Lyne, Lancashire

The Nothe Fort Museum, Weymouth

The Wellcome Library for the History
and Understanding of Medicine,
London

Weymouth Library, Local Studies

Weymouth Museum

Winchester Library, Local Studies

Yeovil Library, Somerset and the inter
Library Laon

Preface

In the early days of this book, I invited a publisher's representative to read a synopsis of it and he commented on the current popularity of these 'little histories'. The expression pleased me greatly, for that is what I feel this narrative is; a little slice, perhaps a mere sliver, of that vast and ever-growing body which is the history of this country. A small incident, but great in significance to those ordinary people whose lives it touched – and altered irrevocably.

Strangely, very little is known, even locally in Dorset, about the tragedy on the Chesil – it is one of so many from earlier days. In any case, it appears that the government of the day tried to cover it up, as a big military expedition was involved. But such a great tragedy in such a small part of the world could not go unnoticed. It passed into local lore. As a boy in Dorset, James Meade Faulkner had heard the story of ships wrecked in the same manner on the Chesil and referred to it in his famous novel *Moonfleet*, published in 1898. And stories have always circulated in the area of relics washed up on the Chesil from wrecks long gone by.

There are many, many voices and events from the past, some extremely distant, many seemingly unconnected, which have conspired in some strange manner to signal the path to the uncovering of the fate of Christian's fleet and the story of the long-forgotten tragedy on the Chesil – and the path was long.

Discussions about shipwrecks with Ian Parry in his famous dive shop on Portland pointed the way to Selwyn Williams, already researching the shipwrecks, and Maureen Attwoll, local shipwreck historian at Weymouth. Thence to Les and Julie Kent, others directly involved in the shipwrecks' history and, much more distantly, to a chance discussion with Robert Isaacs on Grand Cayman in the Caribbean, where, extraordinarily, I first came across the story. Robert, very sadly, was to lose his own life to the sea some years later. Back at home, a copy of an article in a Lancashire Family History Society magazine pointed to the work of yet another amateur historian, Mrs Gladys Whittaker, who had already come across the story of the *Piedmont* in the 1970s whilst researching local registers of baptisms and burials – and to yet another, Mrs Fay Oldland, who had researched and written the history of the Barcroft family. To all these people, I am very grateful for the kind loan of their notes and work. And finally, a very long way from Dorset, there was the discovery of the priceless 'treasure chest' of the letters of William Shrapnell, carefully preserved for over two hundred years and now reposing in the Lancashire Record Office. To this add years of research in the Public Record Office at Kew and many other County Record Offices, museums, archives and libraries, voracious reading of books on military and naval history, the eighteenth century, the French Revolutionary Wars, famous people and places connected with the story; and the end result is an account of the tragedy told in full, for the first time.

For background, I have relied heavily upon the work of military historians and I am, in particular, deeply indebted to Dr Michael Duffy and Professor Roger Buckley whose respective works *Soldiers, Sugar and Seapower* and *Slaves in Red Coats* contributed immeasurably to the background of this story.

I have quoted as fully as possible from the letters and reports written by the people of the time, to capture the immediacy and authenticity of the tale which unfolded over two hundred years ago – and, indeed, why not? They are clear, precise and perfectly understandable – they could not be 'bettered' by paraphrase. Who could improve upon Admiral Thompson's vivid description of the heat and gun smoke during the fall of Fort Matilda in the Caribbean, with the ships of his squadron waiting out to sea to send their boats in under enemy fire and rescue soldiers who had been besieged for months? Or Shrapnell's horror at the gruesome discoveries on the Chesil and his references to the dark and mysterious 'Mrs Burns' who disappeared as mysteriously as she came? Or the drama of her extraordinary salvation from a violent and horrible death, vividly told in Charlotte Smith's narrative? Through their writing, their voices ring clear over more than two hundred years of a changing world. Let them speak for themselves. And, in modern biography too, Derek Jarrett's evocative description of 'First' Minister William Pitt, his utterly lonely personal life, relieved by extreme hard work – and heavy drinking – is unforgettable.

I have not written this book for the *aficionado* of naval stories, who knows his yard arm from his main brace, nor would I presume to write for the academic. I have written for the general reader and lover of history, like myself, and I very much hope that he/she will enjoy it and that, by it, the labour and kindness of Shrapnell and Charlotte Smith, and the bravery and persistence of Hugh Christian and his men, will be remembered.

And, when finally one arrives at the end of this strange, long path of events and discoveries, one realises only too clearly that it could not have been possible to travel along it at all were it not for the encouragement of my family, and the endless generosity, practical and moral support of Peter Nolte, without whom this book might well have remained an unfulfilled ambition.

Edwina Boult
Yeovil, 2003

Chapter 1

Empire

From at least 40,000 BC, man has undertaken voyages across the seas of the world to explore, colonise, trade and raid…

(Sean McGrail, Preface, *The Viking Compass*)[1]

– and Britain was the greatest coloniser of all. Throughout the sixteenth and seventeenth centuries, thousands of men set out each year in tiny wooden ships from this small island, and crossed and recrossed the oceans of the world to take much of it for themselves. They took with them food, drink, clothing, livestock, timber, bricks, barrack blocks, arms and artillery, horses, forges, hospital equipment, medicines – all the resources necessary to support the structure of empire.

In the eighteenth-century world, Britain's trading activities and colonial possessions included fur-trapping in Hudson Bay, Canada, fishing in Halifax, Nova Scotia, tobacco and cotton production down the eastern seaboard of North America to Florida, and sugar from the Caribbean. Across and beyond her possessions in South Africa and India, she traded in tea and silk with China and in spices from the South Seas. Australia, Gibraltar, Malta and the Falkland Islands belonged to Britain. Parts of South America and the northern provinces of India, Kashmir and the Punjab would come under her rule. It is astonishing that such a small country had the resources, determination and stamina to take so much of the world for herself, for her trade, wealth – and her empire.

The empire's greatest resource was her men: Britain had an army whose exotically-named battle honours bear testament to her empire. Britain also had a well-established and meticulously run civil service which oversaw the organisation of transporting, housing, arming and feeding her thousands of red-coated soldiers garrisoned over the world – and a navy.

The empire *was* the navy. It was in equal measure the army but, without the navy, there could be no empire – for seapower was the key to colonial victory.[2] The navy transported the army to the distant corners of the earth where wealth and power lay. It not only broke new ground for the empire, but worked with the army in quelling the resistance of local insurgents who, not unreasonably, did not welcome being dominated by a foreign power, while also fending off the predatory attempts of Britain's colonial rivals, ever ruthless and ready to steal from her what she had gained. 'Zeal', 'vigour' and 'energy' were words in frequent use in the eighteenth-century British army and navy – and her men were judged by these qualities.

One of the navy's most important roles at this time was the transporting and transferring of troops and reinforcements, food and materials to Britain's colonial stations

Outpost of Empire. Fort Royale, Guadeloupe. (National Army Museum, 3940)

around the world. It was a massive and complex operation, given the vast distances involved. It was also extremely hazardous, particularly in time of war, when long-distance amphibious expeditions faced two major dangers: the enemy at large on the sea, and storms.

This is the story of one such expedition which faced – and suffered – one of the worst storms at sea in the eighteenth century. It was at the time of the French Revolutionary Wars and the expedition was on its way to defend the Leeward Islands and St Domingue, in the West Indies, against Britain's fiercest colonial rival, the French. It was the greatest expeditionary force to leave British shores, greater even than that sent in 1777 against the American colonies – and it ended in tragedy on the Dorset coast on the morning of Wednesday 18 November 1795.[3]

This was one of the worst of many maritime tragedies to cast a shadow over the history of Dorset. It was acknowledged as 'the worst incident within historic knowledge of wreck and wrecking on the Dorset coast'.[4] Yet, surprisingly, very little is known about it today and, had it not been for the efforts of two remarkable people of that time to record it, it might have been largely lost in history and forgotten. The events leading up to this tragedy, and the effect it had on those whose lives it touched, are the subject of this book.

Of all her colonies, the West Indian islands gave Britain her greatest wealth. From the 1500s their produce (sugar, coffee, cocoa, spices and cotton) was harvested and shipped to Europe. This was the era of the Merchant Venturers, when the great sugar companies became established and plied their vessels between Europe and the Caribbean. From this, trade spread worldwide and, over the centuries that followed, the islands became the source of immense wealth, not only to England but to France, Spain, Sweden, Denmark and Holland, who also owned 'sugar islands'.

In return, the islands' demand for European goods and American timber and food-stuffs was great. They created a market for the fisheries of Greenland, Britain and America, and took cloth and manufactured goods from Britain. They were the third side of the infamous slave trade triangle between Africa, Europe and the Caribbean. By the end of the eighteenth century, they had become of immense maritime and mercantile importance and were the reason for aggressive colonial competition between their owners – in war and in peace.[5]

The islands were, however, extremely costly to defend. Their remoteness from Europe necessitated expensive and hazardous long-distance voyages by sea; their hot, humid climate and marshy swamplands were the breeding ground for endemic diseases which cost thousands of European soldiers their lives. In war they proved to be an enormous drain of money and men. They had no bearing on the wars fought in Europe by their owners, and what they cost was out of all proportion to any military significance they had. Yet the islands were of the greatest strategic importance, especially to England – the 'Mother Country' grown rich from them.

The Caribbean, c.1790. (From Brian Lavery, *Nelson's Navy*, Conway Maritime Press, 1989)

The 'Mother Country', the hub of this great empire, was, in those days, still peacefully agricultural. Britain was largely self-sufficient in food, her population being around eight million (of whom approximately 750,000 lived in London).[6] There were plentiful supplies of sheep to provide meat and wool, as well as other farm animals and fowl, and linen was widely produced. England also had coal, and wood to build ships. Labourers worked in the fields (or on their own open strips) and wove and spun wool in their cottages. There were few factories in the eighteenth century.[7] Roads were bad and, even with the few turnpikes, travel was virtually impossible in winter.[8]

Yet Britain was on the brink of far-reaching discoveries in science and medicine and was about to embark on an industrial and agrarian revolution which would transform her and the world, and form the basis of the Victorian power and wealth of the next century: the 'dark satanic mills' of the factories and the coal pits of the future.

Colonialism, that tenet of eighteenth-century 'Patriot politics', would continue until the twentieth century, when, even as late as the mid-1960s, a child's stamp album would describe Great Britain as 'the heart of the greatest empire the world has ever known'.[9] But that lay in the future.

In the late eighteenth century, Britain was enjoying the fruits of her colonial riches in an age of burgeoning prosperity. There was an elegance in her social life, music, architecture and painting which has never been surpassed. The great classical country and town houses were built at this time; Stubbs and Gainsborough painted by commission for their rich patrons; the music of Handel was played at Court, in the public gardens at Vauxhall and at pageants on the River Thames.

Yet English society was sharply divided by extremities of social class. The very rich enjoyed sumptuous standards of living, but, for the majority in the English working classes, life was hard. Labourers had little rest to keep themselves above starvation level and, amongst the poorest, there was a very real fear of actual starvation, or being turned out of a rented or tied cottage.[10] Some went poaching, or stealing, for food and risked their necks, or deportation.

Society was not, however, as ruthless as it has been painted. Numerous philanthropic organisations existed, mostly presided over by the Church, but also established by the State, to assist the poor. There were homes for the destitute, which were later combined and organised into the Union Workhouses (being a union of the various parishes of each county) and, in the 1790s, schools were beginning to be built to educate the children of the poor. There were state-funded welfare boards, such as that for Sick and Hurt Seamen, which was set up to support the survivors of disasters of war at sea. There was a fashionable, yet genuine, desire among 'genteel folk' to do good for the less fortunate. This desire existed not merely at home but spread to the distant frontiers of the empire in the movement for the abolition of slavery.

This was also the Great Age of Learning: developments in science and medicine were pushing back the limits of knowledge for human welfare. The astronomer Herschel was expanding the frontiers of knowledge of the universe and the physician Edward Jenner was developing a vaccine to produce an immunity to smallpox which would eventually deliver the world from one of its deadliest diseases.

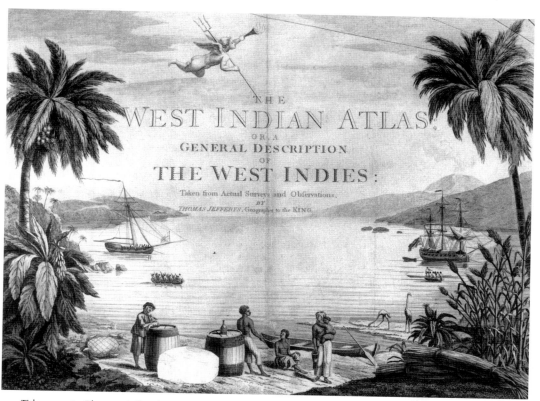

Title page to Thomas Jeffery's *West Indian Atlas*. (By kind permission of University of Bristol Library and Bristol Museums and Art Gallery)

At this time, the county of Dorset was a small, quiet part of the country, largely rural and unaffected by the boom in prosperity caused by a growing international trade, except at her larger ports such as Poole, which was profitably engaged in the fishing trade with Newfoundland.[11] Agriculture was Dorset's mainstay and, as in other parts of peacefully rural England, country sports such as hare or fox hunting, partridge shooting and fishing were a favourite pastime for the well-to-do. Cock-fighting and boxing were popular with the poor.[12] For such people, storms and ship-wrecks upon Dorset's coastline were a common occurrence – a tragic, but soon forgotten, part of life. But even Dorset people were shocked when, on Wednesday 18 November 1795, during a storm of raw and savage fury, six ships were hurled upon the Chesil Beach within the space of one hour and smashed to pieces. Five of the ships were in government service, three of them troop transports, carrying soldiers on the great expedition to the West Indies (the sixth was a merchant trader). Most of the hundreds on board were drowned, half of them men coming from one regiment alone. This expedition, the result of many months of planning, which was to put an end to France's run of victories in the Caribbean, had ended in disaster before it had even begun.

Chapter 2

War

During the eighteenth century, Britain was almost constantly at war. At the heart of these wars were colonial rivalry and territorial expansion. All the major Western European powers had colonies: Spain, Portugal, Holland, Denmark, Sweden, Britain and France, but the two greatest were France and Britain – and between these two great rivals lay the race for supremacy.

The century had started with the resumption of the War of Spanish Succession (1701-1713), ending with the Treaty of Utrecht. Prussian territorial ambitions for Silesia, and British and French trading ambitions, led to war with Spain and the War of Austrian Succession (1739-1748).[1] Britain's superior seapower decided the outcome of the Seven Years War (1756-1763), but that was overtaken by France's newly-developed seapower during the War of American Independence (1774-1783), ending with the Treaty of Versailles.[2]

The French Revolutionary Wars were the fifth of the century. They would last over twenty-two years (with the Peace of Amiens from 1802-1803) and would carry on well into the nineteenth century. They were one of the longest-running wars in British history and were fought across Europe, in the West Indies and in India. They were a truly global conflict and, until the First World War, they were often referred to as the Great War.[3]

In 1789, France had exploded into revolution and the idea of Liberty and Equality for all quickly spread to the slave plantations on the French-held Caribbean islands, incited by the Jacobins, and spies and *agents provocateurs* working for the French National Convention. There were uprisings among slaves in Martinique, Guadeloupe, St Lucia and St Domingue (modern-day Haiti).

The National Assembly in Paris granted full political equality for slaves and then withdrew it, only to grant it again later, thus severely aggravating the unstable situation in the islands. The abolition of slavery was pronounced in St Domingue in August 1793 and in all French possessions in 1794.

The violence of the uprisings (plantations were burnt, whites were murdered) spread fear among the French plantation owners in St Domingue and they appealed to British Home Secretary Henry Dundas for help (in Britain, colonial matters came under the jurisdiction of the Home Office at that time).[4] The British plantation owners also voiced their anxiety at the uprisings: the insurgence could quickly spread to their own plantations – Jamaica was only one day's sail from St Domingue.[5]

Britain was anxious to avoid war with France. After her defeat in the War of American Independence she was, in fact, still largely unprepared.[6] Dundas therefore entered into an agreement with the French plantation owners: he could not yet help but, in the event of war between Britain and France, St Domingue would receive the protection of Britain.[7]

In 1792, France overran the Austrian Netherlands (modern-day Belgium) and threatened Holland. The French National Convention (declared on 19 November 1792) set aside all former treaties France had made with her neighbours and re-opened the River Scheldt in an attempt to establish Antwerp as the major European economic centre in place of Amsterdam.

The British Government had huge reserves in Amsterdam banks and saw this as a threat to British security.[8] British ministers remonstrated against France's actions and France declared war on Britain and Holland in February 1793.[9]

Britain was now committed to helping the French plantation owners in St Domingue – and to protecting her own islands from the spread of slave insurrection. Once more, thousands of red-coated soldiers were to be sent out to defend the old imperial order, but this time against the new: Revolution.[10] The great wastage of lives was about to begin.

War with France was seen by some as a crusade to rid France of revolution, reinstate its monarchy, preserve stability and restore the old established order.[11] Others saw it as the necessary defence of Britain's maritime and commercial interests. Any threat to Britain's fast-growing wealth and prosperity had to be removed.[12]

Britain's astute young 'First' Minister, William Pitt (there was no 'Prime Minister' as such in the eighteenth century), saw it equally as an opportunity to humble a fierce colonial opponent by seizing her rich Caribbean islands, hastening her perceived imminent bankruptcy, winning the war – and colonial supremacy – for Britain. The time was right: France was torn apart by civil war, and a grand coalition of European powers was ranged against her.[13] Britain, Holland, Prussia, Spain and Austria were ready to fight – and the Electoral Dominions of Hanover would fight for their Elector – King George III of Britain.

So Britain's Army was again put into the theatre of war, both in the Netherlands under their commander-in-chief, the Duke of York, King George III's son, and in the Caribbean. The bravery of her men, both in the Army and the Navy, the battles they fought and the hardships they endured became legendary.

When war broke out in 1793, Britain's main Caribbean colonies were Jamaica, St Kitts and Antigua in the Leeward Islands, and Barbados, St Vincent and Grenada in the Windward Islands. France's main possessions were St Domingue, Guadeloupe in the Leewards, and Martinique, St Lucia and Tobago in the Windwards (see map, p.11). The British naval commander-in-chief of the Leeward Islands station was Vice-Admiral Sir John Laforey and the commander of the army there was Maj.-Gen. Cornelius Cuyler.

As in St Domingue, the French plantation owners in Martinique, Guadeloupe and Tobago were strongly against the new French Republic and they likewise appealed to Britain for protection. Dundas straightaway instructed Cuyler to take Tobago, formerly British and ceded to France after the War of American Independence.[14]

With a force of 450 men, a sloop and two merchantmen, Cuyler and Laforey sailed for Tobago in Laforey's flagship, the *Trusty*, fifty guns, arriving on the north of the island on 14 April. They marched across the island to the capital, Port Louis

(Scarborough), and, after a night skirmish, defeated the Republican governor and his army, who had shut themselves up in the garrison. Tobago was once more to Britian.

Meanwhile, a new commander, Maj.-Gen. Bruce, had been sent out from Britain with Admiral Gardner and his squadron of seven battleships, two frigates and a sloop, with instructions to take the islands of Martinique and Guadeloupe, then go onto St Lucia and Marie-Galante (a Guadeloupe dependency). They arrived on 27 April and soon made contact with the royalists of Martinique. On 16 June, Bruce landed 1,100 troops at St Pierre, and they attacked on the night of 18-19 June. It was a disaster, the expected number of royalists failing to come forward. On 22 June, they sailed away, laden with five to six thousand royalist refugees.[15]

A new expedition was formed, this time under the command of General Sir Charles 'No Flint' Grey. Grey was known as a brilliant, ruthless general who did not rest on the merits of his previous campaigns. He had seen active service in the Seven Years War and in America under Wolfe, and had gained the name 'No Flint' in 1777 during the War of American Independence when, during a night attack, he told his men to take the flints from their muskets and use their bayonets only.[16]

For the command of the navy, the Admiralty chose Vice-Admiral Sir John Jervis, sometimes described as a 'dour and ruthless disciplinarian'.[17] Jervis had previously campaigned in the West Indies and had also served with Wolfe. In 1782, he had captured the French battleship *Pegase*, seventy-four guns, without losing a single man on his own seventy-four-gun ship, *Foudroyant*.[18]

The expedition left on 26 November with 7,000 troops, with Grey and Jervis in Jervis' flagship the *Boyne*, ninety-eight guns. They sighted Barbados on 6 January

Grey and Jervis take Fort Royale, Martinique, March 1794. (National Army Museum 8300)

1794 and set out for Martinique on 3 February, which they captured after forty-seven days of siege and battle.[19]

Grey and Jervis now set out straightaway for St Lucia, to the south. The island fell within five days, on 4 April, without the loss of a single man. By 8 April, they were on their way north to Guadeloupe, Grey's force now being substantially reduced by the need to garrison Martinique and St Lucia. On 22 April, Guadeloupe's one remaining fort in French hands, Fort Charles, above the seashore, fell to Grey. The island was now Britain's, together with its dependencies Marie Galante and Deseada.[20]

There remained one final major prize to take: the rebellious St Domingue to the north, France's richest colony – the richest in the world. In the late 1780s, the foreign trade of this colony alone was as great as that of the entire United States of America.[21] Governor Adam Williamson of nearby Jamaica, together with Commodore John Ford, had managed to take about a third of the colony, but could go no further without reinforcements.

These arrived at Barbados on 5 May in the shape of four new regiments. Grey sent three of them to St Domingue, where they captured Port-au-Prince on 4 June. However, they did not succeed in driving out the Republican army or its zealous Jacobin rebel slave leader Toussaint L'Ouverture. The sickly season was now upon the Caribbean islands. Yellow fever and malaria, not warfare, now claimed the lives of British soldiers and the campaigning was for the meantime brought to a close.[22]

Nevertheless Grey's and Jervis' achievements were remarkable. The major French islands had been taken in four months and Jervis was able to write to the Admiralty: 'I have now the greatest satisfaction in informing you of the entire reduction of the French in these seas ...'[23] The French West Indian empire was virtually extinguished – Britain now controlled the Caribbean.[24]

At home, people were jubilant, celebrating Grey's and Jervis' victories, which were added to Admiral Howe's victory over the French at sea on the 'Glorious First of June'. Despite the failure of the king's son, the Duke of York, to capture Dunkirk in the Netherlands campaign, there was buoyancy and optimism for a swift and victorious end to the war. Pitt and Dundas must have been delighted to see their plans coming to fruition.

Then, disaster struck. In June, the month in which Grey's troops captured Port-au-Prince, St Domingue, a convoy of nine French ships got into the harbour at Pointe-à-Pitre, Grande Terre, the eastern half of Guadeloupe. The British troops, unable to defend themselves for lack of numbers, were forced to retreat to Basse Terre, the western side of the island. Grey and Jervis were at St Kitts at the time, preparing for their voyage home. They hastened back with what ships they could muster and Jervis blockaded the harbour entrance.[25] Grey ordered an attack on Pointe-à-Pitre. The force he detached for the job had a long hard march in the dark, through ravines and jungle, and over mountainous terrain. They then found that they were misled by the French royalist guides, who had brought them right in front of the enemy outposts. They nevertheless stormed the outposts and carried on to the town.

The French ships, blockaded in the harbour, had their guns trained on the streets of the town and were waiting for the British soldiers. They opened up. There was chaos as gunfire swept the streets and musket fire rained down upon the British from French soldiers hiding in the houses. There was bloodshed everywhere and losses were high: 543 soldiers and seamen killed, wounded or missing, including many of Grey's best men and the elite of the army. In three weeks, the battle for Guadeloupe had resulted in nearly 2,000 casualties. Grey now saw his army dwindle as food, military supplies and troop reinforcements arrived too slowly and in too few numbers to help – a fate which was to become increasingly common for the British Army in the Caribbean. By 5 July 1794, all of Grey's forces had retreated to Basse Terre, where Grey wrote to Dundas begging for reinforcements. 'You seem totally to have forgotten us' he wrote, despairingly.[26]

The brilliant successes turned to nightmare as tropical diseases such as malaria, typhus and yellow fever, ulcers and sores caused by insect bites and 'jiggers' (a flea, which penetrates the skin), and guerrilla attacks from rebellious slaves drastically reduced the number of soldiers in Grey's army. His men were running out of shoes, clothing and kit, and operating under scorching sun and in drenching rain.[27]

Men had frequently arrived in the Caribbean already weakened by long confinement on crowded and insanitary troopships and poor diet. Exposed to the rigours of the climate, they rapidly succumbed to infections and diseases.[28] Moreover, the hospitals they were billeted in were fever-ridden, crowded and desperately under-manned by medical staff, who similarly fell victims to disease.[29] Barracks were often located in low, swampy areas where mosquitoes proliferated, with the men sleeping on damp, fixed platforms or damp floors, the floorboards 'pervious to exhalations from beneath and to all liquid impurities from above', or on undrained and unventilated ground floors.[30] By 1 September 1794, Grey had only 470 men fit for duty on Basse Terre. By contrast, across the bay at Grande Terre, the Republican–held half of Guadeloupe, the French Commissioner Victor Hugues had augmented his army by conscripting two thousand of the slaves set free by the decree of the French National Convention in June.[31]

Meanwhile, back in Europe, things had started to go very badly too: France had overrun both Belgium and Holland, the allied troops were driven back to the River Waal and the casualty numbers were high.[32] Sickness was rife. In the mud and ditches of Flanders, it was typhus rather than yellow fever which held sway over the troops, who were as ill-shod and ill-clothed as their counterparts in the West Indies.[33]

The demands now made upon Dundas to provide troops came from Grey in the Leeward Islands, Williamson in St Domingue, and from the Duke of York in the Netherlands. In addition, fresh troops were always required to garrison all the other parts of the world where British troops were stationed. Dundas simply did not have enough men. He performed miracles in scraping together what troops he could for the Caribbean, switching regiments from Ireland to Gibraltar and from Gibraltar to the Caribbean in order to send out men already seasoned for the climate.[34]

All that was left now of the British holding in Guadeloupe was Fort Charles above the town of Basseterre, renamed Fort Matilda after it was taken in Grey's and Jervis' glorious victory the previous April (see p.18), which must by now have seemed very far away. Lt-Gen. Robert Prescott, who had been sent by Grey to prepare for his

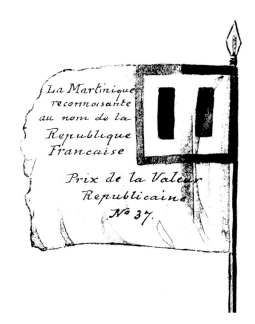

Drawing of the French Republican flag captured by Grey's forces in Martinique. Before the Revolution the French flag bore the *Fleur de Lys*, the emblem of French Royalty. (By kind permission of the Royal Hospital Museum, Chelsea)

arrival in the Caribbean in the previous October, was holding the fort with only one hundred men.[35] Grey put all the troops he could into Fort Matilda and Jervis took the fleet to Basseterre to support him.

Prescott destroyed the town's outer defences, had the guns spiked and magazines blown up, and shut himself in the fort with about four hundred troops. By 20 October, Victor Hugues' guns had forced Jervis' *Boyne* further out to sea, leaving the shallower-drafted *Terpsichore*, thirty-two guns, the fort's only contact with the navy. Isolated in the fort, the men rapidly succumbed to fever in a heat so intense that they could not man the batteries at noon. The water turned foul in the cisterns and the enemy made off with their remaining livestock. Hugues summoned the fort to surrender but Prescott and his men determinedly held on, hoping desperately for reinforcements.

It was into this situation that Vice-Admiral Benjamin Caldwell and Lt-Gen. Sir John Vaughan arrived when they came to relieve Jervis and Grey in November. However, to Prescott's intense disappointment, they brought no troops with them, Dundas having arranged troops to come from Gibraltar.[36] Caldwell was, however, able to supply Prescott with some fresh men. These enabled him to hold out a little longer, but, on the night of 10 December, he evacuated his men under enemy fire to the naval squadron waiting out to sea, which sent boats from their ships to pick them up on the shore below the fort. Sixteen men had been killed in the siege and seventy-five wounded – and Guadeloupe was lost again to the triumphant French.[37] Caldwell reported to the Admiralty:

> From the Ships we could perceive that the walls of the Fort were much shattered and many of the Guns dismounted ... in rowing alongshore to enquire after an out Picket ... Captain

> *Bowen* [of the *Terpsichore*, who was largely responsible for overseeing the evacuation to the ships' boats – without the loss of a single soldier's life] *received a bad wound in the face ... a mate and one man were killed in the* Alarm*'s launch in consequence of her having been thrown on the beach by the Surf ... this was all the loss we sustained altho' the enemy kept up a smart fire of Musketry, and from some of their batteries.*
>
> *Two men from the 60th deserted, being ordered to the waterside, who it is thought gave the Enemy information of our intentions ... The Ships employed in taking off the Troops were the* Vanguard [74 guns], Bellona [74], Theseus [74], Ramillies [74], Terpsichore [32] *and* Experiment [44]. *The* Ganges [74], Veteran [64] *and* Alarm [32] *were called in by Signal and joined about noon.*[38]

The deserters were later re-captured: they were found on a brig coming out of Guadeloupe, stopped by Capt. Cooke of the *Inspector*. The brig was under Swedish colours, commanded by a Swedish major, but armed by the French.[39] 'I do affirm,' Caldwell wrote on 30 January, 'that the Danes and Swedes of St Thomas's and St Bartholomew's are as hostile as an open Enemy, doing everything they can to supply the French ...'[40] The two soldiers were hanged.

After his struggle to defend Fort Matilda, Prescott's health was so poor that his doctors reported to Caldwell he could not last three weeks longer in such a climate.[41] He requested that Caldwell send him back to England by frigate and wrote, somewhat bitterly: 'I trust my presence in England ... [will enable] me to state much more compleatly [*sic*] than can be done by letter as an Old Officer long and well acquainted with these Islands, the real situation of affairs in this Country, perhaps hitherto not so honestly depicted as they might have been.'[42] Caldwell proposed a passage for him in the *Terpsichore* which sailed on 15 January 1795 and Prescott arrived home safely on 11 February.[43]

During the struggle for the islands, the navy fought as valiantly as the army: the seventy-four-gun ships *Ganges* and *Montagu* arrived at Fort Royale (Martinique) on 29 November with only seventeen days' bread left and almost without sails. About thirty leagues (ninety miles) west of Cape Finisterre they had fallen in with the *Jacobin* French ship of war, carrying twenty-four twelve-pounders and two hundred and twenty men. They captured her and brought her with them to Martinique.

Caldwell reported to Admiralty:

> *The* Zebra [16 guns] *returned to Fort Royal on 4 December with the* Carmagnols *French Schooner of ten guns and thirty-five men, ... Captain Robert Faulknor of the* Blanche [32 guns] *... chased an Arm'd Schooner ... and found she was laden with Gun Powder ... the crew effected their escape. He ...*[also] *Chaced a large Schooner into the Bay of Deseada ... she anchored close under a Battery and a long Range of Musquetry on the Shore.* [Faulknor silenced the Battery and brought the schooner out, the crew having abandoned her.] *... a midshipman and one Man was killed and five wounded. The Enemy at the Battery and on board the Schooner suffer'd considerably.*
>
> *Captain Riou of the* Beaulieu [40 guns] *... captured a fast sailing Sloop of ten guns and forty-one men ...*[44]

Included in Caldwell's despatches is a glittering account of a sea battle between the famously valiant Robert Faulknor of the frigate *Blanche* and a French frigate, *La Pique*, with thirty-eight guns and three hundred and sixty men:

> *They laid the enemy on board and twice lashed her Bowsprit to their Captstern, and when* [La Pique's] *main and mizzen masts fell,* [Blanche] *payed off before the wind and towed the Enemy ... the Stern Ports not being large enough, they blew the upper Transom Beam away to admit the Guns to run out and fired into* [La Pique's] *Bows for three hours. Not a man could appear upon her Forcastle until she struck, then the Second Lieutenant and ten men swam on board and took possession of her.* [45]

The battle lasted five hours but Faulknor was killed, struck through the heart by a musket ball fired by a marksman at *La Pique's* bowsprit as Faulknor was lashing her to *Blanche's* capstern.[46]

A postscript to this despatch states: 'There was [sic] many more than three hundred and sixty – many were thrown overboard during the action and numbers fell with her three masts and were drowned. There was [sic] many Americans on board.'[47]

It was a short-lived triumph. In January, Caldwell had another catastrophe to report to the Lords of the Admiralty: 'A Convoy from France under two or three Frigates got into Point-a-Petre [sic] Guadeloupe ... [with] about 3,500 [troops] ... and [1,500] stands of arms ... are informed a Brig carrying four thirty-six pounders got in with them ...'[48]

Caldwell and Vaughan discussed blockading Guadeloupe. They saw little alternative, but knew it would provoke hostility from America.[49] Nevertheless, on 29 January

Blanche captures *La Pique*. Illustration on a nineteenth-century Staffordshire meat dish. (By kind permission of Clevedon Salerooms, Bristol)

PROCLAMATION.

MARTINIQUE

By His Excellency The Honourable Sir
JOHN VAUGHAN K. B. and
Commander in Chief of His Majesty's
Land - Forces, and By His Excellency
BENJAMIN CALDWELL Esq'.
Commander in Chief of His Majesty's
Fleet in the West - Indies.

WHEREAS We have thought it expedient to cause the Islands of Guadeloupe, Marie - Galante and Deseada to be closely invested on all sides by His Majesty's Ships and Vessels of War, and by the armed Cruisers fitted out from the different British Islands, with a view of stopping all supplies from entering the same, We Do therefore by this our Proclamation signify and declare the said Islands of Guadeloupe, Marie - Galante and Deseada, to be in an actual state of Blockade. And all Neutral Nations, and their subjects, are hereby enjoined and prohibited, from attempting to enter any of the Ports or Places of the said Islands with Provisions or Supplies of any nature or kind foever. And all Neutral Ships or Vessels, together with such cargoes, found attempting to enter any or either of such Blockaded or invested Islands, will be dealt with conformable to existing Treaties, and as warranted by the established laws of Nations.

GIVEN under our Hands and Seals at Arms and countersigned
by our Secretaries at Head-Quarters St. Pierre Martinique
this 29th. day of January 1795 and in the thirty fifth year
of His Majesty's Reign.

Signed   JOHN VAUGHAN
Général.

BEN: CALDWELL
Vice-Admiral.

By His Excellency's order
Signed   SAMUEL OSBORNE GIBBES
Secr.

GOD SAVE THE KING.

Printed for P. LE CADRE, SAINT-PIERRE MARTINIQUE.

Proclamation of the Blockade of Guadeloupe. (Public Record Office, WO/1/31, f.99)

they made a Proclamation of Blockade of Guadeloupe and her dependent islands Marie-Galante and Deseada.[50] It was not long before the French riposted with a proclamation of their own, damning Vaughan's and Caldwell's 'laughable blockade' and their 'foolish master Pitt'.[51]

That same month, in Europe, Holland fell to France. The allied armies had beaten a hasty retreat across the River Waal in November after the siege of Nijmegen and established cantonments on the north bank.[52] Then the waters froze – and the French came over. Fighting in the bitter cold, British troops, some of them wearing no more than scraps of clothing and going barefoot, made a wretched retreat across northern Holland towards Germany.[53] Cold and exhausted, hundreds of them froze to death where they fell and, for this reason, the troops were not allowed to halt during the night. Their wake was littered with waggons, guns, dead horses and men.[54]

The sufferings and loss of the Army have been dreadful, a letter in the *Hampshire Chronicle* reported. *When we began our retreat, the number of British only was upwards of thirteen thousand, but now their whole returns of effective men do not amount to half that number. In the march from Amersfort alone, upwards of three hundred soldiers were frozen to death, besides women and children … the miserable victims … [lay] everywhere, dead or dying of cold, famine and fatigue, in the road the army had marched.*[55]

Austria's troops had retreated to the Rhine, and Prussia began negotiations for peace in March.[56] The Grand Coalition against the French was shattered and humiliated.

Back in the Caribbean, in February, French boats slipped the Guadeloupe blockade to bring troops to St Lucia and later to St Vincent and Grenada.[57] Caldwell reported to Stevens at the Admiralty: '... at Pointe-a-Pitre, the Enemy have fifteen sail of vessels, four of them ... Frigates, two Brigs with heavy Canon and the other Armed Transports ... [plus] a number of small vessels in the ports, many of which wear American Colours ...'[58]

French Commissioner Victor Hugues' agents raised insurrection among the slaves on Grenada and St Vincent. On 2 March, Governor Home of Grenada was seized on his way from his estates in the north to the capital, St George's, in the south-west. Under the command of the French Commander, Fedon, Home and forty-seven of the fifty-one British captives were shot, one by one. The slaves massacred every white man at Grenville.[59]

Caldwell reported dismally:

The French ... landed on [the] 2nd at Labaye on the Windward part of the Island ... The Lieutenant Governor was made prisoner in a boat on his way to the Town ... [the] Enemy had summoned the Island to surrender to the Republic of France. The insurrection was General ... no part of the Island except the town and port of St George and that part of the country under the command of the forts, remains to us ... several of the white inhabitants have been murdered and ... they have thirty-three gentlemen of the island prisoners in their camp ... Some houses, buildings and plantations have been destroyed by fire ... The Caribs [of St Vincent] in the night of [the] 9th instant rose and set fire to all the plantations throughout the island and burnt canes ... sufficient to make six thousand hogsheads of sugar, and destroyed several buildings.[60]

LIBERTY. ——— **THE LAW.** ——— **EGALITY**

RESOLUTION.

The Commissaries delegated by the National Convention to the leeward Charibbee Islands.

Considering, that the sentiments of humanity, which have always guided our conduct with regard to our conquered enemies and prisoners of war, have been forgotten by the English in this part of the world who in the impossibility of resisting against the republican bravery, do not cease to force us through innumerable crimes, to use reprisals;

Considering that general Vaughan and Caldwell laughable conduct, is in the nearest resembling, to the foolish design of the famous Pitt (their master) to starve the French nation, at the time when all their beaten and discouraged enemies fled before them, leaving them entire masters over the Belgic and Hollande;

Considering that the event has fully justified our declaration made to the neutral powers, dated the 5d ventôse; since the islands of Saint-Vincent, Grenada and Sainte-Lucie, have been attacked with success by the Republicans, ten days after leaving officially signified the same unto the English, through the means of a flag of truce received by rear admiral Thompson, and in which said declaration he was warned of our intended attack;

Considering that the proclamation of the counsel of the island of Grenada, dated the 4th of march (stile of the slaves), issued by the dishonourable Kenneth Francis Mackensie is an encroachment upon the rights of humanity, of nations and of men, because it puts weapons in to the hands of assassins, by promising twenty joes for every head of our brave and loyal Republicans;

Considering that the cruelties have also been printed and published by the counsel and governors in and over the islands of Saint-Vincent and Dominica, against our friends and faithfull allies the Charraibes;

RESOLVED that whereas the Charraibe nation being in alliance with the French, to which alliance they have been constantly attached, and by virtue of the power with which we have been invested : We have appointed the citizen Duvaley, an officer in the French Republican army, their chief, together with the citizens Torailles and Michel Mathieu, French Republicans, enjoining them, after having signified unto the English this present proclamation through the means of a flag of truce, to use reprisals against them in the islands of Saint-Vincent, ect, ect.

Resolved also that the citizen Noguez, officer in the republican service, is commander in the island of Grenada, and Lagrange, our delegate, shall signify this unto the enemies' commander in chief in that colony; which being done, enjoin all and every officer commanding republican army, as well in the islands already conquered, as in those that might fare after be conquered, to strictly observe the laws of war, in case any Republican should willfully or in cold blood perish by the hands of our enemies, by putting them all to the sword, so as to destroy and blot out, the very name and memory of them in the country where the crime has been committed;

Promising to do the same in all the colonies, where the inhabitants and English chiefs issue and put into execution the like proclamations.

Denouncing to the public opinion and to all nations, Kenneth Françis Mackensie and Mather Byles, having signed the above mentioned proclamation; declaring that the French Republicans, have no occasion whatsoever, to set any sum of money upon such despicable heads, for to conquer and annihilate them.

Port de la Liberté, the 11th germinal, in the 5d year of the French Republic, one and indivisible.

(Signed) Victor HUGUES, GOYRAND and LEBAS.

The French Riposte: Resolution. (Public Record Office, WO/1/31, f145)

To make matters worse, after Holland had fallen, the French started occupying the Dutch-held Caribbean colonies – with Dutch collusion. Vaughan and Caldwell hastened to send troops for their protection and, in what must have been an embarrassing loss of face for them, the Dutch Governor of Demerara informed them he was unable to allow British reinforcements to land in Demerara, Berbice and Surinam.[61] The Governor subsequently escaped from Demerara carrying only a small trunk, in the same British vessel which had brought Vaughan's and Caldwell's request to land troops, and made his way to England.[62]

On 23 April, Capt. Sawyer, Faulknor's successor on the *Blanche*, reported 'sad losses in Souffriere' (St Lucia) and the British retreat from the French there.[63] General Vaughan, who had been a veteran of the campaign in the West Indies during the previous decade throughout the American War of Independence, struggled on to keep control in Grenada, St Lucia and St Vincent.[64] He repeatedly asked for fit and seasoned reinforcements, but his pleas for help were inadequately met. In June, St Lucia fell to the enemy and Vaughan died, fevered and exhausted, a few days later on 1 July.[65]

The following day, Caldwell left for home on board the *Blanche*, having handed over the naval command of the islands once more to Vice-Admiral Sir John Laforey. The man who took Tobago in 1793 had been sent out yet again to cope with an increasingly critical situation. Laforey had arrived at Martinique on 9 June, on board his frigate *L'Aimable*, captained by his son Francis.[66] They had been unable to stop at Barbados, as they were chased off by the French.[67]

A 38-gun frigate of 1770, typical of the naval ships in Christian's Fleet. (C. McCutcheon)

It was not long before Laforey, too, was reporting to the Admiralty that the situation was almost completely out of control:

> *Grenada, St Vincents and St Lucia* [are] *invested by the enemy … St. Kitts* [is] *menaced and under great alarm by an attack from St Eustacia* [sic], *where the French are said to have assembled in great number. They hoist the Dutch and French colours together and fire at any of our ships of war that approach their port…*
>
> *… The Squadron is so dispersed that it is not in my power to send by this conveyance* [a report of] *the state and condition of the ships … they are moved from place to place as the exigency of the moment requires … I found … there were no ships or vessels cruising to windward to cut off any reinforcements the French might send out to Guadeloupe. I have not had one ship to employ on that service, nor do I see a probability while the enemy are so active and worry us so much … The demands upon me from all quarters for protection and assistance have been incessant and far beyond the means I am possessed of to satisfy …*[68]

The situation in the Caribbean now looked worse than ever.

In this same month (June 1795), Spain made peace with France. Holland had made a treaty of alliance with France and Prussia had declared war against Britain in May.[69] An expedition in July by the French Royalists to Quiberon on the Brittany coast, aided by Britain and funded to the tune of over £1 million, had ended in spectacular failure.[70] With her allies failed, Britain now stood virtually alone in Europe (although she had made a treaty with Russia in March[71]). Pitt's hopes of easy colonial conquests in the Caribbean had been dashed. After the disastrous retreat across Holland to Germany in the winter, most of the troops had been evacuated back to England from the Rivers Weser and Elbe. Britain now faced defeat both in Europe and the Caribbean.

'One thing is pretty certain: if we do not conclude a peace, in a short period we shall have no possessions to defend in the West Indies,' cried the *Hampshire Chronicle* of 10 August 1795. But, although the situation was desperate there, it was in fact the only area remaining in which Britain had any hope of negotiation if she were dragged to the bargaining table with France.

On Friday 14 August 1795, the Cabinet met at Downing Street and made a momentous decision: they would send some thirty thousand soldiers from Portsmouth and Cork, the largest ever expedition to leave British shores, to the Leeward Islands and St Domingue, to try and retrieve the perilous situation there and turn it round to some advantage. Pitt described it as 'the great push'.[72] It was now all or nothing.

The general chosen to command this expedition would be Sir Ralph Abercromby, a much respected soldier and veteran of the Seven Years War and the recent campaign in Flanders under the Duke of York. The admiral who would command the fleet, and the man in charge of finding all the ships necessary to transport and convoy this vast number of troops, was the then chairman of the naval Transport Board, a captain, promoted for the expedition to rear admiral. He was Hugh Cloberry Christian.

It was Christian's fleet, which, in November 1795, sailed from St Helens, Isle of Wight, out into the English Channel – and into disaster.

Chapter 3

Slaves, Men and Masters

Hugh Cloberry Christian was descended from the Christian family of Milntown, Isle of Man. His father Thomas was a sea captain, probably serving in the merchant navy (and reputedly killed in a brawl in a gambling-house in 1753). His mother was Welsh and, in probably the only portrait available of him, Christian bears the dark-browed, dark-haired look of a Celt. An only child, he was born in 1747, educated at Charterhouse and entered the navy very young, in about 1761, becoming a lieutenant in 1771. He saw service in the Leeward Islands during the War of American Independence (1774-1783) and in 1778 became master and commander of the *Vigilant*, a hired ship of twenty guns, in action against the French off the coast of North America under Lord Howe. He returned to England in December and was appointed captain of the *Suffolk*, seventy-four guns, after which he returned to the West Indies where he saw 'much active and arduous service' under Admirals Byron, Rodney and Hood.

In 1787 he was appointed to the *Colossus* (seventy-four guns) and in 1790 became second captain of the *Queen Charlotte* (100 guns) under Lord Howe, who was by then in command of the Channel fleet. At the start of the French Revolutionary Wars he still held this position but, in 1794, the Admiralty created the Transport Board in response to the urgent need for supplying ships to transport troops to the many theatres of war in which Britain was now engaged (they also had a Victualling Board, responsible for supplying all the food and stores necessary to undertake long voyages, and a Sick and Hurt Board) and Christian was appointed its first chairman in June of that year.

Twelve months later, when it came to appointing an admiral to take command of the largest convoy of troops ever to leave Britain at that time, Christian seemed, in terms of experience but not in seniority, the most suitable. He was appointed Rear Admiral of the Blue in June 1795. *The Times* wrote: 'Admiral Christian is universally esteemed as one of the most intelligent officers in the British Navy; for to a thorough knowledge of his profession, he possesses a very clear and sound judgement.'

He was a down-to-earth, straightforward man who had little time for Admiralty intrigues, who got over setbacks without blaming others – and got on with the job. 'Only of middle height', 'his slight form full of health and apparent energy', he was, by his own admission, short on temper and he was to find himself driven to extremes of exasperation as he came up against the inflexible and unimaginative attitudes of the naval bureaucracy controlling the preparation of the expedition, both at Portsmouth and Southampton. One admiral, with whom he had a 'run-in'

Admiral Hugh Cloberry Christian. (National Maritime Museum PU 0114)

concerning the payment of troops on board ship, clearly resented his brisk attitude and wrote, somewhat uncharitably, of Christian's 'vehement and untimely warmth' and of 'what may be feared from such intemperance', but, in the opinion of one of the seamen who served with him, he was 'a good, brave and persevering officer'.[1]

Christian had married in 1775 and had five children. The elder son, Hood Hanway, would accompany him on the expedition as a midshipman. The youngest, a daughter, was born only the previous year and, from this time, his wife appears to have suffered continued ill health.

When Christian met his military counterpart for the expedition, Sir Ralph Abercromby, they struck up an immediate rapport. Abercromby was most indignant at the suggestion that Christian was too junior to replace Sir John Laforey, who still held the command of the Leeward Islands station, and would not accept the Admiralty's proposal that Christian should operate in subservience to him. The praise

LIEUTENANT GENERAL ABERCROMBIE.

Sir Ralph Abercromby. (National Army Museum 3588)

he subsequently gave to Christian for the navy's contribution during the West Indian campaign shows the high esteem he had for his admiral.

General Sir Ralph Abercromby was born in October 1734 and educated at Rugby. He studied law at the universities of Edinburgh and Leipzig but entered the profession of a soldier during the Seven Years War (1756-1763). He obtained a cornetcy in the 3rd Dragoon Guards in 1756, and saw active service in Germany under Prince Ferdinand of Brunswick, which gave him good opportunity to observe the strict discipline of the Prussian system. He was promoted to lieutenant in 1760 and captain in 1762. At the conclusion of war, he went with his regiment to Ireland and was stationed there for several years. He was promoted major in 1770 and lieutenant colonel in 1773.

Abercromby was renowned as a man of very firm principles: during the War of American Independence, he had refused to fight the colonists, whom he regarded as his countrymen, and remained with his regiment in Ireland on garrison duty, which cost him professional advancement. After a brief spell in politics, he returned to military life, being made a major general in 1787. In 1793, at the start of the Revolutionary Wars, he took command of a brigade in Flanders under the king's son the Duke of York, who wrote of him to his father: '... there is not in Your Majesty's service a better nor a more honourable man, or one whose military abilities are more universally acknowledged.' When the Flanders campaign took its downward turn into disaster, Abercromby commanded the retreating rear column. These were the troops who, when Holland fell to France, had retreated ill-clothed, ill-shod and in disarray over the frozen ground into Germany. (see p.22) According to the *Dictionary of National Biography*, '...to him fell the real burden of the retreat of the dispirited troops.'

He returned to England at the beginning of 1795 and was made a Knight of the Bath. He was by now regarded as one of the country's best generals and the man most able to get the country out of its military dilemma. Pitt had written to the king: 'General Abercromby ... seems to stand higher than any other officer in general opinion'. He did, however, suffer one significant handicap: he was desperately short-sighted – so badly, that he had either to rely on the sight of his junior officers in the field or use a telescope. General Sir John Moore (of Corunna) wrote of him: 'Sir Ralph is very short-sighted. Without a glass he sees nothing, but with it he observes ground quickly and well. He has the zeal and eagerness of youth, and for his age has much activity both of mind and body,' but, in a later moment of exasperation with him, commented baldly: 'He is blind...'[2]

When appointed, at age sixty, to take command of the great expedition to the West Indies, Abercromby fell to his task with an energy and industriousness which Christian admired, calling meetings at Southampton between all parties responsible for the health of the troops, the sanitation of transports, provision of medical supplies as well as barrack blocks, armaments, rules, regulations and discipline. This was to be the largest of all expeditions, but, for Abercromby, it also had to be the best-equipped.

There were several young officers on this ill-fated expedition who had only just received their commissions and were on their way to take command of six brand-new regiments: the West India Regiments. These were formed in May 1795, and a further two followed shortly afterwards. They were a striking new addition to the British Army and a hitherto-considered unorthodox one. The ranks were formed entirely of coloured soldiers: free blacks, black African slaves and the coloured native slaves of the islands.

Slaves (known as 'fatigue negroes') were used in the army for the heavy duties which the white, European soldiers found insupportable in such a climate and there had long been an established practice in the islands of incorporating free blacks, slaves and coloureds into the militia, to protect the plantations. Slaves had been enlisted into such militias as early as the close of the Seven Years War (1764).[3] During his 1794 campaign, General Grey had embodied the militias of the conquered French islands into his troops, in desperation at the lack of reinforcements from Britain.[4]

However, these militias, or corps, had been intended as defence for the plantations, or the individual islands, only. They were strictly territorial and not intended to counter the troubles that arose after war was declared in 1793, freed French slaves pressed a continual guerrilla-type warfare against the British and incited insurrection amongst the slaves on British plantations.[5] The conspicuously red-coated British soldiers, marching in line and unaccustomed to the heat and sicknesses of the climate, found themselves hard put to cope with the situation:

... in the mountainous, almost inaccessible, and largely uncharted interiors of the embattled sugar islands. Long columns of hundreds of troops moved through hot, airless woods, often along precipitous narrow trails. Soldiers carrying full battle equipment scrambled back and forth across

countless steep and boulder-strewn ravines and up and down rugged peaks in the enervating heat of the tropics ... Under these conditions men and equipment deteriorated rapidly; deaths from heat and exhaustion were not uncommon.[6]

'We seem entirely left to poke out our own way in the dark wilds and fastnesses, not yet having found a guide who knows a yard beyond the beaten tracks...,' wrote Brigadier General Campbell from Grenada ('in a negro hut, on the top of the highest mountain in this rugged island'), '...neither can you get for love of [*sic*] money a person who will venture a hundred yards to gain intelligence; consequently we either fall into ambuscade, or are led to error, through false information.'[7]

When General Sir John Vaughan succeeded Grey in October 1794, he knew that Britain had little alternative but to arm her own slaves. He wrote to the Duke of Portland, now Home Secretary: '... as the Enemy have adopted this measure to recruit their armies, I think we should pursue a similar plan to meet them on equal terms.'[8] Vaughan proposed the formation of permanent black regiments in the islands. They could reinforce his own troops and better counter the guerrilla-type warfare the blacks practised there, for which his red-coated line regiments were no match. 'I am of opinion,' he wrote, 'that a corps of one thousand men, composed of Blacks and Mulattoes and commanded by British officers, would render more essential service in the Country than treble the number of Europeans who are unaccustomed to the climate.' The war in the West Indies could be waged only, Vaughan wrote, by 'opposing Blacks to Blacks'.[9]

Surprisingly, the answer came back as 'No'. There were two reasons for this: the merchants and planters, already alarmed by the number of blacks on the islands who were armed and trained to fight, feared the consequences of having permanent regiments of armed blacks, who greatly outnumbered them, on their plantations. They used their influence to get Vaughan's proposals rejected.[10]

Secondly, back in England, the enlistment of blacks into His Majesty's Army did not accord well with the thinking of the time. Many of those who sat in the House of Commons were merchants and had shares in, or knew people who owned, plantations. Slaves had an intrinsic economic value – they were a capital investment, and their owners were not disposed to have their workforce used in this manner.[11]

Vaughan appealed again, repeatedly, especially after the French reinforcements reached Guadeloupe in January 1795, and when, after they had slipped the blockade and reached St Lucia and insurrection had broken out on St Vincent and Grenada, it became obvious that Britain's loss of the former French islands was imminent. (See pp.21-23)[12]

'So determined are the Caribs of St Vincent's on possessing themselves of the island that, their ammunition being nearly exhausted, they now make use of poisoned arrows dipped in manchineel juice, which occasions instant death,' reported an extract from a letter published in the *Hampshire Chronicle* on Monday 17 August 1795.

Finally, after lengthy deliberation, Dundas authorised Vaughan to raise initially 'two Corps of Mulattoes or Negroes, to consist of 1,000 Rank and File each'. Governor Adam Williamson of Jamaica was authorised to do the same if the situation warranted it.[13] Vaughan received his much-wanted permission just a few days before

Colours of the 4th West India Regiment. (National Army Museum 1321)

St Lucia fell to the French on 19 June. He died, sick and exhausted, only a few days later and the work of raising the slave regiments was continued by his successor, General Paulus Irving.[14] The slaves were enlisted upon payment of the king's shilling, were given a uniform and a wage.[15] The officers were recruited from England.

Several of these young officers, on their way to take their first command, would lose their lives in the storm of November 1795. They were Lts James Sutherland and Benjamin Chadwick, both from the Rothesay and Caithness Fencibles and now in the 1st West India Regiment; Capt. James Abercrombie and Lt David Butle (also of the 1st); Lt Stains, formerly of the Sussex Fencible Cavalry and now in the 2nd; Cornet Benjamin Graydon of the 3rd; and Lt Stephen Jenner of the 6th.[16] Jenner, formerly a marine, was the nephew of Dr Edward Jenner, the pioneer in the discovery of the smallpox vaccine.

It is here that we come to the first of the two people who did so much to hand down to posterity the memory of the tragedy which was to follow. Edward Jenner was a physician at Berkeley, South Gloucestershire. He and his professional associate and close friend, William Shrapnell, administered their services to Berkeley Castle.

In 1768, Frederick, the fifth Earl of Berkeley, had taken the command of the South Gloucester Militia, one of many formed for home defence and, in due course, Shrapnell enlisted as the regimental surgeon. He was commissioned ensign in 1793 and lieutenant in 1795.[17]

In 1795 the regiment was sent to Weymouth for coastal defence in case of invasion, and Shrapnell went with them. He was there when the storm occurred and afterwards worked tirelessly organising the identification of officers and the burial of the dead. To his horror, he discovered that his young friend Stephen Jenner was among those who had drowned. As the expedition's plans had been shrouded in secrecy, he had not realised that Stephen was embarked upon it.

'I have lost a valuable and intimate friend ... and this circumstance has induced me to be more particularly interested than an indifferent spectator,' he wrote.[18] The great efforts he made on behalf of the survivors and the relatives of the drowned extended to writing a full account of the storm, which has come down to us today – over two centuries later.

Also included on the expedition were some 258 men from the 26th Light Dragoons, or mounted cavalry.[19] On the fateful day of 18 November 1795, an officer and twenty-two of these young men, two of them with their wives (six 'lawful wives of soldiers for every company' [100 men] were permitted to accompany their husbands on active service), would die in the storm.[20] The officer was Cornet William Stukeley Burns.

Stukeley Burns, as he was known, came from an American Loyalist family. The Loyalists had suffered greatly for their allegiance to the king during the War of

Officers of the Light Dragoons. (From A. Cardon and S. Lowry, after de Bosset: *A View of the British Army on the Peace Establishment.* RL 760012 The Royal Collection, © H.M. Queen Elizabeth II.)

American Independence and several had been stripped entirely of their possessions. After the war, a Board of Compensation was set up in England to help them, and Burns' mother, a widow, made a petition to the Board from Massachusetts.[21]

Burns came to England having 'no dependence but upon the recompense promised by Government to those who had so suffered,'[22] On 10 June 1795 he obtained a cornetcy in the newly-formed 26th Light Dragoons, and boarded one of the ill-fated transports of Christian's fleet at Southampton, together with his wife, Stephen Jenner, and other officers of the West India Regiments.[23] Burns' wife was one of the few who survived the shipwrecks. The story of her escape is remarkable, but his death left her destitute. At this time, a well-known authoress of romantic fiction was staying in Weymouth, and was deeply touched by the woman's plight. She wrote an account of Mrs Burns' story and published it for her so that she would benefit from the subscriptions. Through her kindness the authoress inadvertently became the second most important source of information recorded about the storm. Her name was Charlotte Smith.

During the debacle of the retreat across Holland to Germany the previous January, Capt. John Charles Ker, the first Baggage Master General to the Waggon Corps in Europe, had had the gruesome experience of witnessing the suffering of the sick and wounded soldiers transported on waggons across the rough, frozen terrain, sometimes with no hospital to take them to.[24] Some were left out overnight and froze to death.[25] When the troops were recalled from Europe, (see p.25) Ker, who was from a well-to-do family on the Scottish Borders, returned with them and was the following year appointed to take charge of another corps – this time for the Service of the Hospitals in the Leeward Islands.[26] He was appointed Military Commandant of Hospitals there and given the rank of major.[27]

Ker must have been particularly pleased with his commission as his young son James was to be sent to the Leeward Islands with the 40th Foot. Aged only fourteen, James had received his commission as ensign and had been 'gazetted' the previous January – a commission which would have cost his family around £400.[28]

James must have been a sickly or weak boy or perhaps simply ill at the time of the embarkation of the 40th. They left without him for the Caribbean in July, as part of a desperate measure by Dundas to prevent the total collapse of the British forces in the islands there.[29] The Monthly Return for the 40th Foot, 'for the Leeward Islands, 11 July 1795' reported him as 'Ensign Kerr – sick.'[30]

In the meantime, James received a new commission as lieutenant (which would have cost his father even more money) and both men embarked on one of the two transports, the *Success* and *Venus*, carrying the Hospital Corps and sick and wounded soldiers from the various regiments on the new expedition.[31] Father and son would die together in the storm. James's body was recovered from the sea. His father's was never found.

The fate of all those who were to perish in the storm was tragic, none more so than the loss of many men from just one regiment – the 63rd Foot. They had all enlisted from a small town in the north-west of England – Colne, in Lancashire –

inspired, it is said, by the magnetism of the man who recruited them, their captain, Ambrose William Barcroft.

Barcroft came from an old established family of landed property in Lancashire and Yorkshire, with a colonial branch of the family in Virginia. He had fought with distinction in the War of American Independence – and bore the scars of battle from it.[32] At Colne, the men rallied to him 'en masse ... the young recruits were drawn up two deep ... [from] the Cross ... to Cabbage Lane.'[33] Approximately one hundred and twenty-six men of the regiment, including their captain, were lost in the storm, on board the troop transport *Piedmont*. (See Appendix 7) 'When the sad news reached Colne ... hardly a home in Waterside but mourned the loss of some dead one,' wrote James Carr in his *Annals and Stories of Colne*.

Barcroft had also recruited for the ill-fated campaign in Europe the previous year:[34] '... no stirring out without being up to ones [*sic*] knees... rain and cold in abundance,' he wrote to his sister Betty.[35] He was one of the last men of his regiment to cross the Waal in the retreat from the French, under heavy fire from the enemy: 'the bridge ... was hacked to pieces. We crossed ... upon simple planks ... up to our knees in water. The town [Nijmegen] was burnt and shattered in the most shocking manner. Many of the inhabitants perished'.[36]

From the mud, freezing cold and typhoid fever of Flanders, they were now to be sent to the burning tropics – although they did not know it. Barcroft wrote to his sister: 'of our Destination ... we are still as ignorant as ever ... we are to encamp near Southampton ... and there to wait for further orders.'[37] His last letter of 11 November, however, gives some intimation of his possible knowledge and betrays some apprehension: 'You shall hear from me every convenient opportunity. God help you all.'[38] They were destined to die, not in the tropics, but helpless on the shore of their native land, in the rage of an overwhelmingly furious storm. Barcroft's daughter, Ellen, was just twelve months old when he died.[39]

These men, and thousands like them, were summoned to their deaths in the name of King and Empire by the leaders of the time. The most powerful of men, they were the Masters of Empire.

At the outbreak of war, Britain boasted two very astute leaders: William Pitt the Younger, the king's 'First' Minister, and Home Secretary Henry Dundas. Pitt was the *wunderkind* of the British economy. When he came to power as Chancellor of the Exchequer in 1782, towards the end of the American War of Independence, Britain was on the verge of bankruptcy. He introduced taxes where none had dared before – on windows, menservants, horses, even wig powder – and turned round Britain's economy from near ruin to affluence and stability in nine short years. In December 1783, he had become the king's First Minister – at the age of twenty-four. Pitt was the second son of a brilliant and powerful man, Lord Chatham, previously a First Minister himself. The boy grew up in the shadow of his great father, who saw the brilliance in his son and sought to exploit and develop it. Pitt had been a sickly child, frequently suffering from sore throats, and his mother, whom he adored, gave him the comfort he needed – fully approving of the port wine the doctors gave him in increasing quantities to relieve his suffering. Profoundly influenced by the colonialist

Caricature of Henry Dundas, William Pitt and Charles Fox. (From A.M. Broadley, *Royal Weymouth 1789-1805, The Court of King George III at the Seaside* (J.G. Commin, 1907)) (Weymouth Library)

policy of his father, he grew into an aloof and deeply solitary man, plunging himself entirely into his work and, when that proved a strain, taking refuge in the comfort of the alcohol which had been given him copiously in his childhood.[40]

Dundas, a highly educated and intelligent Scot, held high office in several areas where his methodical and thorough ways were put to good use. As Home Secretary, he had responsibility for Irish, colonial and military business, was President of the Board of Control for India and had political responsibility for Scotland. But he was a deeply ambitious man and he took on too much – both for himself and the country. He became Secretary of State for War in 1794, overseeing the administration of the army in the Netherlands, the preparation of military expeditions to the West Indies and the garrisoning of troops in all the outposts of Britain's colonial acquisitions around the world.[41] He was driven by ambition – an overweening ambition to capture the possessions of the enemy, be it France or, later, Holland and Spain, to use them to strengthen Britain's hand as bargaining counters in peace negotiations. Like Pitt, he also worked miracles – scraping convoys together when the resources were hardly there, dredging troops from the king's Hanoverian dominions in Germany and subsidising Britain's shaky allies in Europe. At the beginning of the war, he had incurred the king's wrath by allocating troops for the West Indies which the king felt should go to his son to fight the campaign in Flanders.[42] Even when he hardly had the manpower or resources to hold what had been taken, Dundas still forged ahead with plans for fresh expeditions as new enemies entered the war.

Like Pitt, he also drank heavily. Close friends, they frequently drank in each other's company.[43]

When war broke out with France, one of the most pressing needs these men had to address was to stamp out the slave insurrection in the French Caribbean islands before it spread to their own. In addition, to capture France's rich sugar islands would reduce her colonial might and stifle the threat of her sea power. Pitt described it as obtaining 'indemnity for the past and security for the future.'[44]

How they misjudged the enemy! Perhaps neither had anticipated the vigour and determination of a country supercharged by revolutionary fervour – and equally determined to win her rich possessions back. Twenty-two years later, Britain was still at war with a defiant, turbulent France. Dundas had had to struggle with an almost permanently critical shortage of men and ships, which rendered his performance woefully inadequate at times when badly needed.[45] Pitt, weighed down by all the responsibilities of prolonged and sustained warfare, in addition to the management of the country and its economy in difficult times, broke down under an effort which was too great for him. He became exhausted and ill, eventually exhibiting signs of heavy drinking, his face bloated and his hands shaking.[46] Ironically, he too would

Henry Dundas, Secretary of State for War (from *Broadley's Royal Weymouth*, 1789-1805)

die in the service of his country: in 1806, whilst still in office, he died aged only forty-two.

The year 1795 saw high unemployment and soaring food prices, caused by the appalling winters of 1793-1794 and 1794-1795. Snow was followed by widespread floods, crops were withered by the intense cold – and thousands of sheep perished with their lambs in the fields in June.[47] A shortage of bread ensued – and, with it, the ominous stirrings of public discontent.

In October the king's coach was mobbed while he was on his way to open Parliament. The mob threw stones and shattered a window of the coach, shouting 'Peace! Bread! No war! No King! No Pitt!'[48] After that, Pitt introduced increasingly repressive Bills to counter growing social unrest, which amounted to censorship of the press and the prevention of people congregating in 'seditious meetings'.[49]

A wartime government coalition in December 1793, assuring him a position of almost absolute power, enabled Pitt to do this. By the summer of 1794, government opposition had dwindled to just one significant man, Charles Fox, and a handful of his devoted followers, including the playwright Richard Sheridan.[50] Like Pitt, Fox was also the second son of a great and brilliant man, Lord Holland, who had accumulated vast wealth as the Paymaster General to His Majesty's Forces during the Seven Years War and he enjoyed a privileged, extravagant way of life with high connections.[51] However, there was little sign in Fox's childhood of the austere living and hard work ethic of Pitt's.

Fox, the MP for Westminster, was warm, impetuous and expressive; Pitt, the MP for Cambridge University, was cool, austere, shrewd and calculating. Fox supported 'the cause of the people'. He challenged Pitt's repressive Bills in the House of Commons and championed 'legitimate opposition voiced from platform or press'. Pitt's political life depended on the cause of the king – and he defended his authority. Pitt, 'imperturbably self-confident', 'angular and spare', would enter the House of Commons, 'holding himself stiffly upright, his face impassive, his aspect frigid'. Fox, plump and dishevelled, would usually enter late after being up all night gambling or straight from the racecourse, to a chorus of cheers from his few supporters, and would make his way to his seat smiling, shaking hands and being patted on the back.[52]

Fox famously wore a buff waistcoat and blue jacket, the colours associated with the American revolutionaries. He similarly sympathised with the French Revolution and moved many resolutions advocating a settlement with France (but not a restoration of the French monarchy, which he called 'Bourbon despotism').[53] He was Pitt's greatest political adversary and it is significant that this one man, who held no high political office during the French Revolutionary Wars, has come down to us from this era as famous in his opposition to Pitt as Pitt himself. He was the 'warrior for liberty, the champion of good causes', immensely popular and not a man to bear grudges.[54] (Although he carried his eminent father's grudges against the king throughout his life.) Once, when asked by someone in the House, vexed by the verbal excesses of another MP, 'Do you not hate that fellow?' he smiled and replied: 'Ah well, I am a bad hater'.[55]

King George III. (From
Broadley's Royal Weymouth,
1789-1805) (Weymouth
Library)

And so we come to the greatest of all the masters – the one to whom the others (and everyone else) looked up: the king himself, George III. In eighteenth-century England, the king was *the* great master. He literally held the power of life or death over criminals sentenced to death, receiving and considering the details of each case, before approving or quashing the sentence.[56] A deeply conscientious king, George took the keenest interest in the progress of his army and exercised close supervision and control over army affairs. Regimental returns were regularly sent to him, and his son the Duke of York's frequent letters (often more than once daily) from the front in Flanders kept him as informed as his generals.[57] It was with a substantial weight of knowledge that he criticised Pitt's and Dundas' war plans: he saw a huge empire with an army and resources inadequate to protect it. 'The truth is we attempt too many objects at the same time,' he wrote indignantly to Dundas, 'and our force consequently must be too small at each place.'[58]

He was a dutiful king, concerned for the welfare of his subjects. During the food shortages and bread crisis of 1795 he ordered that brown rye or potato bread only was to be served in his household, in order to set an example. He was also energetic and diligent: he rose at 6.00 a.m. and, after horse-riding and Divine Service, was at his desk attending to the affairs of the nation. He wrote all his letters himself (until 1805 when he went blind), each meticulously dated and timed. He lived a homely and simple life, most evenings being spent at home with his family playing cards and listening to music (both king and queen played the harpsichord, and loved Handel).

The glitter and glamour of the Court was maintained for the dignity of the monarchy and the nation but the king and queen preferred the intimacy of their family quarters, where they spoke the tongue of their fathers: German.[59]

George was a devout king. War against revolutionary France, with its godlessness, bloodiness and regicide, was in his view a war that 'every tie of religion, morality and society not only authorises but demands'. Aged fifty-eight (he was born in 1738), George was a large, heavily-built man with a rather florid complexion and slightly bulging blue eyes. He was very fit and seemingly impervious to cold: Lord Glenbervie recalled shivering whilst in conversation with him on the terraces at Weymouth in 1804 in a cold, damp wind but 'The King seemed not to feel it.'[60]

The king's brother, the Duke of Gloucester, had built a house at Weymouth in 1780 and, when George was recovering from his first bout of mental illness in 1789, had placed it at his disposal.[61] Thus began the king's love affair with the little seaside town. From 1789 until 1805, with rare exceptions, he went every year to Weymouth for his summer holidays, buying up three houses adjoining Gloucester Lodge and spending several weeks at a time there. When required, members of the Cabinet removed to the town and Pitt frequently came down 'on business', residing at nearby Kingston Maurward House, Dorchester.[62]

The royal family's holidays were spent in excursions on the frigate *Southampton* around Portland Bill and out into the Channel, bathing in the sea, accompanied by a bathing machine festooned with a banner which read 'God save the King' and containing a small band playing the national anthem, watching pony races on the sand for a silver cup and going on long horserides out into the Dorset countryside. The king and queen, usually accompanied by their daughters, were frequently seen strolling on the Esplanade in the evening, smiling, waving and acknowledging the cheers of the crowds around them. They all clearly enjoyed themselves.[63]

On their first holiday, in 1789, they sailed to Lulworth Cove and Castle, and to Seacombe, Isle of Purbeck. The king looked solemnly upon the treacherous rocks in Seacombe Bay where the great East Indiaman, the *Halsewell*, had sunk three years previously with the loss of nearly all lives, including those of the captain and his daughters.[64]

Six years later, as the ships of Christian's fleet passed this same spot, young Lt Stephen Jenner of the 6th West India Regiment pointed it out to several other passengers on their ill-fated transport the *Catherine*. The following day, they, too, would lose their lives to a raging sea as the *Catherine*, *Piedmont*, *Aeolus*, *Golden Grove*, *Thomas* and *Venus* all foundered within the space of one hour upon that steep and inhospitable bank of shingle called the Chesil.

Chapter 4

The Chesil

The Chesil Bank, or Beach, is a seven-mile-long ridge of pebbles, 50ft high at its southern (Portland) end, facing south-west into the English Channel at Lyme Bay, known in earlier times as the West Bay. Its north-western end is at Abbotsbury (see map p.2). The Bank has long had a grim reputation as a graveyard for ships. Through the centuries tales were told of ships trapped in Lyme Bay in a south-west gale, being rushed on a wild sea towards the Chesil – that fateful lee shore that reaches out like an arm as if to catch them when they have failed to see the lights of Portland, or simply been unable to round the Bill.

To form an accurate idea of this wonderfull [sic] bank of pebbles, I must refer you to any map of Dorsetshire: you will find it connecting the rock of Portland to the Land. It is bounded on one Side by the West Bay and on the other by a backwater, called the Fleet, for an extent of seven miles, where the bank joins the land at the town of Abbotsbury, very near Strangways Castle, the Seat of the Earl of Ilchester', wrote Lt William Shrapnell. It is entirely composed of a very high ridge of pebbles consisting of flints, Jaspars [sic] and other very hard stones. They are many of them valuable and are often collected by the Curious for seals, rings, etc. It wou'd be miraculous indeed if a ship cou'd strike furiously on this bank without going to peices [sic]'.[1]

The Chesil from Portland, showing the Fleet water outletting through Smallmouth into Portland Harbour. (Colin MacFarlane)

A view from the mainland, showing the rope-pulled ferry at Smallmouth, the 'Isle' of Portland in the background and the Chesil Bank on the far right. (Bussell Collection, Weymouth Museum)

...That fatal bank of stones, wrote Charlotte Smith, *which, beginning at the village of Chisle, on the presqu' Isle of Portland, connects it with the coast of Dorset ... has been infamous beyond the memory of man ... for the wrecks that have happened on it ... This extraordinary bank of stones reaches to a place called Burton Cliff, a distance of above sixteen miles, with a singular variation in regard to the pebbles that compose it. At Chisle, in the Isle of Portland, they are as large as eggs, and gradually diminish from that size till, at Becksington, they are not bigger than peas; and, between a place called Swyre and Burton Cliff, they decline insensibly into a fine soft sand.*[2]

A Portland fisherman will assure us that, land him where we please upon the Bank, in a pitch-dark night, he will know his whereabouts by the size of the pebbles, wrote John Coode, the Engineer-in-Chief of the Portland Breakwater in 1838.[3]

The Chesil Bank is indeed a natural wonder: a beach which rises from the sea without land behind it, but instead the Fleet salt-water lagoon. Its origins are not certain. A storm bank, it is believed that it was formed as the sea levels rose after the last Ice Age, some 10,000 years ago. The Fleet water is open at its south-eastern end (called Smallmouth) to the present-day Portland harbour (formerly known as Portland Roads). In the old days, a rope-hauled ferry crossed Smallmouth to Portland, which was effectively an island as the strip of Chesil connecting it to the mainland was impassable except on foot, and then only by the strong and fit.

What is extraordinary about this huge bank is that its pebbles are not local – they have been washed there in their millions by glacier melt-waters and the might of the sea from land further west. Long-shore drift caused their graduation in size from West Bay (Bridport) down to Chesil Cove.[4]

Underneath the pebbles is a firm black clay, which appears when a strong south-east wind blows; the bank is then swept from one end to the other of the stones, and remains only of clay, till

Another view of the rope-pulled ferry. To the left is the church tower at Wyke; to the right the *Magnificent*, seventy-four guns, and the *Southampton* frigate which attended the king and his family on their holidays. (Bussell Collection, Weymouth Museum)

such time as a south-west wind blows, when the sea throws them up and covers the bank again. … to whoever has seen this immense mass of stones, as it generally appears, this account seems incredible, wrote Charlotte Smith.[5]

Incredible though it may have seemed to Charlotte Smith, there are instances, albeit rare, of the bank being swept of its pebbles after a south-east wind. Modern eyewitness accounts have described the sight as 'the barest we've seen it: from the Ferry Bridge to Wyke, it was literally like a solid – I wouldn't call it clay, more like the pebbles embedded in it, like a hard crusty shingle – gravel compressed together … like a grey sort of clay – a gritty, sandy colour.'[6] An account of this phenomenon was also given in John Leland's survey of England made for King John in the 1200s and quoted in Hutchins, *History and Antiquities of the County of Dorset*, Vol.2:

The Saxon name for gravel is Kiesel [= Chesil], Germanic for flint; … a prodigious heap or body of pebbles thrown up by the sea … when a strong north-easterly wind blows it cleaves it asunder and sweeps away all the stones, leaving only a firm black clay that lies at bottom. With a south-west wind, the most violent on this shore, the sea throws up fresh pebbles [and] covers the bank again.[7]

John Coode wrote: *The great elevation of the shingle is to be attributed to the unusual depth of the water close beside it, upwards of eight fathoms … this surprising depth allows the heaviest seas, checked by no shoal water … to fall on the Bank with great violence and throw*

up shingle with a will. The force of the sea on the Chesil Bank during a heavy south-west gale
is tremendous. It often happens that, the water receding from any wave just broken meets that
of the wave next in order in its progress shoreward. The concussion is so great that an enormous
quantity of broken water and spray will sometimes rise perpendicularly into the air to a height
of sixty or seventy feet. Meets of this sort have broken up stranded vessels instantaneously of two
hundred tons burthen ...[8]

Although the Chesil has borne the brunt of ferocious south-westerly gales for probably thousands of years, it is not always a wild and inhospitable place: on a warm summer's day, the biscuit-coloured shingle sweeps in a graceful curve up from Portland, disappearing into a heat haze with the blue of the Burton meres reflected in the sky. 'It is hard to say too much of the extreme beauty of this curve and of the grand view which is to be had of it from the summit of the hill [Portland],' wrote John Coode in Kerridge's *Local Rakings*.

The stones are warmed by the sun, which then radiate their heat, warming air and sea. This warmth has created a microclimate, in which plants from much more temperate zones can flourish – such as those in the sub-tropical gardens at Abbotsbury. The Chesil is a natural barrier, defending the low meadows behind the Fleet, and the Fleet itself is a quiet backwater of rushes and reeds, home to countless seabirds and swans. A variety of waterfowl and sea fish populate its brackish tidal water. Seaward, the bank's steeply-shelving beach and almost saltless water is ideal for the confident swimmer (the warm pebbles ensure that the water is warmer earlier in the year at Abbotsbury than around the Bill at neighbouring Weymouth). However, its notorious undertow must be respected: it can quickly suck the tired or unwary swimmer under.

King George III's bathing machine.
(From Jo Draper, *The Georgians*,
(Dovecote Press, 1998), p.23.
Reproduced by kind permission of
the Dovecote Press)

Moreover, this vast pebble beach is not devoid of wildlife: the brown hare runs here and, in spring, the causeway from Smallmouth to Portland is a mile-long carpet of sea pinks. Bindweed and vetch cover the shingle in patches and sea kale proliferates all along it. Of especial interest is the yellow-horned poppy because it is rarely found in any other habitat, and Portland has a sea spurge unique to it: *Euphorbia portlandia*.[9] Colonies of seabirds, including the little tern, nest here. It is wild – and has a unique character.

At nearby Weymouth, during the Revolutionary Wars, regiments of soldiers were stationed in barracks in the town and in summer camps on the hills above, to counter the threat of invasion by the French. 'Dorsetshire is one of the most vulnerable parts of the Kingdom', wrote the king to his son in 1804.[10]

This brought the South Gloucester Militia to South Down, Weymouth, and with them their surgeon, Lt William Shrapnell. Both the North and South Gloucester Militias, about five hundred men to each regiment, were encamped there throughout the summer – and some of them brought their wives.[11] The 'ladies of the regiment', as Shrapnell described them, visited or accompanied their husbands occasionally, officers' wives staying in the elegant seafront houses which were rapidly going up in Weymouth; others, and certainly women of the lower ranks, residing in the tents with their husbands.[12] Both Shrapnell's wife, who had a small son, Henry, and the Duke of Berkeley's wife, Mary Cole, came to the camp.[13] They mixed with the social life of the town which was particularly busy in the summer, as the king had made it very popular. Fashionable people gathered at the Assembly Rooms, the Baths, and Woods' and Delamotte's Libraries. Social life glittered when the royal family came: there were balls and plays, dinners and fireworks, but despite all this extravagance, when the royal family embarked on an excursion anywhere, they always took their sandwiches with them.[14]

The celebrated authoress of romantic fiction, Charlotte Smith, came to stay at a house on the Esplanade with her son-in-law, a French *émigré* aristocrat called Alexandre de Foville. She was a melancholy, rather morbid soul who had suffered the blows of life and did not carry them lightly. She had, however, a sharp and intelligent mind, and the events she was to describe in the disaster to follow are vivid and mostly accurate in detail. She championed the likes of Fox and his free-thinking, liberal policies, supported the Revolution against oppression in France, yet was unswerving and compassionate in the support and shelter she gave to many desperate, fugitive *émigrés* fleeing the convulsions of their native France – people who would have been her social equals.[15]

At Weymouth the regiments held dramatic and exciting tournaments, on Radipole Common and on the Ridge, towards Dorchester.[16] The Prince of Wales, who was colonel-in-command of the 10th Light Dragoons, took part in one on the Downs, 'where the cavalry had a sham fight. The Prince was very active, riding from post to post and scaling some precipices with great ardour'.[17] The public came and cheered. This was the time when the king, on an excursion into the Dorset countryside, gave a guinea to a woman left all alone working in the fields as she could not afford to go with the other workers to Weymouth to see their king. 'You can tell them,' he said, 'that your King came to see *you*.'[18]

Portrait of Charlotte Smith, from the *European* Magazine, November 1806. (By permission of the British Library, Shelfmark PP5459Z)

The king and queen visited the North and South Gloucester Militias at South Down in August 1795 and were entertained to 'tea, coffee and an elegant collation of fruit, etc.'[19] The king bestowed his 'Royal Approbation' upon them and thereafter the word 'Royal' was added to their title.[20]

The Officers and men of the South Gloucester Militia displayed such an active degree of benevolence upon the late melancholy occasion of the numerous shipwrecks on our coast as render them an honour to their county. The Field Officers contributed 10 guineas each, the Captains five and the Subalterns three. This sum, with the contributions of the neighbourhood, enabled Mr Shrapnel [sic], the Surgeon, to procure coffins for the corpses of every officer, or person above the common rank, and give a decent interment to all others, as circumstances would admit. Mr Shrapnel deserves every praise for his great zeal and activity in this service.[21]

The anticipated invasion never came, but the South Gloucester Militia would be remembered for a different and unexpected service: that which they gave to their fellow soldiers in a tragic accident of war.

Chapter 5

Expedition

When Spain made peace with France in July 1795, Pitt wrote to his brother, Lord Chatham:

> *This varies so much the whole state (of) things… that it makes a new question whether any British force can, without too great a risk, be hazarded on the Continent of France. I incline to think that our plan must now be changed, and that the only great push must be in the West Indies where I trust enough may yet be gained to counterbalance the French successes in Europe.*[1]

The Cabinet Meeting held on 14 August at Downing Street produced the following minute: that a 'prosecution of the war by a vigorous exertion both by sea and land in the West Indies [was] essential'; 'that preparation be forthwith made for offensive operations both in the Leeward Islands and in the Island of St Domingo' (St Domingue was generally referred to as 'St Domingo'); and 'that the conquest of Guadeloupe and St Lucia … must be attempted with the utmost expedition.' The Minute suggested that allowing fifteen thousand 'effective … infantry' for the Leeward Islands would leave no more than nine thousand available for St Domingo and therefore recommended that another three thousand should be taken from the Guards.[2]

Preparations commenced immediately. There were already hundreds of troops encamped at Southampton and Portsmouth, for regular expeditions against the French in Brittany, under the command of the Earl of Moira and Maj.-Gen. Doyle. Moira sent instructions to Doyle, however, warning him that his latest force 'should be considered only as a detachment from this army' as 'I may very speedily after you have sailed be removed from the command on account of the destination of these forces to other operations than those which I was destined to conduct'.[3]

On 24 August, Dundas wrote to Moira:

> *… all the arrangements for the expedition on which [General Doyle] is to proceed are now compleated [sic], and I am authorised to signify to your Lordship his Majesty's permission to resign [your] command… Sir Ralph Abercromby… intends to be at Southampton on Thursday next, in order to superintend the arrangements necessary for preparing the troops for the new service on which they are to proceed…*[4]

When Abercromby arrived at Southampton, one of the very first matters he attended to was to call a meeting of senior medical officers, to draw up a list of 'Instructions for the better preservation of the state of health of the troops', both

Portsmouth in the eighteenth century. (National Maritime Museum BHC 1919)

during the long voyage and on arriving in the West Indies. Conditions on board troop transport ships were notoriously bad. Low between decks, they were cramped and unhygienic, spreading disease and death. Typical measurements were:[5]

Fore hatch	between deck and deck	5ft 7in
	between deck and beam	4ft 8in
Main hatch	between deck and deck	5ft 0in
	between deck and beam	4ft 3in

The medical officers summoned to Southampton recommended that troop transports should be of at least 300 tons, with room to stand upright between decks; the practice of allotting one soldier for every two tons of ship's tonnage should be adhered to and increased if possible to 2 ½ tons per man. Every transport should be cleansed between decks with quick lime; hammocks and deck awnings should be provided, with bellows and wind sails to assist ventilation. No troops should be detained for long on board transports before sailing (this inevitably led to the outbreak of typhus). Fumigation should be carried out between decks daily by vitriolic acid and nitre in a sand bath. Fresh vegetables, including potatoes, should be supplied on board against the risk of scurvy, with two pints of porter a day. There should be a set amount of soup, pearl barley, rice and sugar for the sick. Good discipline, exercise, and personal cleanliness should be enforced, with a bath and clean shirt twice a week. No 'raw and unseasoned' troops should be sent, but preference should be given to men who had served abroad in warm places such as Gibraltar, and the troops should arrive in November, to allow them to become acclimatised during the winter months.

After disembarkation, high ground was preferable for camps; the ground floor should never be slept on; tent boards should be used and the ground frequently changed. Sea bathing was to be encouraged but care exercised that only five minutes was spent in the water. A short-skirted coat, loose cotton trousers and cloth gaiters to protect against the bites of insects should be provided. Each man should have two flannel shirts and flannel drawers. Daily inspection by an NCO and bi-weekly inspection by an MO were advised for insect bites, which were regarded as the cause of sores and ulcers of the legs. Walking barefoot should be forbidden because of the danger of 'jiggers', a type of flea which penetrated the skin.[6] The regulations were to be printed and distributed among the troops in time for embarkation.[7]

Over August and September, Christian and Abercromby conferred with their predecessors Grey and Jervis to discuss preparations and tactics.[8] The two commanders of the previous expedition passed on hints, plans and charts of the islands. Grey recommended that the troops should carry kegs for water and have additional shoes. 'He dwelt much upon the necessity of keeping the windward anchor and not hazarding a day's desertion at Martinique,' wrote Christian.[9]

An enormous amount of medical supplies were to be issued for the expedition, under the supervision of Dr John MacNamara Hayes, who oversaw the provision of medicines, medical equipment, sheets, hospital bedding, regimental and hospital chests and the supplies for the hospital ships. He was also responsible for the selection of men fit for the expedition.[10]

From the start, the enormous demands of this expedition stretched the available resources of soldiers, seamen, transport ships and armaments beyond limit. There had

A West India ship, *Britannia*. (National Maritime Museum BHC2351)

been a continual and pressing shortage of men and arms since the beginning of the war – in October 1794, Maj.-Gen. William Crosbie, the commanding officer of the camp at Netley, near Southampton, had complained that the recruits training there had never fired powder.[11] The shortage of men was in part due to the fact that, at the time, there was no conscription for the army.[12] Although the Militias, into which men were called up by ballot to serve for a limited period only, provided for home defence, men took the king's shilling voluntarily (or were tricked into it by unscrupulous recruitment officers), and recruiting for the regiments could be hard work. Despite the poverty and starvation which prevailed during the 1790s, the English peasant was generally better off than his continental counterpart and did not have the same pressing need to enlist in order to find food and clothing.[13] In France, by comparison, conscription was declared from 1793 by the *Levée en Masse* for the entire male population.[14]

The problem was slightly eased by hiring troops, mainly Hanoverian, from the Continent. Eight thousand foreign infantry were to be sent from Stade on the River Elbe to England 'for service in the West Indies' and French immigrant artillerymen were procured to fight in St Domingo.[15] For the navy, press ganging was a lawful way of recruiting men. There were 'pressing tenders', ships allocated specifically for the purpose of collecting men off serving ships returning to port, or from the ports themselves and press officers and pressmen, paid by government.[16] There was nothing the impressed men could do about it, unless they qualified for exemption.[17] Bounties were also offered to 'Able Seamen' and 'Landsmen' and Pitt's Quota Acts of 1795 provided men from each county, but the shortage of men continued.[18] There was also a chronic shortage of arms and artillery. The arsenal at Woolwich was stretched to full working capacity and, when possible, arms were purchased from the Continent or other dealers. In early June, a large quantity had been bought in Terveer, Holland, and stored at Portsmouth. Although of foreign manufacture and differing in their bore, these muskets were ordered to be put in a state of readiness as soon as possible – without being removed from Portsmouth.[19]

Merchants profited greatly from supplying the War Office for the expedition. Hodson & Hayter, packers, sent invoices for fourteen bales of clothing, six casks of shoes and boots, three of helmets, twenty of saddlery, ten of accoutrements – in all twenty-one tons – for the 21st Regiment of Light Dragoons and the new 7th West India Regiment.[20] Messrs Pearce were requested to provide the clothing for Maj. Ker's Hospital Corps in the Leeward Islands.[21] Thomas Fauquier received an order to do 'everything ... necessary' that clothing and accoutrements for 'Regiment[s] of People of Colour and Negroes' under Col. Lewes [7th West India] and Col. Skerrett [8th] be provided without delay.[22]

There were pre-fabricated barracks blocks to be made, horses and forge carts to be procured, tents – even bricks were to be sent for military buildings on St Domingo.[23] Basket-hilted swords, pistols, light cavalry carbines; horse artillery and draught horses; musket balls, powder, flints; thousands of shirts, shoes, boots, jackets and gaiters – all had to be procured for the expedition. In September, Dundas wrote to Ordnance Master Cornwallis: 'Sir Ralph Abercromby [requires] 5,000 stand of spare arms – and a like number for St Domingo. The first ... to be forthwith provided and placed at

[his] ... disposal at Portsmouth ... The remaining 5,000 stand ... to be shipped on board the ordnance transports ... at Woolwich.[24]

Livestock (live cattle, sheep, chickens) to provide fresh meat had to be obtained and quartered in stalls and mangers on board the ships; water, stored in kegs and barricoes, was required for the long journey. Other victuals, such as 'sour krout', pickled cabbage, wine, potatoes and sugar, all had to be procured and placed upon transport ships. The expenses were enormous – far in excess of any before – and rising:[25]

Expense of Services performed by the Office of Ordnance pursuant to HM Orders and not provided for by Parliament:[26]

West Indies: Brass and Iron Ordnance, Powder, Shot, Shells and other Stores for a Train of Artillery attending HM Forces on an Expedition to the Leeward Islands under the command of Sir Ralph Abercromby: £95,423 5s 9d.

Estimates of the Charge of the Office of Ordnance for the year [to] 1796: Expedition under the Command of Sir Ralph Abercromby on account of the Pay of Engineers and Civil Officers with a Train of Artillery attending HM Forces to the Leeward Islands, also for Contingencies: £10,000 0s 0d.

St Domingo: On account of the Pay of Engineers and Civil Officers with a Train of Artillery attending HM Forces, also for Contingencies: £15,000 0s 0d.

Pay of a detachment of Royal Military Artificers: £964 12s 0d.

£15,964 12s 0d.

Large numbers of hospital staff were required, both on board ships and for the hospitals on the islands: 'every Army Surgeon unemployed and fit for service has been called upon,' wrote Lewis of the War Office in October.[27] Also, chaplains had to be provided: 'Sir Ralph Abercromby does not require more than one clergyman for each Brigade,' Lewis wrote to Cox and Greenwood, Agents of Corps.[28]

When all of the troops, arms and stores were procured, ships had to be found to transport them. The government relied very heavily on the merchant fleet to provide transport for troops and stores. Demand for transport ships was high – and rising with the requirements of this expedition. The Transport Board, Christian's former department, was putting out contracts wherever possible to the owners of merchant vessels for hire to government – and the cost of hire increased with the demand. Ships were hired at a series of different rates. There were tonnage rates, of so many shillings per ship-ton per month, and freight rates, being so much per ton of freight carried, or at a certain rate per man, woman and child. Some transports were also hired by the run, that is a fixed sum paid to convey to the destination.[29] Many vessels, including the ill-fated *Piedmont*, *Aeolus* and *Catherine*, had been in regular charter to the government since the beginning of the war. They were well-worn workhorses, playing a vital part in the constant to-ing and fro-ing of troops to the Channel and foreign stations. They

VI.

All Masters separated from their Convoy, or from the Agent, are to prosecute their Voyages with all possible Dispatch; observing, that, if any Delay be discovered, this Board will not fail to deduct from the Hire of their Vessels, to the full extent allowed by the Agreement in the Charter-Parties; and observing also, that Deductions will infallibly take place, in Proportions suited to their Failure in complying with any of these Articles.

VII.

When Transports abroad may be ordered Home, in Consequence of their being unfit for Service, their Masters are to proceed with the first Convoy, and to make the best of their way to England; observing, that any Delay, on their Part, will be considered by us as a sufficient Proof of the Ship being so unfit for Service, as to justify her Discharge at the Port where she was deemed unfit.

VIII.

All Masters of Transports are to observe, that, if any Accident or Misfortune shall happen to their respective Ships, by which His Majesty may be liable to make good the Loss, no Indemnification will be allowed, unless the Senior Officer of the Convoy, or Agent if not under Convoy, shall certify that nothing was deficient on their Part, or that of their Ships' Companies.

IX.

All Masters of Transports are to observe, that, when Troops are embarked, they are to be victualled agreeably to the Ration prescribed; which is Two-thirds of Seaman's Allowance, in conformity with the Custom of the Navy. Women are to be victualled at Three-fourths of Soldiers Allowance; and Children are to be victualled at the Half of Woman's Allowance. No more Women than the Proportion of Six to every Hundred Men are to be victualled, under any Pretence whatever, without a special Order in Writing, from an Agent of this Board, or from the Commander of a Convoy, in the Absence of an Agent. Masters of Transports are required to pay the most strict Attention to all such Instructions, as they may receive from this Board, or from the Victualling Board, relative to the victualling of Troops. And they are to observe, that any Embezzlement of His Majesty's Provisions or Stores, or any other Deviation from these Instructions, will, if detected, be severely punished.

XII.

When Horses are embarked on Board of a Transport, each Horse is to be allowed, daily, as follows, viz.

Ten lbs. of Hay,
Six lbs. of Oats,
Half a Peck of Bran,
Six Gallons of Water.

A small Quantity of Vinegar is to be daily issued for the Purpose of wetting the Mouths and Nostrils of the Horses.

Extracts from *Regulations, Masters of Ships and Vessels*. (Public Record Office WO/25/3502)

were so desperately needed that government often continued to use them when they were in a barely seaworthy state. The *Piedmont*, which was to take out the 63rd Foot, had run several voyages before, including transporting troops from the 100th Foot to the West Indies the previous September.[30] The 63rd's captain, Ambrose Barcroft, was unhappy about the *Piedmont*'s condition and complained about her in the hope that she might be exchanged – to no avail, and with fatal consequences.[31]

Sixteen East Indiamen, under the command of their original officers appointed by the East India Co., fifty-one of the smaller West India ships and twelve Navy victuallers were initially commissioned for the expedition.[32] (On learning of their desti-

Proportion of Ordnance, Ammunition, Carriages and Stores, for a Particular Service (as specified by Col. Lloyd of Artillery, 31 August 1795).

Brass

Howitzers	8in:	8
	On Strong Carriages	
	5½in, 10cwt:	6
	5½in, 4¾cwt:	9
	On Travelling Carriages	
Guns	12-pounders, medium:	5
	6-pdrs, medium (of 7ft):	6
	6-pdrs, light:	30
	3-pdrs, light (of 3½ft):	5

Mounted on Travelling Carriages and Limbers complete

Hand Carts for Ammunition, complete with Hooks for dragging, with Bail Hoops and Covers, with Shafts: 50, with Poles: 150
Sling Carts with Limbers complete: 4
Drag Carriages of the narrowest construction possible, with very broad low Tracks: 4, to carry Heavy Guns uphill and in rugged, narrow Tracks or Roads.
Platform Carriages to carry an Iron 24-pdr Gun and its Carriage, with Poles: 2
Block Carriage with Pole for conveying Shot & Shells: 2
Forge Carts: 3

Triangle Gyns [sheer legs, for lifting], complete: 3
6ft Scaling Ladders: 150
Grates, complete, for heating Shot: 2

Spare Standing Carriages for 24-pdrs: 1, 18-pdrs: 1
Spare Travelling Carriages and Limbers for 12-pdrs, medium: 1, 6-pdrs, med.: 1, 6-pdrs, light: 4, 3-pdrs, light: 1, 8in Howitzers: 1, 5½in Howitzers of 10cwt, 1; of 4¾cwt: 2

Men's Harness: Draught by Soldiers or Seamen: light at 12 to a Set for Hand Carts: 200 Sets
Draught by Negroes: Tarred Rope, Coils, 3in: 3, 2in: 3 To lash Cross Sticks to the Tarr'd Rope at 2ft distance ea.
Spun Yarn: 2 Coils
Match, Slow, tons: 3, exclusive of the proportion to each Gun

Iron

Guns	24-pdrs:	12
	18-pdrs:	12
	On Garrison Carriages	
Carronades	24-pdrs:	4
	12-pdrs:	4
	On Garrison Trail Carriages	
Mortars	10in:	6
	8in:	10
	On Iron Beds	

Coals, Chaldrons in Casks, for Forge Carts and General Service: 10
Tanned Hides: 50
Wadmill Tilts [wool covering for magazine floor]: 30
Hair Cloths: 10
Shot Gauges, Brass, sets: 2
Brass Callipers, pairs: 2
Copper Powder Measures from 4lb to ½oz sets

Junk [old rope], in Wads, 24-pdrs: 2,000, 18-pdrs: 2,000, 12-pdrs: 2,000; in lengths, tons: 8

Painted Canvas to cover the Ammunition in lieu of Tanned Hides or Wadmill Tilts in proportion to the Number of Pieces of Ordnance and Rounds of Ammunition for the Guns and Infantry

Entrenching Tools for the Park of Artillery
Laboratory Tents, complete
Chests of Tools for Artificers of every Description
Iron for plateing Horses
Horse Shoe Nails
Iron of sorts, cut, for Forge Carts and General Service. A proportion of Spare Handspikes, Spunges and Side Arms to be sent for all the Natures of Iron and Brass Ordnance
Powder: in Whole Barrels of 90lb ea.: 3,000 in Half Barrels of 45lb ea.: 1,000

The proposed Ordnance requirements for the Expedition (Source: Public Record Office WO/1/780 ff475-459)

nation, several of these officers resigned and had to be replaced by naval officers.)[33] A great deal more ships would have to be found to carry the thousands of troops, stores, horses and armaments. Also, Christian had the burden of requisitioning enough navy ships to form a squadron large enough to escort a convoy of such size and, in the event, many of the navy ships took on troops and stores themselves. The huge *Commerce de Marseilles*, 120 guns, a prize taken from the French at Toulon in 1793, was fitted out to take 900 troops, plus their officers, on board, together with an immense quantity of stores. Marvelled at by British seamen for her enormous size, she was armed 'en flute', that is, her lower tier of guns was stowed in her hold, to be used later, when she had discharged her enormous cargo.[34]

On 15 September, Christian raised his flag on board the *Prince George*, ninety-eight guns, at Spithead.[35] The ships initially placed under his command were: *Colossus*, seventy-four guns (Christian's old ship and now the flagship of his second-in-command Rear Admiral Maurice Pole); *Alcmene*, thirty-two guns; *La Prompte*, twenty-eight guns; *Impregnable*, ninety-eight guns; *Irresistible*, seventy-four guns; the *Commerce de Marseilles*, 120 guns; *Lively*, thirty-two guns (replaced by *Undaunted*); *Albacore*, sixteen guns; *Alfred*, seventy-four guns; *Polyphemus*, sixty-four guns (ordered to victual at Cork for Channel service and to Madeira to procure supplies of wine for the expedition); *Leda*, thirty-six guns (ordered to Cork to convoy a merchant fleet to the West Indies); *Babet*, twenty-two guns; gunboats *L'Eclair*, twenty guns, and *Crachefeu*; and bomb vessel *Terror*, eight guns.[36] To these were added *Lion*, sixty-four guns, ('to relieve *Trident*'); *Trident*, sixty-four guns, ('to take charge of loading the transports'); *Undaunted*, thirty-eight guns; armed brig *Requin* (sailed 2 November with dispatches to Laforey); gunboat *Vesuve* and storeship *Etrusco*.[37]

Troops in their thousands now began arriving by land and sea at Southampton and filled the nearby camps on Netley, Nursling and Portsmouth Commons to overflowing. Portsmouth and Southampton were thrown into a frenzy of preparations: '[Romsey] camp contains now about twenty regiments and more troops are arriving here every day; the 3rd and 53rd regiments landed on Friday se'nnight; the 63rd on Saturday, the 31st, 48th and 94th on Monday and the 25th on Tuesday morning. The latter is gone to Netley ... the others to Nursling Common,' reported the *Hampshire Chronicle* of 7 September 1795. 'We have now near 200 transports in our river, from which the following regiments were disembarked on Saturday last, viz. 12th, 14th, 27th, 28th, 57th and 80th, which augments the number now in camp on Nursling common, cavalry and artillery, to near 20,000 men.'

'Our camp on Shirley Common is considerably augmented,' reported *The Times* of 5 August 1795, 'the following regiments are now on the ground, viz. 19th, 33rd, 42nd, 78th, 90th, 103rd, 109th, together with four regiments of cavalry and the flying artillery. The ground is marked out for several more and it is supposed there will be in the whole about 28,000 men.'

'All the regiments of foot now in England, except the 34th, are under embarkation orders,' added the *Hampshire Chronicle* of 26 September 1795. Earl Spencer (First Lord of the Admiralty) and Admiral Hugh Seymour (Lord of the Admiralty) came down from London to supervise the expedition. The troops were formed into six brigades and the process of allocating them to transports, embarking them, feeding and watering them on board began.[38] Many were to remain on board for a long time before departure, contrary to the recommendations of the medical officers at Southampton.

The *Commerce de Marseilles* completed her embarkation on 4 October.[39] At Dundas' instructions, she was to leave immediately with her convoy of seventeen transports as the situation became daily more desperate in the West Indies, but the wind shifted to the south-west and her captain, Smith Childs, missed the opportunity to sail.[40] Christian could barely conceal his vexation: '[The] second wind will not be permitted to excuse him,' he wrote to his friend Huskisson at the War Office. 'This old and worthy man ought not in any point of consideration have been so appointed.'[41]

On 22 October the East and West India ships arrived from the River Thames, where they had been fitted out to carry troops. Christian went to Southampton to arrange the embarkation with Abercromby. He was full of optimism and very impressed with his military counterpart: 'The next week will place us perfectly at liberty to take advantage of the first wind,' he wrote to Nepean at the Admiralty.[42] 'We will not have difficulty when we reach the islands – if I read Abercromby's character I am persuaded he will have none,' he wrote to Huskisson, '[He] has not been wanting in zeal...'.[43]

However, problems *were* to arise – in large numbers, and Christian was to encounter a slowness and lack of co-operation with the naval staff which would test his patience to the limits. He applied to the Victualling Office for barricoes to carry water on the transports. The Victualling Office replied that they had orders not to issue any. He appealed to Admiralty.[44] Admiralty wrote to the Victualling Office and Christian got his barricoes.[45] Capt. Lobb of the *Babet*, one of Christian's ships, applied to have his vessel's bottom examined in dock for the duration of one tide, but was refused. Lobb had to write to Christian and Christian to the Admiralty before, finally, Lobb's permission was granted.[46]

Of a certain Sir Charles, he wrote: 'I am at a loss to account for the persevering industry of this man in his endeavours to impede the success of so important a measure.' (He may possibly be referring to Sir Charles Middleton, the admiral who had questioned Christian's seniority in taking command. See pp.26-27) Christian also refers to the 'persevering obstinacy on the part of Sir M.'[47] He was further frustrated by what he considered as time wasted having to attend a court martial on an officer for disobedience of orders and he was beset by personal worries.[48] His wife was in ill health throughout this time, which caused him constant anxiety, and he had to make frequent trips to her at their home on the Isle of Wight.[49]

'We must not contemplate dificultys [*sic*] but do the best to overcome them,' he had written earlier to Huskisson, but, inevitably, as the problems piled up, his optimism waned: 'Every exertion in my power has been made and difficulty has arisen of every step,' he complained on 4 October.[50]

At Cork, there had been a mutiny in September among the troops assigned for the St Domingo part of the expedition, after their destination became known to them. The 105th and 113th Regiments marched through the city of Cork with loaded muskets. The mutiny lasted from 3-5 September. The offenders were subsequently court-martialled and sentenced to one thousand lashes. One of their leaders was shot. Col. Whyte, who was in charge of the Cork contingent, ordered that troops arriving there should be sent by sea, not land, and disembarked at Spike Island in Cork harbour, to avoid desertion. However, typhus and dysentery broke out in the

AN ADDRESS

From the 105th and 113th Regiments to the Public, and their Brothers in Arms.

Citizens and Fellow Soldiers.

IT is no longer time to fport with our Lives and trifle with our Credulity—We, too, have been Induftrious Citizens till a dreadful and atrocious War had dried up the channels of our Manufactures and caufed us to Roam at large, Idle and Dependent!—Neceffity, dire neceffity induced us to embark in a caufe which our fouls abhorred; but hunger has no Law; fooner than perifh, we had been tempted by large Sums (badly paid) to enrol ourfelves—We did fo, on condition of returning to our homes at the approach of Peace; but what now is the cafe? All faith is broken with us! We are led to be incorporated with Regiments that will never be reduced, except by a formidable enemy and the more formidable climate of the WEST-INDIES! And you, unfortunate and inflaved Natives of Africa, are you to feel our Steel? Are we to be made fhed your innocent blood with our Murderous Arms? Forbid it Heaven! Forbid it Juftice! No, no, perifh firft the man who dare embark for fo horrid a purpofe; Generous Citizens of Cork, do you not fympathife with us? Do you not pity us thus Crimped and Sold by unfaithful Officers? You furely muft; for you cannot be hardened to misfortunes.

As to our Brothers in Arms, they cannot, they will not unfheath the Sword to enforce an Aarbitrary and Unjuft Meafure, Our Fellow Soldiers, are fellow men, and cannot forget what they owe to themfelves—they muft *think*, and then we are all right. Yes, we will defend our Country, our Homes, our Wives and Children, to this we are pledged, and from this we fhall never Flinch.

CORK, SEPTEMBER 4, 1795.

Address from 105th and 113th Regiments at Cork, inciting an uprising against the Expedition. The ringleader was shot; the others sentenced to 1,000 lashes. (National Army Museum, 63305)

cramped and unhealthy accommodation on the island, with the result that five hundred died and three thousand were admitted to hospital.[51]

Meanwhile, the Woolwich Arsenal were working continuously to provide the cannon and munitions for the expedition, but the ships to carry these had to be especially fitted out in the Thames, and this began to cause very serious delays.[52] Dundas wrote in desperation to Ordnance Master Cornwallis, demanding frequent reports on their progress and insisting that transports, once loaded, should proceed immediately to Spithead without waiting to go in convoy. Even those allocated to Cork were to proceed to Portsmouth in order to depart with Christian: they could join the St Domingo contingent later at Barbados. The delay was 'injurious to the Service,' a pained Dundas wrote to the Commissioners for Transports. 'Damn the Ordnance!' wrote Christian to Huskisson.[53]

Christian still had a serious shortage of seamen: 'The squadron under my orders [is] 150 seamen short,' he wrote to Secretary Nepean at the Admiralty. He had requested to Sir Peter Parker, the Port Admiral at Portsmouth, that 'the deficiency in the complement of the ships should be made good, [but] he informs me that he does not possess the means of complying with my request.'[54] The Admiralty directed Parker to complete the complement of ships with landmen.[55]

The transport agents for the merchant ships found themselves up against their own navy in competition for more men. Other fleets, such as the North Sea fleet, were stripped down to skeleton crews in order to provide men for Christian.[56] For the first time the British Navy used lemon juice to prevent scurvy among the crews in the ships of the Channel fleet blockading the French ports, as there was no manpower left to replace them.[57] The press gangs were out night and day. Over 18–19 September, every ship on the Thames from Gravesend to London Bridge was 'visited'.[58] In late October, one East Indiaman, the *Earl of Abergavenny*, on her way to Cork, pressed five men from another, the *Dutton*, as she was passing St Helens – and both were on Christian's expedition. Christian had to protest to the Admiralty and the men were returned.[59]

With such large numbers of troops, the space on board the transports became tighter and tighter. In October, the Transport Commissioner at Portsmouth, Lt John Schank, resorted to squeezing another two thousand troops onto the transports already commissioned.[60]

In late October and early November, stormy weather blew up, which made embarking the troops difficult and dangerous. On 27 October, the gunboat *L'Eclair* was blown onshore whilst taking troops on board. Christian reported: 'The 3rd and 19th Regts. embarked early this day from Stokes Bay and Gosport, it came on to blow [so] exceedingly strong from the south-west it was impracticable to continue the embarkation, which leaves the 8th, 31st and 33rd Regt. to be embarked the first favourable opportunity.'[61] Abercromby requested that the *Commerce de Marseilles'* convoy should be ordered to Cowes Roads to enable their ship-bound troops to land

A typical ship of the line of 1760. (C. McCutcheon)

occasionally on the Isle of Wight. Christian was aware of the difficulty of watering and victualling them at that anchorage and 'did not fail to urge it to the General, but the possibility of desertion was to be considered and guarded against.'[62]

Troops which had embarked on transports on the River Thames were held up trying to get round the Downs (the coastal area east of Kent) and into the English Channel. 'The weather is ... much against us', wrote Charles Patton, the Commissioner of Transports at Portsmouth.[63] The foreign troops were to be similarly delayed from Germany: 'The weather has been so very violent that it has been out of my power to get the ships [hired] from Hamburgh to this place,' wrote Capt. Home Popham, the Commissioner for Transports at Stade, on the River Elbe.[64]

With all the problems at Cork, it became clear that they would not be ready to leave at the same time as the Portsmouth contingent. Christian had been directed to send the frigate *Leda* to Cork to escort the Bristol trade to the Leeward Islands (see p.53) and he requested that regiments boarded on transports at Cork and ready to leave should go in this trade convoy. Both Christian and Abercromby asked that Abercromby should take over the Cork contingent but the request was refused.[65]

During these operations, Christian fell out with Transport Commissioner Schank at Portsmouth over his tardiness in sending the transports with the troops embarked from Southampton to Spithead[66], Abercromby fell out with the medical officer responsible for the supplies and deployment of the hospital ships[67], and the unfortunate Dundas once again fell out with the king over the deployment of troops[68] (see also p.35).

The time passed by and still no departure date was in sight. Dundas wrote a letter of acute exasperation to Abercromby at the number of departure deadlines which had been passed, in which he abandoned his normal cold politeness and reserve: 'I cannot express to you the vexation [your letter] gives me. Having undergone all the Agony I have done under the mortification of the Wind being so long contrary, I had at least the consolation of thinking that everything would be ready the first moment of a favourable wind... there must be blame somewhere...'[69]

Meanwhile, from the Caribbean, desperate reports of defeat and deadly diseases were coming in from the beleaguered Admiral Laforey: '... about eighty men have been cut to pieces in the attack of the post at Ouia [St Vincent] and only one officer escaped,' he wrote on 12 September. 'I am very apprehensive... that an attack is meditating against this island. So many stand of arms could not have been sent to St Lucia but for the purpose of being introduced here.'[70] On 1 October, he wrote that his ship, the *Majestic*, had become sickly: '... a most malignant Fever, she has now lost 110 men. I am now carrying into execution the changing of all her ballast and fumigating, washing with hot vinegar and white washing with lime her hold, where the seat of the infection is thought to lie.'[71] And again on 8 October: 'The troops under convoy of *Scipio* (sixty-four guns) [Dundas' 'stopgap' expedition in July, in which the young James Ker's regiment, the 40th, had sailed (see p.33).] arrived here on 24 Ult. [September] and the greatest part of them were immediately sent to St Vincent. An attack was made upon the Vigiee [*sic*], a strong post that gave access to the town. They gave great resistance until night. However, they evacuated it in the night, when possession was taken of it at the expence [*sic*] of 140 officers and men killed and wounded'.[72]

At last, on 3 November, Christian was able to report: 'The embarkation is this day completed.'[73] It now remained for all the transports to drop down to St Helens, Isle of Wight, from where the expedition would proceed. 'The wind is now in a proper corner,' he had written to Huskisson the day before, 'but I doubt its continuance. Most heartily shall I rejoice when we get from this place. The incessant Bustle will knock me up before I reach the West Indies ... while the Fleet continues in Port, every day starts a fresh difficulty. Abercromby is here and every hour makes me more satisfied with and attached to him. He is a truly sensible, honest man.'[74]

Indeed, the weather did continue to play fair and foul: on 4 November, a calm prevented the Second Brigade and the reserve of the army from dropping down to St Helens and Christian was still waiting for the Third, Fourth and Fifth Brigades. He directed Rear Admiral Pole in *Colossus*, together with *Impregnable*, *Lion* and *Undaunted*, to proceed to St Helens the next day with the available transports and East India ships, whilst he waited at Spithead with the rest of the ships of war for the last remaining transports.[75] Pole and his convoy proceeded on the 5th, but there was a violent gale that night.[76] The East India ships and most of the transports made it to St Helens, but Christian had to report to the Admiralty that 'one transport was sunk by the *Vengeance* getting foul of her, two went ashore and others were damaged.'[77] On the 9th, more transports arrived with ordnance and troops. Christian directed all the ships of war to drop down to St Helens. The wind had become more favourable and he was anxious to go. However, there were still ordnance transports due to arrive and artillerymen to be embarked on them 'but I shall not permit any trifling cause to delay the sailing of the Fleet with so favourable a prospect of wind and weather,' Christian wrote to Nepean.[78]

By 10 November, he would wait no longer for the Third, Fourth and Fifth Brigades, or for the ordnance transports, leaving frigates *Alcmene* and *Prompte* to wait for them at Spithead. He got 'under weigh' for St Helens, proposing to sail the following day, provided the transports had arrived at Spithead and were ready.[79]

Then another mishap occurred. The *Prince George* stranded on the Warner Shoal on her way down to St Helens and lost a cable and an anchor.[80] Christian returned to Spithead for the night. He weighed anchor again the next day. This time, forty of the troop transports and the ordnance transports were caught unawares and failed to respond to his signal to leave Spithead. He had to drop anchor again and get *Alcmene* and *Prompte* to forward them to St Helens. He was now under considerable pressure from the Admiralty to leave and promised 'every possible exertion shall be made on my part to put to sea with the transports under my order.'[81]

Problems continued to dog the expedition right up to the last minute. Gunboats *Vesuve* and *L'Eclair* were both in a bad state. *Vesuve* had no master or surgeon and was deficient in most of her stores, and *L'Eclair* was still in a very bad state of repair after she had been blown onshore in strong winds the previous month (see p.56). Christian supplied *Vesuve* with stores from the *Prince George* but *L'Eclair* was deemed unfit to proceed to sea: she was too weak to carry her load and was leaking very badly.[82] On the 14th, she was ordered back to Spithead.[83] The transport *Elizabeth* was found unfit to sail and the 127 soldiers of the 27th Regiment on board had to

Extract from the diary of John Andrews of Modbury, Devon. showing temperature, wind direction and the sharp drop in pressure over the period 15-20 November 1795. From left to right the column headings are: date; temperature; pressure at 8 a.m.; pressure at 10 p.m.; a.m. wind direction; p.m. wind direction. Also mentioned in the insert is the earthquake which struck on the 18th (see note 75 p.148). (Courtesy of the Met. Office Archive)

be transferred to *Impregnable* as the little transport ships were now so crowded they could not take on any more men.[84] There was still no sign of the delayed ordnance transports – nor had the foreign troops arrived from Germany. But then, on Sunday 15 November, the day dawned fine and clear. Conditions were right, with a north north-easterly wind, backing to north. 'Frosty morning – very fine day – Cold', wrote John Andrews, amateur weatherman of Modbury, Devon, in his diary, as he busied himself amongst his instruments. At 8.00 a.m. his barometer registered a pressure of 30.075in. (The barometric readings Andrews recorded are very significant, showing a rapid and large drop in pressure over the few days to follow). Christian lost no more time in dealing with problems or waiting for tardy transports. He gave the order to weigh anchor. Ships *Alcmene* and *Prompte* would stay behind and escort the latecomers.[85] Anything which arrived after they had gone would have to have escorts provided for them by Schank.[86]

'At seven this morning I made the signal and weighed,' Christian wrote to Nepean on board the *Prince George* off Dunnose, Isle of Wight. 'The Raft ship and some other transports had not last night arrived which I am much to regret but considering the very great importance of the sailing of this Force and the favourable opportunity of wind which is now at north north-east, I trust I shall stand acquitted to Their Lordships for having ventured to proceed to sea without being assured that all the transports had joined.'[87] He also wrote to Huskisson at the War Office: 'This morning at dawn of day I made the signal. The wind is favourable and has the appearance of continuing so but the transports are yet at anchor ... having begun so early I think they will all be out before long ... All frigates are ... pressing them forward.'[88]

With Christian on board the *Prince George* were Abercromby and the French royalist former Governor and commander-in-chief of the French Antilles, the

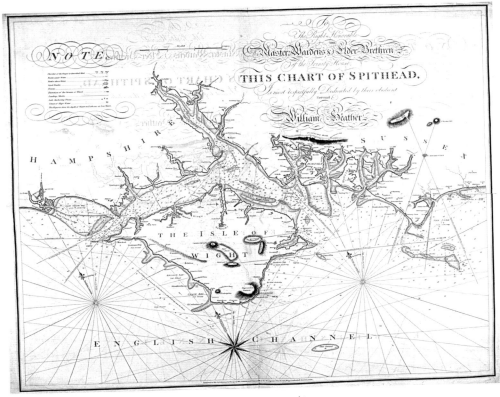

Chart of Spithead, 1797. (Royal Naval Museum, Porstmouth)

Marquis de Bouille, and, in keeping with the practice of bundling as many troops and men as possible onto the ships of war, a party of shipwrights had been boarded on the *Prince George*, bound for the shipyard at Martinique.[89] Their inclusion would prove providential.

'Hove to, the Convoy getting underweigh, *Albicore* [*sic*] and *Undaunted* signalled to keep the Convoy within limits,' recorded the captain's log of the *Prince George*.[90] Slowly, the vast convoy made its way out into the Channel. Hundreds of sails unfurled and filled with the favourable wind. Pennants and signal flags were flying as crews rushed about hauling cables, slipping them from ships' moorings, while anchors broke the surface and splashed from the sea. In the confusion, the frigate *Undaunted* collided with the East Indiaman *Middlesex* and tore her bowsprit off. Christian immediately ordered *Middlesex*'s captain to get the damage repaired and rejoin him as quickly as possible.[91]

'The long expected day is at length arrived, when our proud fleet swells its lofty sails to seek the enemy,' wrote Dr George Pinckard on board the hospital ship *Ulysses*. *Ulysses* was to remain behind in order to join the Cork contingent, which was by now so badly behind in its preparations that it would not be joining Christian, but would be sailing at a later date. This gave the doctor ample opportunity to enjoy the spectacle of the fleet departing and he waxed lyrical in his diary:

The day being fine and the wind from a friendly quarter, the picture was beautiful, as it was grand and animated. On passing round, or, to use the sailor's term, on doubling the point of the Isle of Wight, all the ships seemed to fall into regular succession, forming a line of numberless extent, each elevating her sails into view over the territory of the island as though ... striving to rival the clouds ... It was a pleasing spectacle to every beholder and those who felt as Englishmen ought, derived from it sensations peculiarly grateful. To witness such a fleet full-swelling from our little island into the broad ocean to fight our battles in a far distant country, conveyed ideas of greatness and power, which were calculated to raise a just ambition in every British bosom.[92]

'A more beautiful sight than it exhibited cannot be imagined ...,' wrote Charlotte Smith, '... as that which Englishmen have the greatest pride and pleasure in beholding.'[93]

'[The] convoy [is] coming out,' reported the log of the *Prince George.*[94] Amongst this two-hundred-strong fleet sailed the six small West India ships which were shortly to meet their doom. They were:

The *Aeolus*, 316 tons, a merchant ship of Whitby, owner George Browne, Masters Francis Mead and Isaac Duck. In service to the government since the beginning of the war, she had returned from the West Indies in October with invalid soldiers and had been captured en route by a French corvette. She was released on a promise to exchange an equal number of French prisoners. This time she was laden with timber – masts, 'deals' (planks) and other naval stores, some say with gunboats.[95] She had on board a master, fifteen seamen; a navy lieutenant, Lt Mason, who was also an agent for transports and his brother, a midshipman.

The *Piedmont*, 243 tons, owned by Alexander Davison, Master Robert Frazer. She had on board 138 soldiers of the 63rd Regiment; their captain, Ambrose William Barcroft; his fellow officers Lt Lovett Ashe and Surgeon Luke Kelly; Sgt Richardson and Fifer Ensor. Ashe had been promoted to lieutenant from ensign in September and Luke Kelly, formerly a hospital mate, had been promoted only the previous month to surgeon.[96] The *Piedmont* was a 'very bad vessel', according to Barcroft, and he had tried to get her changed, but, as there were never enough transports available, the unseaworthy *Piedmont* had set out to sea once again.[97]

The *Catherine*, 253 tons, a cavalry transport, owned by George Browne, Master Alex Jolly and Master Cromey. She had on board twenty-three soldiers of the 26th Light Dragoons, including the American Loyalist Cornet Stukeley Burns; Mr Dodd, surgeon, of the hospital staff; two officers of the newly-formed West India Regiments: Lt Stains of the 2nd (Myer's) and Lt Stephen Jenner of the 6th (Whitelocke's); three women, including Burns' wife; twelve seamen; a cabin boy and twenty-eight horses of the Light Dragoons.

The *Golden Grove*, 284 tons, a merchantman bound for St Kitts, laden with bale goods. On board were Capt. William Hodgzard; Lt-Col. Andrew Ross of the 21st Regiment; Dr Stevens of St Kitts and Mr Burows; the master, Robert Bagg; seventeen seamen and two boys.

The *Venus*, 200 tons, hired by Campbell & Co., 8 October 1795. She was an invalid ship, having on board invalid soldiers from the various regiments, several soldiers of the 115th and members of the hospital staff. Also on board were Maj. John Charles Ker, Military Commandant of Hospitals in the Leeward Islands; his son Lt James Ker of 40th Regiment; Lts James Sutherland and Benjamin Chadwick of the 1st West India Regiment (Whyte's); Cornet Benjamin Graydon of the 3rd (Keppel's); John Darley of the hospital staff; Sgt-Maj. Hearne; Capt. Kidd the master and his wife; three other women and twelve seamen.

The *Thomas* of London, some 350 tons, a merchant ship bound for Oporto, laden with bale goods and logwood. On board were the master, Thomas Brown and his son; eleven seamen; the ship's mate; a surgeon; two other male passengers and three women passengers.[98]

'The *Prince George* is nearly without the Buoys',[99] '...and most of the transports following her,' reported Christian.[100] At 2.00 p.m., the order was given to bear up and stand out. Once in the Channel, the convoy altered course to starboard in succession, steering west by north.[101] Very early in the evening, the wind turned northerly.[102] As darkness fell they passed the Needles, at the western tip of the Isle of Wight, and *Alcmene* was signalled to keep ahead during the night and look out.[103]

On board the *Prince George* Christian wrote to Huskisson:

> I am so much jaded that in truth I want the comfort of being at sea … The General is perfectly well, so are all and I trust we shall all do well. Zeal and attention will not be wanting anywhere.
>
> In truth', he had written earlier, 'so much has been done for us that we ought to be satisfied and turn our thoughts and determination to do something with it. I hope to God we shall – and to good effect. I have a presentiment that we shall do so.
>
> Adieu. Your obliged Friend, Hugh Christian. PS – Remember me kindly to Nepean, altho' he has not sent my drafts of Point a Petre [sic]. [Maps passed on to Christian by Admiral Jervis.][104]

'We were about to proceed to a distant climate with one of the most powerful armaments that has ever quitted the British shore,' wrote ship's mate William Dillon, on board the *Prince George*. 'Altogether, the ship had more the appearance of Noah's Ark than a Man of War ... she was deeply loaded.'[105]

'There are upwards of twenty-one thousand troops on board the transports,' reported *The Times* and *Salisbury Journal*, somewhat erroneously, 'and it is altogether the most formidable armament that has been sent out to that part of the world since the American War.'[106]

Altogether 18,740 men, thousands of tons of armaments and stores, and some two hundred ships sailed with Christian that day.[107] The biggest single, long-distance expedition to leave British shores had finally begun.[108]

Chapter 6

Storm

From Portland to the Needles is eleven leagues east by north, from them to St Helens, eleven leagues east... from Portland to Torbay is thirteen leagues south-west ...
(John Hutchins, *The History and Antiquities of the County of Dorset*)[1]

The following morning, Monday 16 November, saw Christian's fleet heading west, along the Dorset coast, in fine weather with a light north-westerly breeze.[2] 'Light breezes and clear,' recorded the log of *Colossus*, '170 sail in company.'[3] Christian noticed, however, that 'the sky had an appearance of uncertainty'. With Portland Bill in sight some eighteen miles to the north-west, thin whisps of cloud streaking over from the south-west would have given the sign of approaching trouble.[4] Christian signalled his squadron to keep the convoy within limits and decided that, if the weather should change unfavourably, they would tack to starboard and make for the anchorage of Torbay in Devon.[5] The frigate *Alcmene* was signalled to look out to the west and south and the gunboat *Terror* fired a shot at the transport *Jamaica* and store ship *Adventure*, which were starting to stray, to keep them within limits.[6]

Further down the convoy, the transport *Catherine* came within sight of the Isle of Purbeck. On board, Lt Stephen Jenner pointed out to his fellow passengers the rocks at Seacombe Bay, on which the East Indiaman, the *Halsewell*, had struck in 1786, and which the king had looked on in sadness six years previously (see p. 41). Jenner had boarded the *Catherine* by luck – as he thought. When he arrived at Southampton, she had already sailed for St Helens. At Southampton, he met Cornet Stukeley Burns of the 26th Light Dragoons, who was due to embark on the cavalry transport *Fowler*, and had already boarded his horse upon her.[7] Burns and his wife decided to board the more comfortable *Catherine* with Jenner, so they hastily hired a hoy to catch her up (smaller craft were constantly passing from ships to shore with messages, men and stores). Once on board *Catherine*, Jenner wrote to his mother how fortunate they had been to have caught up with her.[8]

By evening, the foremost part of the convoy was south-west of Portland. A hundred and sixty-five ships were in sight from the *Prince George*.[9] The north-westerly wind was strengthening and the size of the waves would also have increased. Christian gave the order to stand off on the starboard tack.[10] *Alcmene* fired a shot at the transport *Golden Grove* which was straying from the convoy, and the general signal was given to prepare to tack after the close of day. *Babet* was signalled to keep ahead during the night and carry a light.[11]

'The Evening was such as to mark evident signs of an Approaching Gale ...' Extract from Christian's letter of 18 November 1795. (Public Record Office, ADM/1/317)

By 2.00 a.m. the following morning, Tuesday 17th, the wind had increased and cloud had rolled over. A thick, drizzling rain began to fall. Christian decided to make for Torbay. With his fleet now standing to the west of Portland, in Lyme Bay, he gave orders to tack and stand to the north.[12] Then, in the dark, an accident occurred to *Alcmene*: 'Tacked to the Northward. At ½ past 3, the *True Briton* ran foul of us, carried away our gangway stantion [sic], Fife rail, stove the launch and several guns on the Larboard [port] side of the main deck and broke five or six half ports ... Carpenters employed repairing the damage,' her log recorded.[13]

Daylight broke, and it was still cloudy. One hundred and sixty-five ships were in sight from the *Prince George* as she now headed north-west, up towards Torbay. At noon, they sighted Berry Head (the promontory which forms the southern point of Torbay) eighteen miles to the north-west. The wind by now had backed to the west and blew so hard it headed *Prince George* off the land.[14]

'Fresh Breezes and Squally,' recorded *Prince George*'s log in the afternoon.[15] The sea became rougher. The little transports, overburdened and with less sail-power than the navy ships, started to lag and the convoy began to stretch out several miles behind. The *Prince George* signalled the rearmost ships to make more sail but, underpowered as they were, they could not keep up and started to lose their places in the convoy.[16] The wind became even stronger and hit the struggling ships in squalls. The sea became more turbulent. Christian knew that the ships of war and the big East India ships could reach the shelter of Torbay but the small, struggling transports were by now so far behind, they would not get there by the close of day. He decided that, if the transports had not made enough progress by the afternoon, the convoy would tack again and stand out once more to the south-west.[17] He would stay out with his convoy and face the storm.

The afternoon brought no improvement. The squalls and rain continued. One transport had lost her bowsprit.[18] Another had got into serious difficulty and was lagging far behind. At 4.00 p.m. Christian gave the order to tack again and stand out to the south-west. He signalled *Alcmene* to pass within hail and sent a message by boat to her, detailing her to go to the assistance of the leeward-most transports and to tow the one in difficulty. The *Prince George* signalled the squadron to collect the transports and keep the convoy in company, and the rendezvous signal was made for Torbay.[19]

Berry Head now lay some nine miles to the south-west of the *Prince George*. Night was falling and darkness was closing in, with fresh gales, squalls and rain. 'The evening was such as to mark evident signs of an approaching Gale', wrote Christian to the Admiralty. *Babet* was signalled to keep ahead during the night and carry a light.[20]

On board the *Catherine*, the master came below deck to warn his passengers, who were already feeling the ill effects of a rough sea, of the impending storm. They struggled up on deck and into the gale-force winds to see the approaching storm for themselves. Mrs Burns noticed that, to the west, the sky was 'scumbled and red, with great heavy clouds flying in all directions,' while, to the east, the moon was shrouded in a dull mist.[21] Jenner's previous experience as a marine officer warned him that the storm which lay ahead was a big one.

Further down the convoy, Capt. Drury of the *Alfred* had seen the *Prince George*'s rendezvous signal for Torbay, but the raging wind prevented him from carrying the necessary sail to reach there. He gave orders to bear up for Portland, collecting and taking as many of the transports as possible with him.

In the gathering darkness and increasingly heavy sea, *Alfred* went about, her sails rippling and flapping, and took with her infantry transports *Hope*, *Sally*, *Lady Jane*, victuallers *Marquis of Worcester*, *Fanny*, *Enterprise*, ordnance transports *Firm* and *Harmony*, cavalry transport *Patty*, hospital ship *Juba* and the West Indiaman *General Cuyler*.[22] In the meantime, *Alcmene* had reached the rear of the convoy and the transport in distress: 'Hauled too [*sic*] on the Starboard Tack under his Lee. At eight, strong gales,' her log recorded.[23] 'The wind backed to the Southward and soon after midnight blew hard,' wrote Christian.[24]

As the gale increased in ferocity that night, those on land who had watched the convoy pass the Dorset coast during the day, and had been filled with admiration, now feared for the safety of the ships and men.[25] At Modbury in Devon, John Andrews' barometer had dropped to 29.55in at 10.00 p.m. 'Stormy wind all night,' he recorded.[26]

At Portsmouth, Transport Commissioner Schank (who had patched up his quarrel with Christian just before he left) watched with growing concern as the storm developed, and half expected to see the fleet return, but hoped that Christian had made it to Plymouth or Torbay: '... the best place would be the large ships in Torbay and the small ones in Cattwater [*sic*]' [Plymouth], he wrote to Huskisson.[27]

The following morning, Wednesday 18 November, brought the strongest gales Christian 'ever remembered to have witnessed.'[28] The ships tossed violently in mountainous seas. A thick fog of driving rain and spindrift enveloped them, and their crews could see nothing. Nor could they hear anything but a howling, shrieking wind from the south-west and so strong, it was beating the ships backwards.[29]

Christian knew it would be impossible to continue. He had to turn back. They could make for St Helens or any intermediate port where the ships could put in out of danger. At 7.00 a.m., he gave the order to bear up and make the rendezvous signal for St Helens.[30] They had been within two miles of the shelter of Torbay yet had been unable to reach it.[31]

The *Prince George* bore up, set her foresail, split the main topsail, clewed it up, handed it and handed the mainsail. In the hurricane-force winds, orders were given to strike the mizen topmast, get the mizen topgallant mast down upon deck and balance the mizen.[32]

'Excessive hard Gales and violent Squalls with thick Weather,' recorded her log at 10.00 a.m.[33] 'At eight, bore up. At noon strong gales and thick hazey weather, none of the convoy in sight,' recorded *Albacore*.[34] 'At half past one, lost sight of the *Prince George*,' recorded *La Prompte*.[35] 'Hard gales and squally with rain,' recorded *Alcmene*, as she struggled at the rear of the convoy. She, too, had abandoned the effort to reached Torbay: '...ship labouring much. Standing into Portland Bay under Storm Stay Sails and Fore Sails,' her log reported.[36] For a moment the fog and spindrift lifted and *Colossus*, *Irresistible* and several of the transports were seen astern of the *Prince George* and inshore, to the north.[37]

The transports were desperately struggling to keep with the squadron and be led to safety, but five of them and a merchantman had become lost in the fog. Although they had nothing to steer by, their masters were confident that they had sea room enough. But they were unaware that they had become trapped in Lyme Bay, unable to clear Portland Bill. And the hurricane-force winds were now blowing them directly towards the Chesil – a dreaded lee shore.[38] The *Alfred*, meanwhile, had successfully rounded Portland Bill with her collection of transports and was heading north for Portland Roads, up the east side of Portland, sheltered from the wind by the island. However, in luffing round the north-east end, *Alfred* caught the wind again and a sudden squall split the main topsail and fore topmost staysails. 'Standing for Portland Roads... came too [*sic*] with our best Bower [anchor], but that not bringing her up, let go the small Bower. Struck lower yards. Employed putting the ship to rights,' recorded the ship's log.[39]

Earlier, at daylight, Drury had seen several ships to the south which had been before him in the convoy, now heading east. He realised that Christian must have changed direction to stay out with the convoy, but he decided nevertheless to continue for the shelter of Portland Roads.[40] To the west of Portland, Lyme Bay had now become a maelstrom of howling hurricane-force winds and driving rain, with a thick fog of seaspray. Mountainously high waves lashed the Chesil, leaving a thick white line of heaving surf. With an enormous roar, the sea sucked thousands of pebbles down in its powerful undertow. In such conditions, the lost transports were doomed. At about 10.00 a.m., the *Aeolus*, borne on the crest of waves the height of a house, was rushed towards the Chesil, south-east of the Passage House (the old ferry to Portland). Her crew, utterly helpless, could do nothing but cling, terrified, to any support on deck as *Aeolus* was sucked back and thrown repeatedly onto the beach. Again and again she struck, splintering and breaking with each blow.

Local people had rushed down onto the beach, well aware that such a great storm usually brought a windfall of goods and cargo, to be gathered up by them and hastily carried away. Scavenging of this sort was a capital offence but it was part of life to the people of Portland and, indeed, many of the poor relied on wrecked cargo in order to live.[41] So steeply does the beach shelve, they could stand only fifty yards or so from the furious sea and the stricken ship, without danger. Some of *Aeolus'* terrified crew attempted to jump onto the beach each time she struck. They were overwhelmed by the next gigantic wave which came crashing over them, were sucked away, and disappeared into the roaring undertow.

The local people shouted to the crew to stay on board. They could see that *Aeolus* would eventually be beached and that her crew would be able to get off in safety, but so great was the howling of the wind that it was impossible for them to make themselves heard. They resorted to picking up pebbles off the beach and throwing them at the crew, shaking their fists at them and shouting 'Keep back! Keep back!'[42] And indeed, *Aeolus*, about 500 tons laden, *was* lifted by a gigantic wave and thrown onto the beach with a final, great crash, where she lay on her side. The terrified and exhausted crew struggled down onto the beach, while the locals swarmed round to scavenge what they could.

Up at the army summer camp on South Down at Weymouth, the South Gloucesters were taking a battering in their tents, sitting out the storm. At about

The Look-Out at Weymouth, 1790 (now the Nothe Fort) from where *Aeolus* was first sghted. In the background, Portland and the Chesil where *Aeolus* struck. (Dorset County Museum)

11.00 a.m., a naval lieutenant rushed into the camp to tell them that a frigate had run aground on the Chesil. The lieutenant was aware of the plundering nature of the local people and was anxious that the ship and her crew should be protected. The regiment's Maj. Austin immediately organised a guard of men to march to the Chesil, saying he would go with them himself. The regimental surgeon, Lt William Shrapnell, had never seen a shipwreck before and his curiosity was aroused. He asked to go with them. He was unaware at the time how much his services would be needed.[43]

With Austin and Shrapnell, the guard, under Capt. Symonds, marched three miles through the storm-force winds towards Portland. When they rounded the bend at Sandsfoot Castle which turns directly to the west, they were knocked back by the force of the wind and they could only continue bent forward.[44]

They arrived at the ferry at Smallmouth and saw the masts of *Aeolus* sticking up above the Chesil, to their right. Suddenly, as they watched, another mast appeared obliquely above the Bank, and sank down again quickly. They hastily took the rope-drawn ferry across Smallmouth and arrived over the top of the Chesil to see *Aeolus* lying on her side with the waves still crashing over her and people rushing around, mixing with the confused and injured crew, gathering up the cargo which had spilled from the stricken ship. Austin's men moved in to make order.

LOSS OF THE CATHERINE AND FIVE OTHER VESSELS.

Mrs Burns on the broken *Catherine*, from *Chronicles of the Sea*, 1838. (By permission of the British Library, Shelfmark 88076D26)

It was soon learned that *Aeolus* was not a frigate but a merchant ship in the service of the government and that the local people, whilst not entirely innocent of plunder, had in fact assisted many of the crew to escape safely – as a letter subsequently written to the local newspaper by some of the crewmembers testified.[45]

At this point, Lt-Col. Ross of the 21st Regiment, who had been on board the *Golden Grove* transport, struggled over the beach to make himself known to Austin and Shrapnell. They then realised that the mast they had seen rising and falling suddenly above the Chesil had been that of the *Golden Grove* as she made her one, fatal, impact with the beach and sank immediately. Ross had managed to jump to safety with seventeen of the crew. The rest had perished, along with passengers Dr Stevens of St Kitts, Mr Burrows and two boys.

Shrapnell was shocked at the extent of the destruction and injury he saw. He set about helping the injured survivors. Whilst doing so, he did, however, receive one pleasant and welcome surprise: he met his professional colleague and friend Mr Bryer, the surgeon from Weymouth, who was also attending the injured.[46] The two men worked together to help the casualties while Austin's men kept order. All were unaware at the time that, four miles further up the beach, a scene of even greater destruction and death was unfolding.

Four miles to the north-west, on board the *Catherine*, her master Cromey and his crew were in the same desperate situation as *Aeolus* and the *Golden Grove* had been. Lost in thick fog, and borne aloft on gigantic waves, they suddenly heard breakers pounding onto a beach and the roar of an undertow. The *Catherine* was being rushed towards the Chesil and there was nothing they could do about it. A later report, by Capt. Drury of the *Alfred*, suggests that she may have tried, in vain, to anchor.[47]

A ship's mate rushed below deck to warn the passengers, most of whom were still lying in bed, too tired and ill to move from the night's storm. 'Save yourselves!' he cried, 'Save yourselves – if you can!'[48] The weary passengers struggled to their feet, hastily threw on what garments they could find and went up on deck.

An account of what happened next by a survivor, the wife of Cornet Stukeley Burns, was recorded by the writer Charlotte Smith:

It was about ten o'clock in the morning of the Eighteenth when the Mate looked down into the cabin and cried: 'Save yourselves, if you can!' The consternation and terror of that moment cannot be described: I had a loose dressing gown on and, wrapping it round me, I went up, not quite on the deck but to the top of the stairs, from whence I saw the sea break mountains high against the shore, while the passengers and soldiers seemed thunderstruck by the sense of immediate and inevitable danger; and the seamen, too conscious of the hopelessness of any exertion, stood in speechless agony, certain that in a few minutes they must meet the destruction which menaced them. While I thus stood surveying, in that kind of dread that no words can convey an idea of, the scene around me, Mr Burns who was near me and had come up in his shirt, called to Mr Jenner and Mr Stains for his cloak. Nobody, however, could attend to anything in such a moment but their own preservation.

Mr Jenner, Mr Stains and Mr Dodd the Surgeon now passed me. Their countenances sufficiently expressed their sense of the situation we were all in. Mr Burns spoke cheerfully to me;

he bade me take courage – and Mr Jenner observed there was a good shore near and all would do well.

The gentlemen then went to the side of the ship with the intention, as I believe, of seeing if it was possible to get on shore. The Master of the ship alone remained near the companion [stairs], when suddenly a tremendous wave broke over the ship and struck me with such violence that I was for a moment stunned and, before I could recover myself, the ship struck with a force so great as to throw me from the stairs down into the cabin, the Master of the vessel being thrown down with me. At the same moment, the cabin, with a dreadful crash, broke in upon us and beams and planks threatened to bury us in ruins. The Master, however, recovered himself. He left me to go again upon deck and I saw him no more.

A sense of my condition lent me strength to disengage myself from the boards and fragments that surrounded me and I once more got up the stairs I hardly know how. But what a scene did I behold! The masts were all lying across the shattered remains of the deck and no living creature appeared on it – all were gone! I knew not then that they were gone for ever. I looked forward to the shore but there I could see nothing except the dreadful surf that broke against it while behind the ship immense black waves rose like tremendous ruins. I knew that they must overwhelm the ship and thought there could be no escape for me.

Believing my death immediate and unavoidable, my idea was to regain my bed in the cabin and there, resigning myself to the will of God, await the moment that was approaching. I could not, however, reach my bed and was awhile insensible. Then the violent striking and breaking up of the wreck roused me again to recollection. I found myself near the cabin window, but the water was rising round me. It increased rapidly and the horrors of drowning were present to me – yet I remember seeing the furniture of the cabin floating about.

I sat almost enclosed by pieces of the wreck and the water now reached my breast. The bruises I had received made every exertion extremely difficult and my loose gown was so entangled among the beams and pieces of the ship that I could not disengage it.

Still the desire of life, the hope of being welcomed on shore, whither I thought my friends had escaped, and the remembrance of my child all united to give me courage to attempt saving myself. I again tried to loosen my gown but found it impossible. The wreck continued to strike so violently, and the ruins to close so much more around me that I now expected to be crushed to death.

The water, as the ship drifted higher on the stones, rather lessened as the waves went back, but, on their return, continued to cover me and I once or twice held my breath and, for a moment, my recollection. When I had power to think, the principle of self-preservation still urged to me to exertion. The cabin now broke more and more.

Through a large breach I saw the shore very near me and, amidst the tumult of the raging waves that dashed upon it, I had a glimpse of the people who were gathering up what the sea drove towards them. I thought they could not see me and from them I despaired of assistance. I therefore determined to make one effort to preserve my life. I disengaged my arms from the dressing gown and finding myself able to move, I quitted the wreck and felt myself on the ground. I attempted to run but was too feeble to save myself from a raging wave that overtook and overwhelmed me. Then I believed myself gone, yet, half-suffocated as I was, I struggled very much and I remember I thought I was very long dying. The wave left me – I breathed again and made another attempt to get higher upon the bank, but then, quite exhausted, I fell down and my senses forsook me.

By this time, some of the people on the bank saw me and two men came to my assistance. They lifted me up. I once more recovered some faint recollection. As they bore me along, one of them said the sea would overtake us, that he must let me go and take care of his own life. (This man, it is believed, saw at that moment a quantity of goods driven on shore which he wished to share and therefore would have left the poor sufferer to her fate.) I only remember clinging to the other, and imploring him not to leave me to the merciless waves.

But I have a very confused idea of what passed till I saw the boat which I was to be put into, to cross the Fleet water. I had then only strength to say 'For God's sake, do not take me to sea again.' I believe the apprehension of it, added to my other sufferings, helped to deprive me of all further sensibility, for I have not the least recollection of anything afterwards till I was roused by the remedies applied to restore me in the farmhouse where I was carried and heard round me a number of women who asked me a great many questions which I was unable to answer. I remember hearing one say I was a French woman, another that I was a negro and I was so bruised and in such a disfigured condition that the conjectures of these people were not surprising.

When I recovered some degree of confused recollection and was able to speak, I begged they would let me go to a bed. I did not ask this with any expectation of life, for I was now in such a state of suffering that my only wish was to be allowed to lie down in peace and die.

[The *Hampshire Chronicle* reported that she remained for several days 'delirious, at times waking to a recollection of her situation, only to add to her misery.'[49]]

Nothing could exceed the humanity of Mr Abbot, the inhabitants of Fleet Farm House, nor the compassionate attention of his sister Miss Abbot, who not only afforded me immediate assistance but continued for some days after I got to Weymouth to attend me with such kindness and humanity as I shall always remember with the sincerest gratitude.[50]

A 28-gun ship of the line of 1794. (C. McCutcheon)

Mr Abbot and his sister sent immediately for Mr Bryer, the surgeon at Weymouth, to attend Mrs Burns' dreadful injuries.

Shrapnell recalled seeing the wreck of the *Catherine* the following day: 'She was driven very far on the land. I saw [her] whole stern windows but, in a few hours, they were broken up for the iron ... the other parts of the ship were dashed to atoms.'[51]

Mrs Burns and a young cabin boy were the only survivors of the *Catherine*. The boy had been swept off the deck by the great wave which had knocked her and the master down the companion stairs. He scrambled desperately up the beach, and, from the safety of the summit, watched the *Catherine* being smashed to pieces in the waves below.[52] Twenty-two soldiers of the 26th Light Dragoons, two soldiers' wives, twelve seamen and all the horses drowned. The officers lost were Lt Stains of the 2nd West India Regt., Lt Stephen Jenner of the 6th, Cornet Stukeley Burns of the 26th Light Dragoons and Mr Dodd of the Hospital Staff.[53]

Now the same terrible fate lay in store for the troop transport *Piedmont* and 138 soldiers of the 63rd Regiment, their captain, Ambrose William Barcroft, Lt Lovett Ashe and Surgeon Luke Kelly. Those on the shore could hear their pitiful cries above the roar of wind and waves. All save Sgt Richardson and eleven privates lost their lives, either in trying to jump to safety or when the *Piedmont* was dashed to pieces on the beach. Four of the crew were saved – the rest lost. In trying to jump to the shore, one old soldier had his leg broken and crushed by a piece of the smashed ship. In agony, he dragged himself up and over the summit of the beach and took shelter under an upturned fishing boat by the Fleet water. A fifer named Ensor jumped – and found himself unhurt. Running in terror from the sea, he suddenly swung back again and rushed back down the beach to try and save his wife. He plunged into the sea – and was never seen again.[54]

Next in this macabre sequence it was the turn of the invalid transport *Venus*. She struck the beach and went to pieces, taking down with her most of the seventy-four invalid soldiers on board, the passengers and crew. Maj. John Charles Ker, the new Commandant of Military Hospitals in the Leeward Islands, was drowned, together with his son Lt James Ker of the 40th. The ship's master, Thomas Kidd, and his wife; three officers from the West India regiments: Lts James Sutherland and Benjamin Chadwick (of the 1st), Cornet Benjamin Graydon (3rd); three women passengers and eight crew were also drowned. Those saved were Sgt-Maj. Hearne, twelve soldiers, four seamen, a boy, and John Darley, a hospital mate.

Darley must have been a strong man. He disappeared right under the broken, sinking *Venus* yet still managed to haul himself out from the waves that sucked him and the drowning victims down, and drag himself up the beach. Exhausted, he fell at the top of the bank, where he looked down the landward side and saw the Fleet, and the many little boats passing to and fro over it to the mainland, carrying salvaged cargo, tightly held in the arms of those who had found it. He went down and asked a boatman to row him and other survivors from the *Venus* across to the mainland. The boatman initially refused – so busy were they ferrying their booty across the Fleet that they had no time for soaked and cold survivors – but changed his mind in the face of considerable, probably physical, persuasion from Darley, and rowed them over.[55]

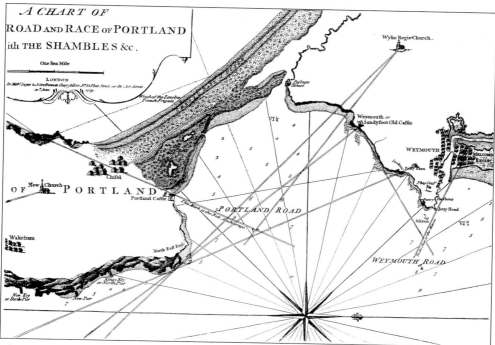

Chart of Portland Roads, 1779. (Dorset Record Office)

Finally, the merchant ship *Thomas*, bound for Oporto with bail goods, logwood and 'coppera' (probably 'copperas', another name for ferrous sulphate, used for water purification) struck the Chesil, east of the other ships.[56] Her master, Thomas Brown, and his son had been swept off the deck into the sea by huge waves.[57] The mate and four seamen had jumped to safety, but all the other passengers drowned, save one, a boy by the name of Smith, a fifteen-year-old, on his way to Oporto to collect letters from his parents in the East Indies.[58] Smith was left all alone on the ship, paralysed with fear and unable to jump, as the ship tossed violently in the mountainous waves and broke up around him. The terrified boy finally screwed up his courage and jumped with the next big wave that sent the *Thomas* crashing and splintering onto the beach. He made the beach and scrambled up to safety. Again, Charlotte Smith takes up the story:

Weakened as he was, and encumbered with his wet cloaths [sic], he got on the other side of the stony bank … On looking around him over the dreary beach, his first idea was that he was thrown on an uninhabited coast. At length he saw a fishing boat and, approaching it, heard the groans of the unhappy old soldier [who had crawled under it from the Piedmont] … whom he attempted to relieve. But he could do nothing alone and it was long before he saw any assistance near; till at length he perceived a man at some distance, to whom he hastened and enquired if a Surgeon could be procured for a poor creature with a broken limb, who lay under the boat.

The man shewed no great alacrity for Master Smith found it necessary to [give him] half a guinea, which he imagined would engage him to seek for a surgeon. The man pocketed the half-guinea with the greatest composure, then, saying he was a King's Officer, and must see what bales of goods were driven on shore, he hastened away without giving himself any farther trouble than telling Master Smith that there was a ferry about four miles off by which he might get to Weymouth.[59]

A four-mile walk on shifting shingle would have been exceptionally arduous in any conditions – in these, it must have been dreadful. In the driving rain and bitter cold wind, the young Smith trudged east towards the Passage House, near where the *Aeolus* had been beached. He arrived, soaked and exhausted, a very pathetic sight indeed. There, Lt Richard Wilkinson, master of the local Revenue Cutter *Greyhound*, who had come down to keep an eye on the crowd around the *Aeolus*, took pity on the boy, took him home and looked after him.[60] The old soldier of the 63rd died alone and in agony, under the upturned boat.[61]

In the meantime, Shrapnell and Bryer had left the *Aeolus* and returned to Weymouth, having done all they could for the injured seamen, and feeling themselves unable to withstand any further the cold wind and rain. As soon as he arrived back, Bryer was summoned to the Fleet Farmhouse, 'to attend a Lady who was saved from one of the ships, and sheltered' there. It was, of course, Mrs Burns. On his way to the farmhouse, Bryer came across several survivors from the other ships wandering on the road, soaked and exhausted – some severely injured. He billeted them in cottages at Chickerell and other villages nearby. His partner, Mr Warne, who was Agent for the Board of Sick and Hurt Seamen, sent them clothes and procured lodgings for John Darley, the hospital mate from the *Venus*. Bryer sent Darley to Shrapnell, who was happy to 'offer [his] feeble assistance'. Shrapnell also befriended the young boy Smith, who survived the *Thomas*: 'I was with him a good deal during his stay at Weymouth and was much pleas'd with his interesting observations. His forward mind at the age of fifteen was much superior to his years, and his affecting

'Lost a Man Overboard ...' Extract from log of the *Prince George*, Wednesday 18 November. (Public Record Office, ADM/1/317)

tale endeared him to the respectable Inhabitants of this place ... his Father and Mother are in the East Indies and his journey to Oporto was with the view of meeting letters from them. He is Nephew to Mr Orme, who wrote the History of Indostan...'.[62]

Back at Portland, Capt. Drury on board the *Alfred* had reached the anchorage of Portland Roads, with the transports he had collected. Most of them were badly damaged: torn sails, broken tackle and timbers – some with their sails blown clean away. He was soon joined by Capt. Brown on the *Alcmene*, who arrived bringing other transports, all substantially damaged: 'At 10 came to in Portland Roads with the best bower in 8 fathoms water ... came in here and anchored HM ship *Alfred* with eight sail of the Convoy,' recorded *Alcmene's* log. Brown had seen the *Prince George* stand out to the south the previous evening and had also seen the rendezvous signal for St Helens that morning, so he was able to confirm to Drury that Christian had indeed changed orders and was heading back for safety.[63]

Drury and Brown had to stay at Portland for the duration of the storm, and longer – to allow the transports the time needed to repair their substantial damage. It was not long before Drury received a report that two transports had gone down on the Chesil 'at the back of Portland.' He sent an express to the Admiralty and then set about preparing a report of the ships lost and damaged that day.[64]

In the meantime, Christian was still battling with the storm at sea, where conditions were atrocious for the *Prince George* and the remainder of the convoy. They were steering south-east by south towards St Helens and the gale was increasing.[65] Many of the ships were flying signals of distress.[66]

Christian was in desperate trouble: the *Prince George's* rudder, which had been under immense strain running before the gale in heavy seas, had broken from its lower fastenings, which would have put her dangerously out of control. The rudder was striking violently against the stern post, 'shaking the whole ship in the most alarming manner.'[67] To make things worse, she had a second, iron, tiller of considerable length which was now out of control and cutting a wild swathe across the wardroom on the middle deck, lethal to anyone who came into contact with it: '... this iron machine [was] sweeping right across the ship, tearing up everything with which it came into contact,' wrote ship's mate William Dillon. 'It [was] only with extreme difficulty that we could steer her through the sea,' wrote Christian. He had to press on: 'I was constrained to haul off under such sail as the ship could carry.' 'At half past eleven, hauled to the wind, handed the Fore topsail and set Storm Staysails. Reefed the Foresail and set it,' recorded *Prince George's* log. 'Got down the Top Masts on Deck and housed the middle deck guns,' the captain's log recorded. Almost inevitably, struggling in hurricane-force conditions, another accident was to follow: some fifteen miles west of St Catherine's point, the southernmost tip of the Isle of Wight, one of the carpenter's crew, Archibald Boyle, fell overboard and was drowned.[68]

At 6.00 p.m., now in pitch darkness and with the weather continuing to be atrocious, the *Prince George* was still battling with her faulty rudder up-Channel, when she was struck by a violent squall with heavy rain. The wind, which had been south-west by south, shifted to the west north-west – and very suddenly became calm. Christian's relief was only momentary for, in that time, the rudder, which had been under strain for so long, finally broke from its fastenings and fell away into the sea.[69] 'At half past seven, lost our Rudder, and with it the Iron Tiller', recorded the ship's log.[70]

Christian ordered the crew to drop anchor immediately, haul up the foresail, bring down the staysails and make the signal of distress. Anchoring with the best bower in thirty-four fathoms (204ft), the *Prince George* veered to a whole cable's length (200yds). She fired a gun every five minutes until 8.30 p.m., when *Impregnable* passed within hail to help her. Christian directed *Impregnable*'s Capt. Thomas to anchor nearby and be prepared to take them in tow in the morning.[71]

At this point, it was the taking on of the shipwrights bound for Martinique which proved a godsend. Christian immediately ordered the ship's company to lay hands on any material they could find and construct a temporary rudder, 'upon Captain Edward Pakenham's principle', as fast as possible.[72]

In the meantime, the wind had risen again, now blowing from the west north-west.[73] In the dark, the ships were all in the greatest danger of running into each other, being on different tacks. The frigate *La Prompte* was run foul of by a three-decker, which stove in her starboard quarter gallery.[74]

The ships anchored overnight, battered by squalls and rain, until the darkness should pass and they could see by daylight the extent of the damage and the state of the convoy. One of the worst days in seafaring history had come to an end – and still they did not know what the next day would bring.[75]

Chapter 7

Aftermath

As dawn broke on Thursday 19 November, the sorry consequences of the storm were clearly visible: the convoy was scattered, ships broken and damaged, the length of the English Channel from Torbay, Devon to the Downs, off the east coast of Kent.[1] Dead bodies were washed ashore at Dover.[2]

Two transport ships, the *Hope* and the *Firm*, lay dismasted in Weymouth Bay, four others lay to the east of Weymouth: the *Hannah*, the *Harmony* (which had run foul of *Hannah*) near Hills Harbour, the *Pitt*, west of St Aldhelm's Head, and the *William Pitt* at Chapman's Pool, Isle of Purbeck.[3]

At Portsmouth, five ships were driven on shore: two with troops, two merchant ships and one cavalry transport.[4] The transport *Commerce* was totally lost on shore but her crew and passengers saved, and the transport *Britannia* was badly damaged but all hands saved. One transport was totally lost off the Isle of Wight and all lives lost save two.[5] Several transports had come into Portland Roads, some with their masts lost, others with their sails torn or blown away. Nearly all were damaged. Capt. Drury of the *Alfred* sent out boats to examine their state – *Alfred's* own main topsail yard was sprung.[6]

As for the Chesil, upon this steeply shelving bank now lay the shattered remains of the five transports and the little merchantman *Thomas*. 'The *Mary Ann*, my ship, luckily weathered it with the loss of only some of her sails, and after beating about without a single ship in sight until Thursday the 19th in hopes of getting into Torbay, I insisted upon our Master bearing away for Portland Roads in which we anchored the same evening,' wrote Lt-Col. Paget to his father, the Earl of Uxbridge.

And now prepare to hear what has come under my knowledge within the space of about ten leagues. About four leagues to the eastward of Weymouth one ship struck and is completely lost with all hands. In Portland Roads are seven or eight transports the most of which are totally dismasted. The Alfred *and* Alcmene *are both here, the former has sprung her main mast. To complete the whole I yesterday went to witness a sight that I think beats everything I ever saw before. In the bay to the westward of Portland Roads are the remains of seven [sic] transports so completely knocked to pieces by the violence of the surf that in no instance could I discover two timbers that had not been separated … You may guess my anxiety for the remainder of the Fleet … This catastrophe, I fear, will prove fatal to the grand expedition.*[7]

Still out in the Channel, some twenty-one miles south-east of Dunnose, Isle of Wight, lay Christian's flagship, the *Prince George*, at anchor and rudderless, still tossing in heavy seas. Four miles to leeward of her lay *Impregnable*, her main yard torn away.[8]

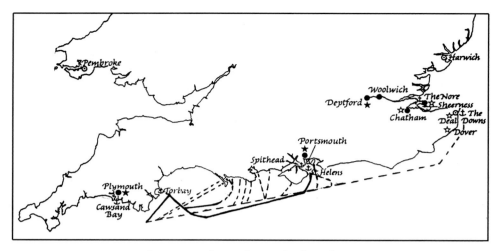

Christian's Fleet 15th – 20th November 1795

15-18 Nov. ⟵ westbound

18-20 Nov. – – – – – – – – – –

⟶ eastbound

Route of Christian's Fleet 15-20 November 1795. (*The Age of Sail*, Conway Maritime Press, 2003)

She had been run foul of by the East India ship *Sullivan*, which was also severely damaged.[9] The East India ship the *King George* had lost her mizzen mast.[10] The storm had by now somewhat abated, but there were still 'fresh breezes and squalls with rain.'[11] Only sixty-two ships were in sight.[12]

In reviewing the situation, Christian wrote: 'I venture to hope that the *Alcmene* was enabled to gain the anchorage of Portland and that the missing transports may have worked inshore and gained Torbay, or possibly have run last night for the Downs.'[13]

At Portsmouth, Schank was already making preparations for gathering up the scattered transports and bringing them back: 'I have sent a Lieutenant with orders to call at every port between this and Plymouth to give immediate assistance to any of the transports that may have met with any misfortune...', but even he was not aware of the extent of the disaster: 'I am certain they must be in Torbay,' he wrote.[14]

On board the *Prince George*, the shipwrights had been working throughout the night to fashion a new rudder but it was still not ready. As *Impregnable* was disabled, *Colossus* came forward to take the *Prince George* in tow and, at 9.00 a.m., the ships recommenced their arduous passage towards St Helens.[15]

Back at the camp at Southdown, Weymouth, Shrapnell was again visited by John Darley, the hospital mate who had survived the *Venus*. 'He was anxious to revisit the fatal spot in hopes of finding the bodyes of some of his friends and if any part of his property had been driven on shore,' wrote Shrapnell.[16] Charlotte Smith adds: 'He earnestly wished to know what had been the fate of Major Ker, and to find his body if he had perished, which could not yet be known.'[17]

Shrapnell offered to procure a horse for Darley and, in the event, both he and Bryer rode with Darley back to the beach, via the cottages in which the other survivors had been billeted.[18] In a cottage in Chickerell they found survivors of the *Piedmont*: Sgt Richardson of the 63rd Regiment, with the ten privates who had escaped with him and the one soldier from the 115th. Two of them were nursing fractured legs and almost all the rest had wounds and bruises.[19] In this house, Shrapnell also saw some women's shoes and silk stockings which had been washed up on the beach and bore the names Mrs Seilswell, Mrs Ailiff and Mrs Nash. It was not known on board which ship these women had perished. Next, they called upon Mrs Burns at the Fleet Farmhouse. She had a wound in her foot and was very badly bruised and cut.[20] Bryer attended her injuries while she gave an account of those on board the *Catherine*.[21] Then she mentioned Stephen Jenner. Shrapnell was shocked. He realised, with horror, that he had lost his friend in the storm:

> *I did not know how much I was interested in her tale untill* [sic] *her description of the officers convinced me that* [her] *Lieut. Jenner was my valuable and intimate friend, whose embarkation (being only a few days previous) I had not yet been informed of and had little suspected, as he had been but one month married to an amiable and accomplished woman.*[22]

Shrapnell undertook to try to find Mrs Burns' husband. He was also anxious to trace Jenner, and he, Darley and Bryer left for the beach, furnished with a description of Cornet Burns' distinguishing features.[23]

They crossed the Fleet water to the Chesil and came over its summit and into the roaring wind, with the sea still turbulent below. What lay before them must have been one of the most appalling sights of their lives: for a distance of two miles the beach was strewn with the wreckage of ships and the corpses of men, women, horses and other animals. In the violently tossing sea floated more bodies, the waves occasionally heaving them up onto the beach to join the others. The bodies were stripped naked of their clothes, either by the sea or by scavengers, the skin ripped and bruised. They made an horrific sight: mutilated and injured beyond recognition, some no longer had faces, so terrible was the damage of shingle and turbulent sea. And amongst these corpses, local people moved about, still scavenging implacably for goods.

> *No celebrated field of carnage ... ever presented, in proportion to its size, a more fearful sight than the Chissel* [sic] *bank now exhibited*, wrote Charlotte Smith. *The sight filled the newly-arrived spectators with grief and amazement.*
>
> *On the poor remains of these unfortunate victims death appeared in all its hideous forms and indeed the particulars cannot be given − either the sea, or the people who had at first gone down to the shore, had stripped of every article of cloaths, those who had probably ventured, or been thrown by the shocks into the water with their cloaths on, as some of the officers certainly were cloathed at the fatal moment.*[24]

Shrapnell described the sight as 'Scenes which no vicissitudes of my future life can ever erase.'[25]

Shrapnell and Bryer realised immediately that a mass burial was needed urgently, before disease could spread – the putrefaction of so many rapidly rotting corpses was too dreadful to contemplate. Together with Darley, they set about trying to identify the officers, but the bodies were so badly disfigured and barely clothed that they could hardly distinguish them from the ordinary soldiers. They had little means of identification other than by looking at their hands, those of the officers being generally smoother than the hands of those accustomed to hard labour.[26]

Shrapnell later wrote to the aunt of Capt. Barcroft, one of the victims:

> It would be painful ... and distress your mind too severely to describe a small part of the horrid shore we were about to explore. Suffice it to say that pieces of wreck and dead bodyes covered this dreary beach for an extent of two miles. We came to it about the centre and after trailing up and down each way, I singled out and marked the bodies of several officers.[27]

After their gruesome labours on the beach, Shrapnell returned to the Fleet Farmhouse to see Mrs Burns again. He had been unable to identify Burns, but 'offered her the protection of our officers and endeavoured to check her anxious mind with the promise of every comfort we could procure' – a promise which he was to fulfil handsomely.[28]

He then returned to the South Down barracks and informed Maj. Austin of the situation. After procuring the authority of a magistrate to bury the dead, Austin organised a work party of forty men to go to the beach the next day to bury the corpses. In the hope of finding Jenner's body, Shrapnell offered to command them, and Austin was 'so good as to accept [his] offer.'[29]

In the meantime, out in the English Channel, *Colossus* was south-west of Selsey Bill (the large promontory east of Portsmouth), struggling in squalls and rain north-west up towards St Helens.[30] The smaller, seventy-four-gun ship was still towing the larger *Prince George* and their progress was painfully slow. Christian wrote: 'We are now in tow of *Colossus* and standing on but, unluckily, as we near the land, the wind in squalls draws [us] off...'.[31] At 2.00 p.m., *Colossus* sprung her jib boom and had to re-set it.[32] Christian continued: 'The utmost I expect to effect this day will be to get into such a situation as to enable me with tomorrow's ebb to reach over to St Helens when the rudder may be fixed and answer the purpose of steering the ship into the harbour.'[33]

Prince George signalled *Colossus* to cast off the stream cable and anchor. She herself anchored with the small bower, veering to a third of a cable, and signalled *Trident* to shorten sail and close, stay by and attend the ships in distress.[34] They would spend another night at anchor, this time waiting upon the tide.

Ninety-five ships of the convoy had been counted that day – about one half of the total size of Christian's fleet when he left St Helens four days earlier.[35] The following morning, Friday 20th, when the flow of the tide was favourable, *Prince George* and *Colossus* weighed anchor again. They gained a more secure anchorage south-east of Dunnose and at 10.00 a.m. *Colossus* cast off the towrope. *Trident* anchored nearby while the shipwrights worked on finishing the temporary rudder.[36] By early afternoon the rudder was completed and brought to the sternpost. It was fixed successfully at 3.00 p.m. After that, the ships made their separate ways towards St Helens, no doubt much to Christian's great relief.[37] They anchored again that evening and finally came to at Spithead the following day.[38]

That same morning, Friday 20th, the first working party of the South Gloucesters arrived over the Chesil to begin burying the dead. Shrapnell wrote: 'I had been furnished with marks to distinguish the remains of Major Kerr [sic], Lieut Kerr [sic] his son, Adjutant Creighton [sic – Graydon], Lieut Jenner, Lieut Sutherland and Cornet Burns.'[39]

He was successful in finding the body of Capt. Barcroft, whom he identified by the scars of 'wounds he had received in the service of his country', in the American War of Independence.[40] 'I well remember the features and was much struck with [his] firm and manly appearance even in death,' he wrote to Barcroft's aunt, Mrs Wilson. 'The few remains of covering which the impetuosity of the waves had not divested the body were part of a black silk handkerchief round the neck, some parts of grey worsted stocking and a small remnant of trowsers [sic] or pantaloons on one leg, these were not taken off – I particularize this circumstance as most of the bodies were quite naked.' In a moment of deep respect for this man whom he had never known, Shrapnell

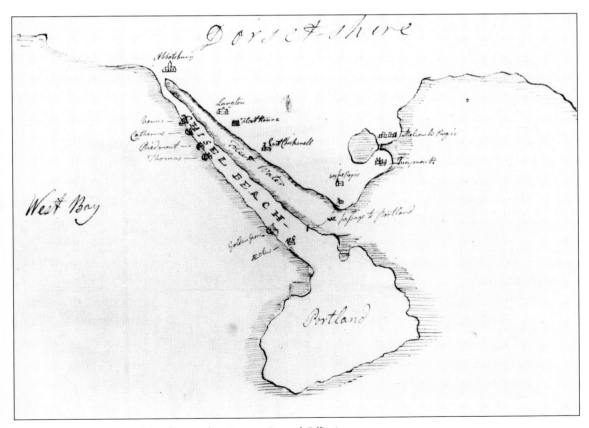

Shrapnell's plan of the shipwrecks. (Preston Record Office)

covered the nearly naked body with a scrap of sail he found nearby.[41] He continued: 'I thought his age appeared rather more than you describe but perhaps the difference from circumstances deluded my judgement.' He had cut off a lock of Barcroft's hair which he sent to her, commenting: 'You will find the hair much darker brown than the pattern [sic] you sent me, this may in some measure be owing to the sea'.[42]

For six days the South Gloucesters continued their gruesome and laborious task on the beach. Each day they struggled on six miles of shifting pebbles to reach the bodies, which lay scattered over the beach for a further two miles, then carried them up and over the summit and down to the Fleet, where they buried them by the waterside, raising a pile of stones over each grave to mark where they lay. Two hundred and eight soldiers and seamen were buried in this way. Shrapnell wrote: 'The labour I and my party have gone through, I look back upon with astonishment, but almost think it miraculous. The cause supported us.'[43]

Day after day he searched for the body of Stephen Jenner but, as the bodies were so horrifically injured, he was unable to identify his friend positively: 'I selected a body much like my friend in size, height and, as I thought, features and preserved it with the bodies of two others, which I thought resembled him also.'[44] The young Jenner's family had been devastated by the news of his death, which they received on 25 November. Stephen's father wrote to Edward Jenner: 'The situation of the poor widow is indeed truly deplorable.'[45]

The *Prince George* under tow, this time in battle. The frigate towing her is *Triton*. (Battle of the Saints, 1782) (National Maritime Museum, PAH 7816)

The bodies of Capt. Barcroft, Cornet Burns and other identifiable officers were set aside, to be buried at the local churchyard at Wyke, with military honours.[46] Mr Warne, the agent for the Sick and Hurt Board, sent twelve coffins for the bodies of women drowned, who would also be buried at Wyke. In the event, only nine women's bodies were found, so the officers of the South Gloucester clubbed together and ordered fourteen more coffins, to contain the bodies of all the seventeen officers found.[47] Capt. Barcroft's family had offered to help with the burial expenses but Shrapnell wrote to them: 'With respect to funeral expences [sic], there can be none to an individual. Private subscription from the officers of our regiment enabled us to act the part of friends when more interested relatives could not be near, however desirous, and we hope you will not repeat any further wish of this kind.'[48]

'I gave poor Mrs Burns the satisfaction that I had identified the body of her husband. His marks were so particular that nobody could be deceived,' Shrapnell wrote to Edward Jenner, 'I also found the bodies of Captain Creighton [sic – Graydon], Lt Sutherland and Lt Kerr [sic]. These we are all sure of.'[49]

The young Lt James Ker's remains were delivered up to his family, who came down to bury him separately in the churchyard at Wyke. Those of his father, Maj. John Charles Ker, were never found.

On the following Monday, the 23rd, two horse-drawn waggons went down to the side of the Fleet water and were loaded with the coffins in which the shrouded bodies had been placed. The loaded waggons made their laborious way up and over the hill to Wyke Regis church, where they were uncoupled and left outside the churchyard, under a guard, throughout the cold and gloomy November night.[50]

The funeral took place the following morning, Tuesday 24 November.

> *A party of the* [South] *Gloucester*[s], *consisting of a Captain, subaltern and fifty men, preceded the seventeen coffins; Master Smith appeared as chief mourner* [at Shrapnell's request]. *The body of Lt Ker, attended by his friends, made part of the mournful procession, which was closed by the soldiers and officers of the South Gloucester, following as is usual in military funerals.*
>
> *In a large grave, close to the north side of the tower of Wyke church, the officers were interred with military honours ... at the south-west corner were committed to the earth the remains of the nine women, whose coffins had been deposited in the church during the ... ceremony,'* Charlotte Smith wrote.[51]

Young James Ker was buried by his family near the south side of the tower. As his father's body had never been found, the family erected a memorial stone over the young man's grave commemorating both father and son.

The Rector of Wyke, Samuel Payne, recorded that he also buried Mr Dodd of the Hospital Staff, who had been on board the *Catherine*, Mr Brown, the master of the *Thomas*, and his son that day.[52]

Approximately 296 lives were lost on the Chesil that Wednesday 18 November, and some seventy-one saved.[53] (See Appendices 1 and 2, p.106.) A total of two hundred and thirty-four bodies were recovered from the beach.[54]

Meanwhile, Mrs Burns, still badly injured, remained in the care of Mr and Miss Abbot. She had, unfortunately, become the curiosity of the neighbourhood and people were continually visiting the Fleet Farmhouse to take a look at the woman who had so miraculously survived the storm. Concerned that she needed rest to recuperate, Shrapnell persuaded her to come to Weymouth. He sent a post-chaise to collect her and she was brought to the house of Dr Bryer. 'My wife and the other Ladies of the regiment, together with Mrs Bryer, were happy in rendering her any service in their power,' Shrapnell wrote to Barcroft's aunt. He continued:

> *I am sorry to say she has lost her all, has no friends living in England and Mr Burns' sister is not in a situation to afford her any assistance – Mr Burns himself was a distressed man … she has one child six months old at nurse in London. The subscription for her by the visitors and inhabitants of this place has been liberal, but can only be a temporary relief. She is young and accomplished and offers herself as the only means of permanent support to attend as companion to some lady. I heartily wish her success and am using my endeavours for that purpose amongst my friends.*[55]

Of the other survivors, Sgt Richardson of the 63rd and the soldiers who were unhurt had set out the following day by road for Portsmouth, disobeying orders to re-embark and go by sea. 'I cannot blame their terror of the sea, but I should imagine Richardson has by this time been reprimanded for his disobedience,' wrote Shrapnell.[56]

Three of the 63rd, Trigge, Bristow and Edwards, remained in Weymouth until late January. Darley, the hospital mate, had gone by December. He had been recommended to the Surgeon General and to Sir Ralph Abercromby, and Shrapnell presumed (and hoped) that he had got another appointment in the Hospital Corps.[57]

Debris from the storm continued to be washed up onto the beach for many weeks. Shrapnell recovered a seal of Cornet Burns and what he thought to be an epaulette belonging to Maj. Ker.[58] Although he tried for a long time, he was unable to identify positively anything which had belonged to Barcroft:

> *I rode yesterday to the beach accompanyed* [sic] *by some officers who were not present at the wreck. The sight called up the dreadfull* [sic] *remembrance of it … even at this distance of time* [February 1796], [the local people were] *collected together to watch the bounty of a wave at the coming in of the tide. I enquired what they had collected and the largest portion of wealth obtained by anyone that day was four leaden bullets and an old nail.* [They] *will neglect any employment in hopes of rings, watches, etc. and dreams of gold… Most of the things now thrown up are so mutilated as to be good for nothing. A set of itinerant Jews monopolised the first gleanings…*[59]

Safely anchored at Spithead on 21 November, Christian had reported the situation to the Admiralty. Reports had by now come in from *Alcmene*, *La Prompte* and many others of the disaster on the Chesil.[60] Christian commended the shipwrights on board *Prince George* for 'their great steadiness and perfect good conduct … I am in a

A 74-gun ship of the line from 1794. (C. McCutcheon)

principle [*sic*] measure to attribute the expeditious fitting of the temporary rudder to the great exertion of these men in the construction.'[61]

Further damage to the ships of war had now become apparent. The huge *Commerce de Marseilles* – marvelled at by the seamen for her size (she was 'the largest ship that had ever been seen in England') had been so overburdened with armaments, troops and stores that she was right down in the water and had been 'shaken almost to pieces' by the storm. Her 1,050 troops were transferred to four forty-four-gun ships and she was taken to Plymouth, where she was used as a receiving ship and then subsequently broken up.[62] The *Sherborne and Yeovil Mercury*, Monday, 23 November 1795 reported:

London, November 21. It is with much concern we have to announce most dreadful details of the late violent gales which are rendered the more calamitous from the temporary discomfiture which the West India expedition has consequently experienced. Yesterday morning an express arrived at the Admiralty Office from Portsmouth with an account of the loss of five transports, laden with troops for the West Indies, and of every soul on board having perished [sic]. The ships of war and the remainder of the convoy have been driven into different ports in great distress, as will be seen by our letters from Weymouth, Portsmouth, etc. This intelligence was considered of so alarming a nature by the Board that Earl Spencer, Lord Hugh Seymour and Mr Dundas set out yesterday afternoon for Portsmouth, to ascertain the nature and full extent of the misfortune.

Watercolour of Wyke Church, copied from the Chevalier de Foville, showing the officers' grave in front of the tower. (Preston Record Office)

Dundas had gone to Portsmouth to oversee repairs and get the expedition off again as soon as possible.[63] Desperate to get something of a force over to the Leeward Islands, he wrote on 23 November to Abercromby, instructing him of a change of plan: as the Cork contingent, bound for St Domingo, had been unable to sail with Christian, it should now sail as soon as possible and go direct to Barbados. There was a general anxiety that the French would get wind of the disaster and hurriedly send out fresh troops to the islands before Abercromby could get there.[64]

In the meantime, Christian had hoisted his flag on board *Irresistible* and was optimistic about reforming his squadron and putting to sea again promptly. He stressed the importance of collecting the convoy at St Helens as early as possible:

> *I ... dispatched an express to Torbay, directing the masters of all the transports at that anchorage to repair without loss of time to St Helens.*
>
> *The* Alfred, *with such transports as might be ready to accompany her, may be expected to arrive from Portland Roads this evening ... Captain Drury ... shall leave the* Alcmene *for the protection offshore* [of those vessels] *that are not immediately ready to put to sea. I am already able to account for all the convoy, a very small number excepted, and I hope in a day or two, when my returns are compleat* [sic], *I shall be able to give Their Lordships a more satisfactory account...*[65]

On 24 November, the day of the funeral at Wyke, the *Alfred* and *Alcmene* arrived, bringing the repaired ships from Portland. *Alfred* herself required a new carpenter, the other being 'sent to sick quarters without a possibility of returning'.[66] Dundas had earlier written to the Admiralty whilst Christian was struggling in the storm that, if Christian should put back to St Helens, the ordnance transports bound for Cork from there should join him and all should sail together direct to Barbados. Also, the transports with the foreign troops for St Domingo should leave with him as well, but that Christian 'must be positively instructed not to wait for them, or any other transports whatsoever,' in putting back to sea.[67]

The Admiralty instructed Christian that he was to 'avail [himself] of the earliest moment of putting to sea ... the moment wind and weather shall be such as to admit of your departure'. If his entire convoy was not ready, he was to leave the unfinished transports behind, leaving part of his squadron of naval ships to escort them later.[68]

On 30 November, Christian hoisted his flag on board the *Glory*, ninety-eight guns, and wrote to the Admiralty that 'though much retarded by unfavourable weather ... the expedition will be wholly ready tomorrow' to proceed to St Helens.[69] On 4 December, from St Helens, he reported that the wind had continued westerly and detained the squadron so long that the replacement and refitting of the transports was almost complete and it would not be necessary to leave any of the troops behind, or any part of the squadron to convoy them: '... the squadron and transports are in a state to sail, so soon after a fair wind may spring up,' he wrote.[70]

On Wednesday 9 December, Christian finally weighed anchor again: 'The wind being at north-east this morning, at eight I made the signal to weigh and stood out in the *Glory* and I have the pleasure to add that the greater part of the convoy have weighed and are now standing out to join me so that I hope to be enabled to shape a course down Channel before dark.'[71]

This time, part of the Cork contingent were ready and was ordered to move out the following day to join him.[72] His fleet was even greater than before: some 218 ships (Richardson on board *La Prompte* recorded '380 sail altogether'[73]) and nearly twenty thousand men sailed with Christian on his second voyage.[74]

And that would have been that, save for an intriguing sequel to this story – an incident which set society tongues wagging in Weymouth, caused great consternation to Shrapnell, and called upon all his qualities as an officer and a gentleman to extricate from a delicate situation the lady who had by now come to occupy a substantial amount of his attention.

Chapter 8

Scandals

On 4 January 1796, an anonymous announcement appeared on the front page of *The Times*:

> CAUTION to the Public against an IMPOSTER, who, in order to excite compassion, has personated the Widow of the late Cornet Burns. This is to inform all persons that Mrs Burns was NOT on board the ship at the time of the accident.

At the same time, a public letter was sent to John Crouch, the Mayor of Weymouth:

> Boston, January 2 1796. Worshipful Sir, I must entreat your pardon for the liberty I take writing to you, but my wrongs call loudly for justice … the person, Sir, who now addresses you is the injured and afflicted wife of the late Cornet Burns who was lost in the fatal storm of the 18 November last … a vile woman, who was on board at the time of the accident, has taken the advantage of no other being saved, has usurped my name and impersonated me. Many … subscribed large sums of money [and] what they intended for a virtuous and indigent widow has been obtained by a licentious abandoned adulteress …
> The letter was signed 'Ann Burns'.

Strong words, and it cannot at first have been known what to think – or whom to believe. The writer went on to allege that:

> [This]… bad woman… had the temerity to make application at the War Office with intention to defraud me of the Widow's pension, but they have discovered the chief end and the business is now settled… She cannot say he deceived her, she has seen me with him in the House where she was a menial servant [and] therefore knew he was married.[1]

The real Mrs Burns (she had enclosed a copy of her marriage licence to validate her claim) asserted her right to the sums of money collected on the survivor of the *Catherine*'s behalf. This had by now amounted to a very considerable sum. The kindness of the officers and men of the Royal South Gloucester Militia, together with donations from the people of Dorchester and Weymouth, and a ten-guinea draft sent by Capt. Barcroft's aunt, Mrs Wilson, had produced a sum of £250 for 'Mrs Burns', which she had invested in stock.[2] Furthermore, all the costs of the officers' funeral were eventually paid by the Sick and Hurt Board, and the money for this had been added to 'Mrs Burns'' little fortune.[3]

Mr Bryer, the surgeon in whose house this imposter now resided, already knew the true situation: 'Mrs Burns', the woman who had survived the wrecking of the *Catherine*, had told him of her real position shortly after the storm.

Burns *was* married to another woman. When he came from Massachusetts to pursue the Loyalist claims of his American family, he was penniless (see pp.32–33). He married a Miss Trueman of Boston, Lincolnshire, but the marriage was unhappy and they parted after eleven months, during which it appears that he met the survivor of the *Catherine*.

They lived together as man and wife, having undergone 'a form [of marriage] to satisfy her scruples'. They were very poor and, eventually, Burns was put into the Fleet prison in London for debt for nine months. 'Mrs Burns' supported him there 'by the use of her needle'. 'Mrs Burns' claimed that she did not find out about Burns' real marriage until shortly before his release from prison. By then she was pregnant. She had no friends and no one to protect her. She was completely devoted to Burns and, although she now knew their marriage could not be legal, he had acknowledged her as his wife at all times and she did not leave him. Soon after, she gave birth to a son 'which [Burns] directed should be Baptized after his own name in the church of St Clement Danes...'.[4] Not long after that, Burns obtained his Cornetcy in the 26th Light Dragoons and, with it, the fateful posting to the West Indies.

Now came the dilemma of a separation. Although six 'lawful wives of soldiers for every company' (100 men) were permitted to accompany their husbands on active service, Abercromby had specified that as few women (and as little baggage) as possible should be taken on the expedition, because of the extreme shortage of space. 'General Abercromby proposes to take none or at least very few/not more than two per Company,' the War Office wrote to General Whyte at Cork, commanding officer of the 1st West India Regiment. It is probable that children were not permitted at all – the Return of Regiments, men, women and horses, shows no children on the expedition.[5]

Faced with this dilemma, 'Mrs Burns' found she could not leave Burns. She was slavishly devoted to him, to the extent that she could leave, and effectively abandon, her own child 'at nurse in London' (a very dubious fate for an illegitimate child in poverty in the eighteenth century) with the near certainty that she would not see him ever again, or know how he would fare.[6]

After the storm, when she knew Burns was dead, all she wanted to do was to lie down and die herself but, when she was fighting for her life on board the *Catherine*, it was the thought of him and her child which drove her on to save herself. Ironically, the ship which they should have boarded, the cavalry transport *Fowler*, upon which Burns had already boarded his horse (see p.63), put back to Spithead in safety after the storm.[7] All this she told to Mr Bryer while in his care. Bryer wrote to Burns' sister, presumably asking for help. (It may be the reply to this letter which prompted Shrapnell to tell Mrs Wilson that Burns' sister was not in a situation to help her, see p.84.) The sister then contacted her real sister-in-law: '...language cannot express my surprise and horror...' Ann Burns wrote, as she plunged the survivor of the *Catherine* directly under the harsh spotlight of public scrutiny.[8]

So, what to do about the 'virtuous and indigent widow' and her claim? Shrapnell discussed the matter with Bryer and others. Their conclusion was swift and firm: 'Mrs Burns' 'did not obtain any subscription under false pretences ... the money collected was for her use and no other person ... her very respectable and exemplary behaviour during her remaining with us at Weymouth has sufficiently convinced the Inhabitants, and must soon convince the world, that she is not that abandon'd character which the ... letter represents her.'

Moreover, the real Mrs Burns lived 'with a Batchelor Brother reported to be in affluence, had a thousand pounds settled on her on her Marriage and now enjoys the pension from the Widows of Officers who are killed'. Shrapnell concluded: 'God forbid that I should judge ill of anyone. My sole motive of this account is the uses of Humanity.'[9] So, the 'Mrs Burns' scandal died down, as quickly as it had arisen.

It was at this point that Shrapnell first considered writing an account of the whole tragedy: 'to vindicate the cause of a friendless and unfortunate woman.'[10]

There was also another reason: the scandal, as he saw it, of a cover-up by government of the tragedy on the beach. 'I have had many hints,' he wrote, 'that Government endeavoured to stifle the affair by every plausible means, but such a catastrophy [sic] cannot pass unnoticed.'[11] 'This unparalell'd [sic] loss seems to have been hushed up in an extraordinary manner, and the friends of Lt Jenner have desired me to make it known through the medium of some periodical publication generally read.'[12]

Certainly Pitt and his Cabinet would not have wanted the French to know of their intended 'Final Push'. They had used the Earl of Moira's expedition to Brittany as a 'blind' for Christian and Abercromby's expedition. (see p.46) There were spies everywhere and the country was in a state of alert for a possible invasion.[13] Secrecy was demanded at all levels.

The disaster may also have been concealed for the sake of national morale, which was particularly low at the time: the fall of Britain's allies in Europe, her defeats in the Netherlands and retreat to northern Germany were well known; unpopular legislation was being introduced to suppress 'seditious' meetings and publications, which were increasingly calling for an end to the war and the seeking of peace with France; food prices were impossibly high after another harsh winter and cold summer, and unemployment was high. The people were hungry and clamouring for bread – and peace. This tragedy might fuel the clamour of the mob still further.

However, Shrapnell was right – such a catastrophe could not pass unnoticed. The horror of the scene on the beach after the storm was reported in all the local newspapers and was frequently exaggerated to gross proportions, describing thousands dead.[14] Shrapnell intended to send his account of the storm to *The Gentleman's Magazine*.[15] He sent a draft to his friend the physician Edward Jenner, whom he described as 'a Gentleman of Genius and extensive literary acquirements,' who would 'correct and amend my humble attempts to describe the direfull catastrophy [sic].'[16] 'I am sorry the task falls on me,' he wrote, 'as the friends of the deceased will find much in it to wound their already afflicted feelings. Notwithstanding this, I must suppress much of the horror I was witness to.'[17]

' . . . tossed about for near six weeks and driven back by stormy weather . . . ' Christian, on board the *Glory*, and his second fleet, December 1795 to January 1796. (National Maritime Museum PAH7891)

Shrapnell and other friends of 'Mrs Burns' were still trying to procure a position for her as a lady's companion. 'We are endeavouring to seek a situation for her and hope soon to succeed, as it had been better for her to have perished in the waves than to become again exposed to the guilty measures of artfull [*sic*] and designing men.'[18]

He wrote to Miss Wilson, acknowledging receipt of the ten-guinea draft for 'Mrs Burns': 'She is very thankfull [*sic*] and says she will procure some honest method of supporting herself and child in a sober obscurity. The little income allotted her will serve to alleviate the moments of sickness or the unavoidable casualtys [*sic*] of this uncertain life.'[19] 'Her behaviour is very modest and exemplary. She is a very little woman with delicate features, fair, and by some thought very handsome, with the most jet black hair I ever remember to have noticed and black eyes, her whole figure strikingly particular.'[20] Mrs Burns had certainly found her champion in Shrapnell.

Meanwhile, Christian was in deep trouble again: his fleet had run into fierce gales just five days after leaving St Helens.

Glory at Sea, 14 December, Lat. 48 deg 35 min N., Long. 9 deg 50 W. The continuance of the easterly wind enabled me to get with the squadron and transports as far to the westward (as) Long. 11.03W (west of the Scilly Isles). On the 12th, being then in the Lat. of 48.35N... the wind shifted to the south-west at 8 p.m. and increasing blew a very severe gale.

> *The* Glory *shipped a considerable sea and was compelled to bear up in the height of the gale and was for some moments in danger ... the* Alfred *[has] lost her main and mizen masts ... the* Hermes *transport has lost her foremast and bowsprit ... material damage has happened – great quantity of wreck has been floating near us ... the* Undaunted *parted company ... and has not been seen ... from whence I entertain apprehension respecting her safety ... having only the* Alcmene *and* Prompte *with me, I am much limited in the power of keeping the convoy collected.*[21]

The *Sherborne and Yeovil Mercury* of 21 December 1795 reported that:

> *... the outward bound West India fleet, which lately sailed from Portsmouth, was overtaken by a violent gale of wind on Sunday last, fifty leagues (150 miles) west half-west from Scilly, by which they were separated and some of the fleet damaged ... the* Alfred, Undaunted *frigate and* Favourite *sloop of war ... put back here on Wednesday ... the frigate* Undaunted *with the loss of all her masts and bowsprit, all which were rolled overboard during the gale ... several of their crews are said to be killed and wounded.*
> *(Extract from a letter from Plymouth, 19th December)*

The newspaper also reported the following week that the Admiral's flagship *Glory*, ninety-eight guns, had been in the most imminent danger of foundering. She had been struck by a sea which went completely over her and filled her with water: 'nothing short of the greatest exertions and skill could have saved her.'

Battling out the storm on board *La Prompte*, seaman William Richardson wrote:

> *One night, it being as dark as pitch and the sea running mountains high, and our ship lying to under a storm mizzen stay-sail, the* Vesuve, *a large gun-brig, lying to under a close-reefed main topsail, drove slap up against our weather quarter, which alarmed everyone exceedingly. One minute she was higher than our mast-heads, and the next we thought she would have fallen on us; and we expected nothing else than both of us would soon knock each other to pieces and go to the bottom. However, by throwing her main topsail aback she dropped astern without any other damage than leaving her bower anchor sticking in our quarter near the water's edge, and when it dropped out by the rolling of the ship the water came in so fast that many thought she was sinking ... One of our 'mids' named King, a fine young man, on his first trip to sea, was terribly alarmed and wanted a pistol to shoot himself; being asked the reason, he said he was afraid of drowning, but by shooting himself he would be out of pain in an instant.*[22]

Christian's troubles continued: '*Glory* at Sea, 16th December ... the *Lively* and *Alexander* transports [are]... leaking and unfit to keep the sea, the former having on board 130 soldiers of the 28th Regt. and the latter 195 troops of 27th Regt.'

Capt. Crawley of the *Lion* took the *Lively* in tow, but the sea was so rough that *Lion*'s boats had great difficulty in taking the men off her. *Colossus*, *Impregnable* and *Irresistible* took the men of the 27th off the *Alexander*. Christian continued: 'In the night of the 15th [it] blew again with such violence from the south-west that we could not carry sail. The fleet has merely held its situation.'[23]

A Return of Ships in Sight on 26 December showed a huge number of ships missing: one hundred and twenty-five, among them five of the big East India ships, thirty West India ships and the forty-four-gun ships *Charon*, *Expedition*, *L'Etrusco* and *Crachefeu*, which had not been seen since the twelfth. Christian wrote: 'I am... determine[d]... to continue at sea as long as may be practicable and to proceed with such forces as I may be enabled to keep together. In this opinion, Sir Ralph Abercromby perfectly concurs.' At Latitude 48.40 north, Longitude 11.00 west, he wrote that he would press forward and endeavour to collect the scattered transports by crossing south and west, but he was strongly inclined to think that the greater part of the ships had put into port.[24] He 'pressed forward' throughout January. Still the gales continued, beating the struggling ships back and scattering them far and wide.

On 18 January, one of the transports, the East Indiaman *Dutton*, carrying some six hundred troops including three hundred and fifty men of the First Grenadiers, flew the signal to denote having sick on board. Abercromby ordered her into Plymouth, together with the *William Beckford* transport, carrying two hundred and forty men of the 88th Regiment.[25]

The story of what happened to the *Dutton* became local history and was frequently recounted, and embellished, in naval history books. She entered Plymouth Sound on 25 January, anchored and waited to enter the safer Catwater. This was before the construction of the breakwater (Plymouth was then an unprotected sound).[26] During the night, the gale continued with increased fury from the south-west, driving the *Dutton* towards the rocks of Mount Batten. At about 9.00 a.m. the following morning, the crew slipped the cables to run for Catwater, but the buoy which marked the reef off Mount Batten had been set adrift by the gale and the *Dutton* crashed against the rocks stern first and lost her rudder.[27] Out of control, she was then blown onto the rocks below the Citadel, near the Barbican, 'the sea continually breaking completely over her, which occasioned her to roll ... prodigiously.'[28] 'Her masts were cut away and, although they fell towards the shore, were useless as a bridge, being broken by the heavy sea.'[29] The captain and officers got safely on shore but the seamen, soldiers and their wives and children remained on board, many of the soldiers drunk and riotous with fear.[30] 'The shore was crowded with ... pilots, boatmen and other sea-faring men ... the gale every moment increased and one and all were appalled.[31] '... boats from the ships of war in port ... tried in vain to approach (the stricken ship, but) had to run for safety to the inner harbour.'[32]

Onto this scene of imminent catastrophe arrived Capt. Edward Pellew of the frigate *Indefatigable*, which was in Plymouth for repairs. Pellew 'saw that the loss of nearly all on board was imminent ... a single hawser only having been run from the ship to the shore.'[33] He gave instructions to be strapped into a harness on the hawser and was hauled through the rough seas towards the *Dutton*. The hawser alternately slackened and tightened as the *Dutton* rolled on the rocks and Pellew was 'at times high above and at others under the water.' 'He was sorely bruised thereby.'[34] Once on board, Pellew, with sword drawn, assumed command. He sent a hawser to the shore, 'to which travellers and hawling lines were affixed,' and several on board were enabled to make their escape by this way.[35]

The sinking of the *Dutton* at Plymouth, January 1796 (Plymouth Art Gallery)

The Times stated that the *Dutton*'s captain 'was hauled on board again at 2.00 p.m., by a rope lashed around his waist. About 3.00 p.m. the storm abated and shore boats were able to go to the seaward side of the ship. They took out about 300 soldiers, grenadiers of the 2nd, 3rd, 10th and 37th Regiments, as well as eighty sick, women and children. The ship was lost, although parts of her were subsequently salvaged and sold.'[36] Pellew received the freedom of the City of Plymouth for his bravery.[37]

Christian had battled against fierce storms for six and a half weeks – and got nowhere. 'We often wished and often looked to see the signal up on board the *Glory* for the remainder of us to bear up for a British port,' wrote William Richardson on board *La Prompte*.[38] On 24 January, 'after unexampled perseverance and having experienced the dismal effects of violent gales of wind for so long a time,'[39] Christian gave up: 'At last ... the wished-for signal was made, after we had been tossed about almost in continual storms for forty-seven days; and of our 360 sail [*sic*] there were not now above fifty of us together,' Richardson recalled. Christian returned to St Helens, anchoring at Spithead on the 29th where Richardson observed: '... by the ship [*La Prompte*] being so continually wet the green grass was growing on her sides and on her decks under the gun-carriages'.[40]

Christian struck his flag on 3 February. He made an application to the Admiralty for an allowance to the officers and ship's company of the *Glory* for all the damage they had sustained to their property in the storm. It was refused. He then distributed hundreds of pounds out of his own pocket amongst the crew – which won him all hearts.[41] Not all the surviving ships returned to Spithead with Christian. The masters of the transports had sealed orders, to be opened after departure, to the effect that, in the event of separation from the Admiral's flagship, they were to continue to Barbados. Several continued without him and arrived at Carlisle Bay, Barbados, in February.[42]

In April and May, Pitt and Dundas faced a lambasting in the House of Commons from the Opposition for the scandal of their failure to get reinforcements out to the West Indies in time and for the loss of soldiers' lives on board the transports during the many delays and storms. The playwright Richard Sheridan demanded that all the papers concerning the preparations for Christian's and Abercromby's expedition be produced and swore that he would prove ministers' incompetence was to blame for the delay and loss of lives as much as the storms. Fox denounced the King's ministers for their misconduct in the handling of the war and accused them of being 'influenced either by arrogance or ... infatuated ambition'. But the majority of Sheridan's motions were negatived on the grounds of security and Dundas stated repeatedly to the House that only four ships 'were found to be missing' from Christian's fleet and that sixty-seven had safely arrived, containing above seven thousand regular troops. His statement went unchallenged.[43]

What an ill-fated Fleet was Admiral Christian's! wrote Shrapnell to Miss Wilson. *They are now returned, much disabled, to Spithead. Surely some particular vengeance of Almighty God awaits the unfortunate 26th Regiment* [of Light Dragoons]. *I am just informed that the bodyes* [sic] *of another troop from the same regiment are thrown on shore on the coast of Cornwall.*[44]

The Times, 30 January 1796 (Marazion, Cornwall, 26 January)
Yesterday morning, about four miles to the eastward of this place, great quantities of wreck floated on shore, supposed to be some of the West India convoy. There were many horses with D26 [the brand mark of the 26th Light Dragoons] *burnt on their hoofs; men, women and children, cloathes, etc. In the evening, we learnt that about 150 men and women were washed on shore ... On the blade of an oar is stamped 'Fowler of Scarborough'.*

This was the cavalry transport which Cornet Burns should have boarded instead of the *Catherine* – and which had put back in safety after the first storm.[45]

Chapter 9

Conclusions and Consequences

Although Shrapnell had intended to publish his account of the storm in *The Gentleman's Magazine*, his plans were changed when the writer Charlotte Smith approached him.

> *An opportunity has offered of altering our purpose to some advantage – and for the pecuniary benefit of the unfortunate Mrs Burns (for she must still retain that name),* he wrote to Miss Wilson.[1]
>
> *Mrs Charlotte Smith, who... is well known in the literary world, is now at Weymouth and has very humanely offered her endeavours to assist the unfortunate woman ... and intends writing the narrative in a seperate* [sic] *publication.*[2]
>
> *Mrs Smith will publish it at her own expence* [sic] *and give Mrs B. a certain number for sale, which I shall have the receipt of.*[3]
>
> *I have furnished her with the story and she has seen the spot, as well as every attending scene we could describe. She seems to think the pamphlet ... will sell at two shillings, or half a crown... and with* [her] *descriptive fancy, it must soon have a rapid sale.*[4]

Shrapnell also had another object in mind. It was his ambition to place a memorial, or tombstone, over the grave of the seventeen drowned officers at Wyke: 'I am now about to settle the plan of a small plain marble stone, simply relieved, just big enough to contain the names of nine officers, the date, and occasion, to be erected against the Tower of Wyke Church, over the grave. I think this will be but a very small expence.'[5] It is most likely that Shrapnell proposed naming only nine officers because of the simple fact that he could not identify the others. He was later to write in a letter: 'I wish I could ... specify the names of all the deceased officers...'[6]

Shrapnell subsequently changed his mind about using marble and decided that the memorial should be of Portland stone: 'The churchyard stands on an eminence and is very much exposed to the weather ... I doubt if the best monument could outlive a hard Portland stone and, if done up a little tasty [sic], I would prefer to marble.' He proposed 'inserting simply the names, rank and regiment of the different officers, the number of men and women and then say Perished by Shipwreck on Portland Beach on Wednesday the 18th of November...' and he hoped to have the stone erected before the king came to Weymouth: 'He may then see (as he frequently walkes [sic] to Wyke) that the plans of Ministry are not always infallible.'[7]

Shrapnell would, in fact, run into difficulties over the stone, and time was running short. Soon, the South Gloucesters would be receiving their orders to march from Weymouth: 'The stay of our regiment at Weymouth is very uncertain,' he wrote to Mrs Wilson.[8]

In the meantime, the female relatives of Capt. Barcroft had shown their appreciation of all Shrapnell had done by sending him a ring as a keepsake of their drowned brother and cousin. Shrapnell was greatly touched: 'I shall treasure [it] in remembrance of a family for whom I have concieved [sic] the highest regard, and am happy in the idea that my poor services could have rendered them the smallest consolation.'[9] Shrapnell sent in return a print of Wyke Church: 'I have marked the place of the grave with a pencil. It was close to the north side of the tower and, at the head of it, close to the tower, I have concluded to put up a plain Portland stone with [a] simple inscription.'

He had arrived at a final decision on the tombstone with the help of Dr Jenner, who also thought that stone was preferable to marble, which he thought would be too costly. Also, the family of the young Lt Ker had erected a Portland stone over his tomb, and a stone memorial to the officers would be more in keeping with that.

'...the Stonecutter's bill will amount even in this plain way to the sum of seven pounds, including a guinea fee to the Rector, with halling [sic] and erecting it, the letters at three halfpence each and the stone three guineas.'

The Barcroft family must have offered to pay for the stone, as Shrapnell continued:

Dr Jenner will gladly join you in the expense. He asked: *Please to give me your alteration or approbation of the following:*

To the Memory of
Captain Ambrose William Barcroft | Lieut. Ash – & | Mr Kelley – | Surgeon | Of the 63 Regiment of Infantry – | Of Lieut Stephen Jenner of the 6th West India Regt. | Lieut Stains of the 2nd West India Regt. | Cornet Wm Stukeley Burns of the 26th Light Dragoons | Cornet Benjamin Graydon of the 3. West India Regt. | Lieut. Sutherland – | Ensign Chadwick | 215 Soldiers, Seamen etc. | and nine women | who perished by shipwreck on Portland Beach | on Wednesday the 18th of November | 1795 [10]

He added: 'I cannot make out the Christian names of all the officers [or] the names of the Regts. which Lt Sutherland and En. Chadwick served in.' Difficulties of identification aside, Shrapnell now ran into vexatious problems with the Rector of Wyke, Samuel Payne, who demanded a payment of 5 guineas to have the tombstone erected in the churchyard. Shrapnell was scandalised at such a mercenary attitude coming from a man of the cloth, and wrote indignantly to Barcroft's family:

I did not suppose that I should be under the necessity of disclosing the following fact, nor will you expect to hear my proceedings obstructed by the rapacity of a person whose sacred profes-

The officers' tombstone at Wyke. (By kind permission of Mr Robert Oldland)

sion ought to ensure the most upright conduct but, as you must be informed why I have made so enormous a demand on you, I cannot avoid describing his conduct.

At the time of the funeral, at a time when every spark of compassion and humane assistance was demanded for the protection of the unhappy sufferers who survived the wreck, and to cover a little earth over the remains of those who perished, the virtuous *Rector of Wyke modestly demanded half a guinea each for his fee for opening a grave in the churchyard to contain twenty-six coffins.*

He actually received upwards of twelve guineas … from the Agents for the Sick and Hurt Board, who … took it off from our subscription that we might be enabled the better to assist the survivors.

On my applying for leave to erect the stone … he sent me word that he should only demand five guineas as a fee, and seemed to hint that it was a favour, as so many were interred there, and that he should expect the money before the stone was put up…

I feared a sudden route [departure] for the Regt might prevent my performing my promise to you [so] I paid him his unjust demand … and saw the stone erected the day before yesterday. [26 March 1796].

After several scathing references to the bad reputation and exorbitant demands of the Rector, Shrapnell set out the fee for the tombstone in full:

	£	s	d
16 feet stone at 3s	2	8	–
498 letters at 1½d	3	3	3
Foot stone	–	7	6
Carriage to Wyke and setting up	–	8	–
Clerk's fee	–	1	6
Unjustly exorbt. fee for the Parson	5	5	–
	11	**13**	**3**

'The (half) sum you will find (is) £5 16s 7½d.'

Still indignant, Shrapnell added: 'I shall not fail to beg Mrs Smith to remember the circumstance in a note to her pamphlet,' and, indeed, she did make a scathing but oblique reference to the mercenary Rector of Wyke.[11]

Time was running out for Shrapnell and the South Gloucesters at Weymouth – the regiment were under orders to march to Chelmsford in Essex.[12] On 30 March, he told Mrs Wilson: 'We shall leave this place the first week in May,' and expressed anxiety over completing a memorial for Wyke Churchyard in time. This suggests that he planned a second, more detailed, memorial stone:

> *I wish I could so far compleat [sic] it as to specify the names of all the deceased officers and the Regts., [but] at this distance from the seat of information, I have not been able to succeed as yet.*
>
> *I do not know the Christian names of Lieut Ash [sic] or Mr Kelly, of the 63rd., of Lieut. Stains, Lieut Sutherland and Cornet or Ensign Chadwick. These were all, I believe, of West India Regts but I do not know [the] number [of the Regiments].* He continued: '*It is very possible that I am not accurately informed by the poor people who were saved, but they all told me what they believed and I have written what they asserted.*

Shrapnell asked if Mr Wilson, whilst residing in London, could make enquiries at the War Office for him, adding:

> *For this publick [sic] memorial, we cannot be too accurate … we have now but very little time to lose and I had better mention only their names than delay the business much longer.*[13]

One memorial stone only, with the full names of the nine officers identified and the numbers of their regiments, stands to this day in the churchyard at Wyke.

June 1796 saw the publication of Charlotte Smith's Narrative:[14]

> *A | Narrative | Of the loss of the | Catharine, Venus and Piedmont | Transports | And the | Thomas, Golden Grove and Aeolus | Merchant Ships | Near Weymouth | On Wednesday the 18th of November Last | Drawn up from Information taken on the Spot | By Charlotte Smith | And published for the Benefit of an unfortunate Survivor | From one of the Wrecks, and her Infant Child.*

Shrapnell busily set about persuading people to buy copies, priced two shillings. He achieved a substantial list of subscribers, among whom were Mrs Barrett of Yeovil; Lt-Gen. J. Leveson-Gower, the commanding officer of the 63rd Regiment (he came down to Weymouth after the storm and 'very feelingly regretted the loss of Capt. Barcroft as a general calamity and spoke in the highest tones of his military character'.[15] He also wrote a letter of condolence to Capt. Barcroft's family[16]); Colonel the Earl of Berkeley, South Gloucester Militia; Miss Barcroft of Otley, Yorkshire, and the Misses Elizabeth and Barbara Barcroft; Dr Edward Jenner (five copies); the Revd H. Jenner (Stephen's father, three copies); Lt William Shrapnell, South Gloucester Militia (four copies); Mrs Shrapnell; Mrs Wilson, Manor House, Otley, Yorks (five copies); Miss Wilson and Miss Ellen Wilson; Maj. Austin, South Gloucester Militia (five copies); Mr Abbot, Fleet Farmhouse; Mr Bryer, surgeon, Weymouth; Miss Burns; Mr Crouch Junior, Mayor of Weymouth; Capt. Symonds, South Gloucester Militia.

In a final letter to the Barcroft family, Shrapnell sent a drawing of Wyke Church, executed by the son-in-law of Charlotte Smith, the Chevalier de Foville. He mentioned that 'Mrs Burns' had not yet procured a situation, 'but has many friends anxious for her welfare.' He again thanked them for their gift and sent his 'most respectfull Compts. [sic] to my excellent correspondent Mrs Wilson.'[17]

Shrapnell and his regiment left Weymouth in June, not for Chelmsford, but for Blatchington Barracks, near Seaford in Sussex.[18] He had done all he could for 'Mrs Burns', the other survivors and the dead. When receiving the gift of the ring and plaudits of praise from the Barcroft family, he had modestly written: 'I am not conscious of having merited the encomiums you are pleased to pass on my humble labours during the late shipwreck, as the duty of one individual to another demanded those endeavours which it would have been brutal to neglect,'[19] but perhaps the enormous efforts he made had worn him out: he confessed to Mrs Wilson that he would be glad to leave Weymouth, especially after the tragedy and the dismal winter there: 'I rejoice at the prospect of leaving this dreary Coast ... whose neighbourhood contains the most brutal of the human race,' he wrote bitterly.[20] He had not forgotten the behaviour of those who had looted and plundered the wrecks and corpses which lay, broken and defenceless, on the Chesil after the storm.

'Mrs Burns' went back to London when her injuries (and Mr Bryer) permitted her, was reunited with her son and brought him back to Weymouth to live. It was not long before she entered into another common-law marriage, changed her surname once more – and vanished into history. Ever the gentleman, Shrapnell had always been ready to believe her innocence in the bigamy scandal: 'I am of the same opinion, that she was deceived by Cornet Burns in her first connection with him,' he wrote to Mrs Wilson.[21] Doubt may linger over that issue, but a survivor she certainly was.

After his second defeat by storms, Christian's morale was very low. Ship's Mate William Dillon commented that Christian's health had been affected by his enormous struggle.[22] Earl Spencer, First Lord of the Admiralty, wrote to the king that Christian felt somehow to blame for their failure to reach Barbados, although he had battled against the storms for six and a half weeks.[23] Certainly there was no

NARRATIVE

OF THE LOSS OF THE,

CATHARINE, VENUS, AND PIEDMONT

TRANSPORTS,

AND THE

THOMAS, GOLDEN GROVE, AND ÆOLUS

MERCHANT SHIPS,

NEAR WEYMOUTH,

ON WEDNESDAY THE 18TH OF NOVEMBER LAST.

Drawn up from Information taken on the Spot,

By CHARLOTTE SMITH,

And published for the Benefit of an unfortunate Survivor from one of the Wrecks, and her Infant Child.

Una Eurufque, Notufque; ruunt, creberque procellis
Africus, & vaftos volvunt ad littora fluctus.
Infequitur clamorque; virum ftridorque; rudentum
Eripiunt fubito nubes cœlumque diemque
. . . . ex oculis, ponto nox incubat atra.
Intonuere poli, & crebris micat ignibus æther
Præfentemque viris intentant omnia mortem.   VIRG.

. . . . . . Vagæ ne parce malignus arenæ,
Offibus & capiti inhumato
Particulam dare.   HOR.

London :

PRINTED AND SOLD BY
SAMPSON LOW, BERWICK STREET, SOHO;
AND C. LAW, AVE-MARIA LANE.
ALSO MAY BE HAD AT DELAMOTTE'S AND WOOD'S
LIBRARIES, WEYMOUTH.
1796.

Title Page, Charlotte Smith's *Narrative.*

question of blaming him at the time. On the contrary, after the second storm, Lord Spencer stated that Christian and Abercromby deserved only praise for their efforts.[24] (However, the northerly route Christian had insisted on taking *was* later questioned.[25])

In his narrative, Shrapnell had referred to the ships' masters' fatal mistake during the first storm in trying to get back to St Helens on the morning of Wednesday 18 November, '...for, instead of clearing the Race of Portland ... they had not cleared the West Bay...'[26] and Charlotte Smith had written that they thought 'they had sea room enough'.[27]

In standing out to remain with his convoy and face the storm, had Christian placed the six ships in this dangerous situation? Or did their position in the convoy dictate their fate? With no technical means of forecasting weather in those days, much reliance had to be placed on the 'feel' of the wind and a good 'weather eye'. Christian demonstrated that he certainly possessed both in that he was able to foresee trouble well ahead – and plan evasive action. In his letter of 18 November, he stated that, on the Monday morning (16th), 'the sky had an appearance of uncertainty' – yet the storm did not strike in all its ferocity until late on the Tuesday night and throughout the Wednesday.[28] He had already tacked in order to make for the shelter of Torbay at 2.00 a.m. on the Tuesday morning.[29] The circumstances which followed must have made it unavoidable that some of the convoy would suffer and that some would be lost – but Christian's ability in handling the situation was never called into question.

Moreover, a subsequent attempt in February 1796 by another admiral, Cornwallis, suffered similarly, with storms splitting the fleet in two and Cornwallis facing a court marshal for not continuing to Barbados. The divided fleet struggled on without their admiral and arrived in the West Indies in April.[30]

In February 1796, Christian was invested with the Order of the Bath upon a recommendation by Pitt to the king.[31] The king, who knew all about Christian's efforts throughout the storms, was happy to invest him.[32] It was a gesture of support and kindness.

Christian came back to undertake his third attempt on 20 March 1796. He hoisted his flag on board *Thunderer*, seventy-four guns, and headed a convoy of six warships, forty-one transports and over five and a half thousand men. Once past the storm-belt, he transferred to the faster frigate *Astrea* and arrived at Carlisle Bay, Barbados, on 21 April 1796.[33]

At Martinique, Sir John Laforey, who had waited so long for reinforcements, handed over command to Christian on 24 April and set sail for England on board *Majestic*, seventy-four guns.[34] But he was destined not to live in his native land again. On 14 June, two days before his ship reached Portsmouth, he died of yellow fever. He was buried there with full honours on 21 June.[35]

Abercromby had already arrived in the Caribbean on board the frigate *Arethusa* on 17 March.[36] Reunited with his admiral, he re-took St Lucia in June, establishing Brigadier General John Moore as commander-in-chief there for a year.[37] They went on to take Berbice, Demerara and Essequibo, the Dutch-held colonies on the South American coast, which had in part agreed to put themselves under British protection after Holland fell to the French, and restored Britain's hold in St Vincent and Grenada.[38]

They did not, however, retake Guadeloupe and, although reinforcements were sent to St Domingo, it was a forlorn hope (and a measure of Dundas' huge ambitions) that the British Army could keep control there. In 1798 the troops were withdrawn from that island.[39] Nevertheless, within a year, the French-inspired slave rebellions throughout the Caribbean were over and Britain's predominance in the Leeward and Windward islands restored.[40] Although Dundas continued to send large numbers of troops out to the Caribbean, there were no further massive military expeditions such as Christian's and Abercromby's. It is estimated that, in 1795, half of the entire British Army's line regiments were allocated for deployment in the Caribbean. During the first half of the war, to 1802, approximately ninety thousand men were sent there. Some forty-five thousand lost their lives and fourteen thousand were discharged as sick. To these must be added the lives of seamen lost, both naval and merchant. An estimate based on available records puts this in the order of nineteen to twenty-four thousand deaths among naval and transport crews.[41]

Christian left the Caribbean in the frigate *Beaulieu* with his second-in-command Rear Admiral Pole in October 1796, having handed over command to Rear Admiral Harvey (the man who had commanded the Earl of Moira's 'cover' expedition to Brittany with General Doyle in August 1795) in the *Prince of Wales* on 23 June 1796. Abercromby had left in early July.[42]

Christian and Pole arrived back in England on 17 November 1796 – exactly one year after the storm which left two hundred and thirty-four dead on the Chesil changed for ever the lives of many struck by the tragedy and bequeathed a sombre legacy to Dorset history.[43]

Abercromby was sent back to the Caribbean almost immediately in November 1796. Spain had declared war on Britain on 8 October and Dundas ordered two expeditions to capture the Spanish colonies of Trinidad and Buenos Aires. Abercromby was to lead the Trinidad expedition. In this he was successful, but later faced defeat at Puerto Rico.[44] The Buenos Aires campaign took place some years later. In 1797 he was sent as commander-in-chief to Ireland from which position he resigned on a matter of principle and, in 1799 commanded an expedition to the Helder, Holland. Greatly respected by his fellow officers and men, he refused the peerage he was offered for his service there. In 1801, while in command of the Mediterranean troops at Minorca, he served in Egypt, where he died, victorious, at the Battle of Alexandria in March of that year. He was buried at Malta.[45]

Lt William Shrapnell retired from the army and returned to Berkeley, Gloucestershire, where he continued to practise medicine with Dr Edward Jenner. He also assisted the Countess of Berkeley, Mary Cole, in the collection and arrangement of the archives at Berkeley Castle.[46]

Shrapnell's son, Henry, who was only three years old at the time his father was encamped at Weymouth, followed in his father's medical footsteps and became a junior partner of Jenner's. He also became the informal curator of Edward Jenner's collection of fossils and other specimens of natural history and was in part responsible for the erection of Jenner's statue in Gloucester Cathedral.[47]

Shrapnell died at Berkeley in 1817, aged fifty-two.[48] Through his unstinting efforts after the storm and meticulous care in writing to bereaved relatives, he established an affectionate and enduring relationship with the family of the drowned Capt. Barcroft. He sent them pebbles from the Chesil, pictures of Wyke church and a plan of the wrecks on the beach.[49] His letters remained in the hands of Barcoft's descendants for a hundred and fifty years and were given to the Lancashire Record Office in 1946.[50]

Charlotte Smith died in 1806. Although herself suffering straitened circumstances throughout her life – '...she was a very unhappy woman ... embarrassed in her affairs ... and ... enduring the pangs of penury...' – she gave her time ('all I have to give') 'to assist the unfortunate person' 'Mrs Burns'. Her kindness and generosity to a

'Tippoo's Tiger', captured by the 33rd Regiment at Seringapatam, 1799, and now in the Victoria and Albert Museum. (2545 IS)

woman in distress resulted in one of the few contemporary accounts available of the storm. 'The motive which led to this publication did honour to the humanity of the fair authoress,' wrote the *European Magazine*, which described her as 'a very elegant writer.'[51]

Christian was promoted to Rear Admiral of the White and sent as assistant commander-in chief to the Cape of Good Hope in 1797, with his son Hood, who had accompanied his father throughout the fateful storms. There he received intelligence of the hostile intentions of the Indian Sultan Tippoo Sahib, the 'Tiger of Mysore', who was intriguing with the French against the British in India.[52] Christian vigorously set about making preparations to provide the transports to convey between two and three thousand troops from the Cape to India, to join those already there. He assumed the command of the Cape in 1798 but died there suddenly in November of the same year, aged fifty-one. He was buried at the Cape.[53] His wife, who had been in poor health for some years, survived him by only a few months and died, unaware of his death, on the Isle of Wight, where she is buried.[54]

Abercromby wrote of his former colleague: 'Rear Admiral Sir Hugh Christian, and the Royal Navy, have never ceased to show the utmost alacrity in forwarding the public service. To their skill and unremitting labour the success which has attended His Majesty's arms is in great measure due.'[55] The *Naval Biography* wrote: 'it is said by those who knew him, that it would be difficult to find another possessing more calmness or real courage ... by his death, his country lost an officer of untarnished honour and fidelity.'[56]

Two young officers who had battled it out in the storms of 1795/96 went on to achieve lasting fame and eminence for themselves during this war. When Christian and Abercromby left Brigadier General John Moore in command of St Lucia (he arrived in the West Indies on 13 April 1796, in Admiral Cornwallis' 'divided' fleet (see p.102)), he made a study of the black and native soldiers of the West India regiments and, like General Vaughan before him, came not only to the conclusion that they were better suited to the climate than whites but that, with their abstemious qualities (they avoided alcohol and meat), conscientiousness and attention to duty, they compared very favourably with the debilitated, feverish and often drunk and disorderly redcoat.[57]

The West India regiments had been intended as 'light', skirmishing companies to counter the guerrilla tactics of the French and insurgent slaves and Moore wrote to Abercromby that they were invaluable.[58] Moore subsequently developed his ideas for the training of 'light' infantrymen.[59] His recommendations, and the general experience of the service of the West India Regiments, were influential in the forming of the Light Brigade of the British Army in 1803.[60]

Moore died at the Battle of Corunna, Spain, on 16 January 1809 in a last stand against the French, having successfully brought his troops to safety after a twelve-day strategic retreat across frozen Spanish terrain, in an attempt to deplete the resources of the pursuing French Army.[61] Acknowledged as 'the Father of the Light Brigade' he became a legend in military history.

In the aftermath of the storm of 18 November, some of the transports, badly battered, put in to Lymington, Hampshire, where the troops were sent to recover from their ordeal. Among them was one young man from the 33rd Regiment, who had only recently purchased his commission of lieutenant colonel. His aristocratic mother had once said of him, somewhat dismissively, that her son was only fit for cannon fodder: Arthur was 'food for powder and nothing more.'[62] Sick and feverish, the young man took leave to travel from Lymington to his family seat in Ireland where he recuperated and pursued his social and political life – although he remained bitterly frustrated in his ambition to court the woman he would eventually, much later, marry.[63]

In his absence, his regiment were issued with new orders: they were not to go out with Christian again to the West Indies but were to proceed to India and, indeed, they embarked without him, in April 1796.[64] He joined them later by fast frigate at the Cape of Good Hope. Their later campaigns against Tippoo Sahib, the 'Tiger of Mysore', became famous in history.[65] The young man was Arthur Wellesley, later the Duke of Wellington, whose victory at the battle of Waterloo in 1815 finally put to an end the greatest and most far-reaching conflict with the French in British history.

Ships and Men Lost and Saved on the Chesil, 18 November 1795

The extent of our loss, in the late storm is now known accurately by the returns to the public offices. It amounts to 293, including 15 officers, and this is the total of the drowned; and two transports still missing. This is very different from 2,000 or 1,500, first reported to be lost.
Sherborne and Yeovil Mercury, Monday 30 November 1795

Aeolus of Whitby

		Drowned	Saved
Weight	316 tons	Lt. Mason, his brother,	The Master,
Master	Isaac Duck/Francis Mead	7 seamen	8 Seamen
Load	Masts, deals and other stores	**= 9 drowned**	**= 9 saved**
Passengers	2		
Crew	15		

Golden Grove, London

		Drowned	Saved
Weight	284 tons	The Master,	The Captain
Master	Robert Bagg	Dr Stevens,	(W. Hodgzard),
Load	Bale goods	Mr Burrows, 2 boys	Lt-Col. Ross,
Passengers	3		17 seamen
Crew	17	**= 5 drowned**	**= 19 saved**

Piedmont

		Drowned	Saved
Weight	243 tons	Captain, 11 seamen,	4 seamen,
Master	Robert Frazer	126 soldiers and officers	14 soldiers
Load	138 soldiers and officers	(inc. Capt. Barcroft,	
	of 63rd Regt	Lt. Ashe, Surgeon Kelly)	
Passengers	–	**= 138 drowned**	**= 18 saved**
Crew	–		

Venus

		Drowned	Saved
Weight	200 tons	The Master, his wife,	14 soldiers,
Master	Thomas Kidd	73 soldiers, Maj. Ker,	4 seamen, a boy
Load	Invalid soldiers and officers,	Lts Ker, Sutherland,	
	Hospital Corps, 3 officers of	Chadwick,	
	West India Regts	Adj. Graydon,	
Passengers	5 women	4 other women,	
Crew	12	7 seamen	
		= 91 drowned	**= 19 saved**

Catherine of Montrose

		Drowned	Saved
Weight	253 tons	The Master,	Mrs Burns,
Master	Alex Jolly, Master Cromey	22 soldiers of	a cabin boy
Load	23 soldiers of 26th Light	26th Light Dragoons	
	Dragoons,	and Cornet Burns,	
	2 officers W.I. Regts,	Lts Jenner and Stains,	
	1 Hospital Staff, 3 women	Mr Dodd, 2 women,	
Passengers	–	11 seamen	
Crew	–	**= 40 drowned**	**= 2 saved**

Thomas, of London

		Drowned	Saved
Weight	350 tons	The Master,	The Mate,
Master	Thomas Brown	his son,	1 passenger
Load	–	7 seamen,	4 seamen
Passengers	2 male, 3 female	1 male passenger,	
Crew	12	3 female passengers	
		= 13 drowned	**= 6 saved**

Total: **296 drowned**   **71 saved**

NB: Figures based on reports of the time, which varied (see Appendix 2). The highest figures were taken in each case.

Details of the Ships and Men Lost and Saved on the Chesil, 18 November 1795

The notes are taken from Admiralty and War Office records, local and national newspapers, *Lloyd's Register*, *Lloyd's List*, W. Shrapnell's *Narrative*, C. Smith's *Narrative*.

Aeolus

R. & B. Larn, *Shipwreck Index of the British Isles*, Vol.I, Sec.6: *Piedmont*:
London-Jamaica; Port: Whitby; Cargo: Wood (unspecified), Masts, Naval Stores (unspecified); built 1777 Philadelphia.

ADM/49/127:

Date of Contract	Time of Entry into Pay	Tons	Parts	Owner	Master
5/8/1793	11/8/1793	316	86	George Brown	Francis Mead

DDB/61/43 Shrapnell Narrative, with letter to Mrs Wilson, Weymouth, 21 December 1795:
'...Merchant Ship, laden with timber, etc. ...' (p.41)
'...the circumstance of the Aeolus remaining on the bank was owing to the very great height to which it was driven up, a circumstance unparalelled [sic].' (p.47)

CO/318/18 *A Return of Transports Lost in West Bay and about Portland:*

Ships' Names	Masters' Names	No. of (?) Horses/Foot	What Regiment
Aeolus	Isaac Duck	Loaded with Gunboats, Masts and other Stores	

How many Sailors Saved	How many Soldiers Drowned	Officers Saved	Officers' Names Drowned
Captain and ten men	–	–	Lt Mason and his Brother

(Sgnd) Nathaniel Stuart, Weymouth, (?) November 1795.

ADM 108/148 Ship's Ledger: *Eolus*, 316 tons transport for owner George Browne. Francis Mead master

ADM/108/158 Freight Ledger:

Aeolus, 316 86/94 tons, Francis Mead master.

Date of Charter	Entry into Log	Time Employed	Rate/Month	Discharge
5 Aug. 1793	11 Aug. 1793	27 mos, 8 days	13/ (pounds?)	18 Nov. 1795, lost on Port-land Beach

	£	s	d
Sum	5616	0	[illegible]
Disc	225	10	[illegible]
	5841	**10**	

ADM/1/1717 *List of Vessels belonging to the Convoy under the Command of Rear Admiral Christian that are arrived in Portland Road with those that are stranded:*

Ship's Name	How employed	Agent	Master	Lading	Damages, etc.
Aeolus	Transport	Lt Mason	Lake (?)	Materials for boats	Stranded at the above place (Portland)

Lt Mason and 8 men drowned. (Sgnd) Thos. Drury (HMS *Alfred*).

WO/1/798 (Transport Office):

f 175 Lt Skipsey, Agent of Transports. BOUGHT of John Wilkey '*Tierces*' of Moist Sugar for: ....*Eolus*: 5 1 14. Attested Alex Whitehead (Sec. to transport Board), Plymouth 1794. f 177 Scheme for the Distribution of Sugar at the rate of half a pound each man per week for two months, being troops destined for foreign service, under the direction of Capt Geo. Rice, Principal Agent.

Ship	Troops	?Sugar	Women	Children	Sugar	Casks
Eolus	147	588	3	1	14	4
(January 1795)						

PRO Cust 59/20: *Aeolus* of Whitby, Isaac Duck master, bound to the West Indies partly laden with masts timber and deals, which we suppose will be saved. A Lieut and midshipman of the navy and seven seamen were drowned, the master and eight seamen saved.

The Times, Monday 5 October (*Portsmouth, 2 October*):

> *Thursday passed by the homeward bound West India fleet under convoy of Montague, 74 guns, and a sloop of war. Eight transports with invalid soldiers are arrived here. One, the Aeolus, Capt. Isaac Duck, having been captured in Lat. —, Long 69 by the French corvette Brutus but was released on the Captain giving an order for the exchange of an equal number of French prisoners. The captain of the French corvette behaved partic-ularly civil*[ly], *considering the situation he was in.*

Sherborne and Yeovil Mercury, Monday 23 November (*extract of a letter from Weymouth, 19 November*): 'The *Aeolus* transport, Isaac Duck, master, with masts and other naval stores; part of the crew are saved.'

Sherborne and Yeovil Mercury, Monday 30 November *(Weymouth, 24 November)*: 'Particulars of the Loss of the Ships, and of those that have received Damage, on Portland Beach and on this Coast, on the 18 Instant, in a violent Gale of Wind at S.S.W., Weymouth, 24 November 1795'.

> *The ship* Aeolus, *belonging to Whitby (a transport), Isaac Duck, master, bound to the West Indies with masts and other naval stores; a Lieutenant of the navy, a midshipman and seven seamen were drowned; the master and eight seamen are saved. The ship sets a whale – On Portland Beach.*

Sherborne and Yeovil Mercury, Monday 28 December 1795 *(Sherborne, 21 December)*: 'Copy of a Letter from the Mate and others saved out of the Ship Aeolus, which was unfortunately cast away in the late Gale of Wind.'

> *Sirs, Having had the misfortune to be wrecked on Portland Beach, in the Aeolus trans-port, and being informed of the appearance of a scandalous paragraph in the papers, concerning the Portland people, stating that they have not only plundered the property of the distressed seamen, in spite of the soldiers, but were instrumental to their death! In gratitude, we do hereby assure you, Sir, of the contrary, but that we have experienced the most hospitable treatment, we could have expected in any part of the world, and that they actually hazarded their lives to preserve those who were in danger.*

(Sgnd) W. Lloyd, Master; James Hannah, Carpenter; Samuel Cock, Seaman. Portland, 3 December 1795. (NB: authenticity of this letter is called into doubt as the name of the Master here is quite different from that given anywhere else.)

Smith's Narrative: The *Aeolus* Merchant Ship, laden with timber on account of Government. There perished Lt Mason of the Navy (who was also an Agent for Transports) and his Brother a midshipman. A number of men were also drowned...

Lloyd's Register, 1795: Bg (Brig); sC (sheathed with copper); 94 (year repaired); J. Norris, builder; 155 (tons); SDE (single deck); Philad; some repairs; 77 (year built); 12 (foot draught); Lo-Jamai (London-Jamaica).

Lloyd's List (The Marine List) No.2769, Friday 20 November: The Aeolus (Transport), Duck, is on Shore on Portland Beach. Ten men drowned.

Aeolus of Whitby, 316 tons transport. Owner: George Browne (NB: he also owned the *Catherine*). Masters: Francis Mead, Isaac Duck. Date of Charter: 5 August 1793, bound to W.I. with mast timber, deals and other naval stores (much of it salvaged).

The *Aeolus*, of Whitby, Isaac Duck, master, Frances Mead, master.
Lost: Lt Mason, Navy Agent for Transports and his brother, a midshipman. Duck, Capt.

Golden Grove

R. & B. Larn, *Shipwreck Index of the British Isles*, Vol.I, Sec.6:
Golden Grove, London-St Kitts; built 1783, Southampton; armament: 16 x 6-pounder cannon; Capt: Hodgzard.

DDB/6/43 Shrapnell Narrative, with letter to Mrs Wilson, Weymouth, 21 December 1795:
'The *Golden Grove* Merchantman, bound to St Kitts with a very valuable cargo. Lt Col. Ross (a passenger) and some others were saved from this ship.' (p.41)

CO/318/17 *A Return of Transports Lost in West Bay and about Portland*:

Ships' Names	Masters' Names	No. of Horses/Foot	What Regiment
Golden Grove	Uncertain whether a Transport	Everyone drowned.	

(Sgnd) Nathaniel Stuart, Weymouth, (?) November 1795.

ADM/1/1717 *List of Vessels belonging to the Convoy under the Command of Rear Admiral Christian that are arrived in Portland Road with those that are stranded*:

Ship's name	How employed	Agent	Master	Lading	Damages, etc.
Golden Grove	Do.	-	-	Unknown Stores	Gone to pieces & (illegible) lost at the back of Portland.

Master and four men drowned. (Sgnd) Thos. Drury (HMS *Alfred*)

WO/1/798 f669 *List of East and West India ships, common Transports, to carry 16,276 troops..*:
Golden Grove, 200 tons, 110 men expected from the River.
(Sgnd) John Schank, Portsmouth, 15th Oct. 1795.

WO/6/168 Dundas to Treasury, Horseguards, (?) November 1795:
'...the vessel on board of which Lt-Col. Ross of the 21st Regiment had embarked was wrecked and the whole of the baggage and stores belonging to that officer totally lost...'

Golden Grove of London. Wm Hodzard. Robert Bagg, Master.
Lost: Dr Steven of St Kitts, Mr Burrows.
Saved: Lt-Col. Ross. Wm Hodgzard, Capt.

PRO Cust 59/20: *Golden Grove* of London, Robert Bogg [sic] Master, bound to St Kitts, laden with sundries, of which but a small part is saved. The Purser, 2 passengers and 2 boys were drowned. The master, 17 seamen and a Lt-Col. Ross were saved. NB: The ship went to pieces.

Sherborne and Yeovil Mercury, 23 November 1795 (*extract of a Letter from Weymouth, 19 November*): 'The *Golden Grove*, Robert Boss [sic], master, bound to St Christopher's, laden with sundry goods; soon after she struck went to pieces.'

Sherborne and Yeovil Mercury, Monday, 30 November (*Weymouth, 24 November 1795*): 'Particulars of the Loss of the Ships and of those that have received Damage on Portland Beach and on this Coast, on the 18th Instant, in a violent Gale of Wind at S.S.W.'

The Golden Grove *of London, Robert Bagg, master, bound to St Christopher's, laden with bale goods; the master, two passengers and two boys were drowned; Lt-Col. Ross and seventeen seamen saved; the ship went to pieces – Lost on Portland Beach.*

Smith's Narrative: '... the *Golden Grove* Merchant Ship. Dr Stevens of St Kitt's and a Mr Burrows were lost; Lt-Col. Ross escaped to the shore.'

Lloyd's Register, 1795: SsC (Copper sheathed); 91 (year repaired); Proudfoot (builder); 284 (tons); Soton (Southampton) 83 (year built); W. Hodzard; Miles & Co.; 15; Lo-Africa. (NB: This appears to be incorrect, as the voyage out is given as Africa.)

Lloyd's List, 20 November 1795 (*Marine List*) No.2769: The *Golden Grove,* Hodzard, from London to St Kitt's, is wrecked on Portland Beach. Very little of the Cargo saved.

Lost: Robert Boss, master, Dr Stevens of St Kitts, Mr Burrows, 2 boys
Saved: Lt-Col. Ross, 17 Seamen

The *Golden Grove* of London, 284 tons. Masters: Robert Boss/Bagg Proudfoot, William Hodzard. Bound to St Christopher/St Kitts, laden with sundries of which but a small part saved.

Piedmont

ADM/49/127:

Date of contract	Time of Entry into Pay	Tons	Parts	Owner
23/3/1793	6/4/1793	230	-	A/D Fraser

DDB/61/43 Shrapnell Narrative, with letter to Mrs Wilson, Weymouth, 21 December 1795: '(One of) The ships which went to pieces opposite these Villages [Chickerell, Langton and Fleet]; the *Piedmont*, Capt. Frazer, with Capt. Barcroft, Lieut Ash & c.' (p.47)

CO/318/18 *A Return of Transports Lost in West Bay and about Portland.*

Ships' Names	Masters' Names	No. of Horse/Foot	What Regiment
Piedmont	-	150	63

How many Sailors Saved	How many Soldiers Drowned	Officers Saved	Officers Drowned
4	139	none	Capt. Barcroft, Lt Ash, Mr Kelley, Surgeon, and the Master of the Ship

(Sgnd) Nathaniel Stuart, Weymouth, (?) November 1795.

ADM 108/148 Ship's ledger: *Piedmont* transport 243 7/94 tons. This ship was re-examined by Navy Board Office at Deptford and Purfleet to be 243 7/94 tons (subject to be re-measured). Date of press into service 23 March 1793 for total of 32 months 13 days. (For) owner Alexander Davison. Robert Frazer, Master.

ADM 108/158 Freight ledger:

Piedmont (re-measured by Navy Board Officers at Deptford) 243 7/94 tons.

Date of Charter	Entry into Pay	Discharge	Time employed
23 March 1793	6 March 1793	Lost on Portland Beach 18 Nov. 1795	32 mos 13 days

£	s	d
5123	9	3
218	8	7
5341	**17**	**10**

ADM 1/1717 *List of Vessels belonging to the Convoy under the Command of Rear Admiral Christian that are arrived in Portland Road with those that are stranded*:

Ship's name	How employed	Agent	Master	Lading	Damages, etc.
Piedmont	Transport	-	Unknown	-	Stranded at the above place.

[unclear] soldiers, all the officers and crew drowned. (Sgnd) Thos. Drury (HMS *Alfred*).

WO/1/798   f 25 *List of Transports at Spithead, ready to proceed under Captain William Hollanby*:

100th Regt total   (3 Div. Lt. Stevens)   *Piedmont*, 243 tons
600 rank and file   *Success*, 270 tons
     (Dated August 1794)

f 651 Embarkation List

Ships' Names	Tons	Troops
Piedmont	243	120

f 669 *List of East and West India ships, common Transports to carry 16,276 troops* ...

Piedmont, 243 tons, 120 men at Portsmouth and Southampton

(sgnd) John Schank, Portsmouth, 15 October 1795.

WO/12/7243 63 Muster: Surgeon Kelly dead 18 Nov. (Corporals ?) James Challis, John Somervill, James McKenzie.

WO/17/183: On 6 transports at Spithead. Barcroft's company consists of: 1 Capt. 1 Lt., 5 Serjeants, 2 drummers and fifer and 74 fit men, 1 in hospital, 1 on command, total 76. 24 rank and file waiting to complete. Return dated Dec 95. 'On the coast – great part lost' 65 of Barcroft's dead, 9 (ord.) seamen. 21 of James Alston's troop. 9 which were saved from the *Piedmont* transport on their way to the Isle of Wight by the *Brunswick* (see Appendix 5, pp.128-129) (H.C. Wylly, *History of the Manchester Regt*, p.120).

PRO Cust 59/20: *Piedmont ... bound to the West Indies, with troops, 138 soldiers and sailors were drowned (including the master) and 18 soldiers and sailors saved.*

DDB/70/8 Letter accompanying attested copy of Capt. Barcroft's Will, dated 27 November 1793:

> *Capt. Barcroft sailed from Spithead about 15th or 16th Inst. with a Fleet of Transports, Men of War, etc., destined for the West Indies, on board the Piedmont transport, a very bad vessel, as he informed me by letter of 7th inst, in so much that he had represented his ...[illegible] ... Government and hoped she wo'd be exchanged, (sgnd) (?) I.W. Bolton.*

W. Rhodes, 'A Night of Horror on the Chesil Beach', *Dorset Evening Echo*, Saturday 6 October 1962:

> Piedmont, *dismasted. Aboard her were 138 soldiers of the 63 Regt, commanded by Capt. Ambrose Barcroft... Sgt. Richardson... 11 soldiers and 4 seamen... saved. One soldier, his leg smashed, died upon the beach. Fifer Ensor attempted to swim back to the sinking ship. He died.*
> Piedmont, *Frazer capt. 63rd regt.*

Sherborne and Yeovil Mercury, Monday 23 November *(extract of a letter from Weymouth, 19 November)*: The *Piedmont* transport, bound to the West Indies with troops on board, the Captain, greatest part of the crew and of the troops are drowned.

Sherborne and Yeovil Mercury, Monday 30 November *(Weymouth, 24 November 1795)*: 'Particulars of the Loss of the Ships and those that have received Damage on Portland Beach, and on this Coast, on the 18 Instant, in a violent Gale of Wind at S.S.W.'

> The Piedmont *(a transport) bound to the West Indies, with troops; the master, 138 soldiers and seamen were drowned, 18 soldiers and seamen are saved. The ship went to pieces – Lost on Portland beach.*

Smith's Narrative:

> *On board the* Piedmont *were one hundred and thirty-eight soldiers of the 63rd regiment under the command of Captain Barcroft, Lieutenant Ash and Mr Kelly, Surgeon of the same regiment. Of all these, only Serjeant Richardson, eleven private soldiers and four seamen reached the shore alive – the rest perished ... [inc] Fifer Ensor.*

Lloyd's Register 94 and 95: *Piedmont*; S.s (spruce ?); J. Hall; Hull; 84 (year built); 232 (tons); SRP (some repairs); 90 (year repaired); Burstall & Co. (builder); 13 (foot draught); Hl-Str'ts; c (constant trader).

Lloyd's List (The Marine List) No.2769, Fri. 20 November 1795: The Piedmont (Transport) with Troops, is wrecked on Portland Beach. Only ten Men saved.

Piedmont 243 tons transport, owner Alexander Davison. Master Robert Frazer. Date of charter 23 March 1793. Examined by Navy Board office at Deptford and Purfleet. Bound to W.I. with troops, 63 Regt.

Piedmont. Drowned: Captain Ambrose William Barcroft (age 36) 63rd Regt; (total 138 soldiers); Lieut. Harry Ash; Mr Kelly, Reg. Surgeon; Fifer Ensor of 63rd went back to find his wife and never seen again. Saved: Serg. Richardson, 11 private soldiers, 4 seamen.

Venus

DDB/61/43 Shrapnell Narrative with letter to Mrs Wilson, Weymouth 21 December 1795: [One of] *the ships which went to pieces opposite these villages* [Chickerell, Langton and Fleet], *the Venus, Capt. Kidd, with Major Kerr (Commander of the Hospital Staff in the Leeward Islands), Lieut. Kerr, Lieut. Sutherland and Adjutant Creighton* [sic – Graydon], *several soldiers of the 115th Regt. and of other Regts. appointed to the Hospital Corps. From this ship Mr Darley was saved.' (p.47, 48.)*

CO/318/18 *A Return of Transports Lost in West Bay and about Portland*:

Ships' Names	Masters' Names	No. of Horse/Foot	What Regiment
Venus	Thos. Kidd	64	Invalids

How many Sailors Saved	How many Soldiers Drowned	Officers Saved	Officers' Names Drowned
4	52	Mr Darley, Surgeon	Maj. Ker, his son Lt Ker, Adj. Grayton, Lts Sutherland and Chadwick of a Black Corps

(Sgnd) Nathaniel Stuart. (?) Smith, Weymouth, (?) November 1795

ADM 108/158 Freight Ledger:
Venus 200 tons. J. Kidd master. (Hired of Campbell & Co. to carry troops etc. to the W.I.)
1795 Oct 8. To Bill 351 No.
Dist 2/2 8 15 6 1537 359 15 6
The ship having been wrecked on Portland Beach whilst prosecuting her voyage and 11 men only saved the account is directed to be closed per minute 29 Jan (18? – date unclear).

ADM/1/1717 *List of Vessels belonging to the convoy under the Command of Rear Admiral Christian that are arrived in Portland Road with those that are stranded:*

Ship's name	How employed	Agent	Master	Lading	Damages, etc.
Venus	Transport	-	Kidd	-	Stranded at the above place.

(Unclear) soldiers, 4 officers and eleven seamen drowned. (Sgnd) Thos. Drury (HMS *Alfred*)

WO/1/798   f 651 *Embarkation List:*

Ships' names	Tons	Troops	Regt	Officers	Sgts	Drms	Women
Venus	181	90	-	-	-	-	-

WO/12/5319 40th Regt. Muster. privates: Dead 18 November 1795 William Fuller.

PRO Cust 59/20: *Venus* of London, – Kidd Master, bound to the West Indies with troops. 81 soldiers and sailors (including the master), Major Kerr [sic] and son, Adjutant Grayton, Mess. Sutherland and Shaddick [sic – Chadwick] and five women passengers were drowned and sixteen soldiers and sailors and Mr Darley, surgeon, were saved. NB: the ship went to pieces. Major John Charles Ker, Military Commandant of Hospitals in the Leeward Islands.

W. Rhodes, 'A Night of Horror on the Chesil Beach', *Dorset Evening Echo*, Saturday 6 October 1962: *Venus*, 96 men and boys, 19 men and 1 boy were saved.

Sherborne and Yeovil Mercury, Monday 23 November (*Extract of a letter from Weymouth, 19 November 1795*):

> The Venus transport, bound to the West Indies, with troops on board; the Captain drowned; a part of the crew and of the troops are saved.

Sherborne and Yeovil Mercury, Monday 30 November (*Weymouth, 24 November 1795*): 'Particulars of the Loss of the Ships and of those that have received Damage, on Portland Beach, and on this Coast, on the 18 Instant, in a violent Gale of Wind at S.S.W.'

> The Venus of London (a transport) bound to the West Indies with troops; the master, Major Kerr and son, Adjutant Grayton, Messrs Sutherland and Shaddick [sic – Chadwick], five women, 81 soldiers and seamen were drowned; Mr Dafly [sic – Darley] Surgeon and sixteen soldiers and seamen are saved; the ship went to pieces – Lost on Portland beach.

Smith's Narrative:

> On board the Venus were Major Ker, appointed Military Commander of Hospitals in the Leeward Islands, his son, Lieutenant James Ker of the 40th Regt., Lieut. James Sutherland of Col. Whyte's West India Regt., Cornet Benjamin Graydon of the 3rd West India Regt., Lieut. B. Chadwick of Col. Whyte's West India Regt., Mr Kidd the Master, his wife, three other women, seventy-four soldiers and twelve seamen. Of all these (ninety-six persons) only Mr John Darley of the Hospital Staff, Serjeant-Major Hearne, twelve soldiers and four seamen and a boy were saved.

Lloyd's Register 1795: Ss (sheathed); 93(year repaired); T. Kidd; 230 (tons); N. Sco. (Nova Scotia (?)); 91 (year built); Willock; 13 (foot draught); Lo-Antig (London-Antigua).

Lloyd's List (The Marine List) No.2769, Fri. 20 November 1795: The Venus (Transport) of London, is wrecked on Portland Beach. Only eleven men saved.

Venus of London, 200 tons, hired of Campbell & Co. Master: J. Kidd. Bound to W.I. with troops (invalids) 115th reg., 40th reg., 3rd W.I. reg., Colonel Whyte's W.I. reg.

Venus of London. Kidd master. 115 reg. and other regs.

Venus Drowned: Maj. John Charles Ker (aged forty); son Lt James Ker (aged fourteen), (40th Regt); Lt James Sutherland (Col. Whytes's W.I. Reg.); Lt B. Chadwick (Col. Whyte's W.I. Regt); Cornet Benjamin Graydon (3 W.I. Regt); Mr Kidd (Master) and his wife; three other women, seventy-four soldiers and twelve seamen.

Saved: Mr John Darley of hospital staff; Sgt-Maj. Hearne; twelve soldiers; four seamen and a boy.

Catharine/Catherine

ADM/49/127:

Date of Contract	Time of Entry into Pay	Tons	Parts	Owner
6/9/1793	7/12/1793	253	92	George Browne, Alex Jolly

ADM/108/148 Ships Ledger: f113 *Catherine*, 253 tons, Cavalry transport. Owner: for owner George Browne. Alex Jolly master. Impressed cleared 1797, p.9.

DDB/61/43 Shrapnell Narrative with letter to Mrs Wilson, Weymouth 21 December 1795: 'One of the ships which went to pieces opposite these Villages [Chickerell, Langton and Fleet]; the *Catharine*, with Lieut. Jenner & cc.' (p.48, 49-52)

CO/318/18:

A Return of Transports Lost in West Bay and about Portland

Ships' Names	Masters' Names	No. of Horse/Foot	What Regiment
Cathrina [sic]	-	28	26th Light Horse

How many Sailors Saved	How many Soldiers Drowned	Officers Saved	Officers Names Drowned
1 boy	28	Mrs Burns, a Cornet's wife	Cornet Burns; Lts Jenner and Staynes; another name unknown going to join a Black Corps; Mr Dodd, surgeon

(Sgnd) Nathaniel Stuart, Weymouth (?) November 1795.

ADM/108/158:

Freight Ledger: Catharine Alex'r Jollie master. Tonnage 253 92/94.

Date of Charter	Entry into Pay	Discharge	Time Employed	Rate per Month
6 Dec. 1793	7 Dec. 1793	Lost 1795	23 mos 12 days	13/

	£	s	d
Sum	3862	1	10
Disc	196	3	-
	4058	4	10

ADM 1/1717 *List of Vessels belonging to the Convoy under the Command of Rear Admiral Christian that are arrived in Portland Road, with those that are stranded*:

Ship's Name	How employed	Agent	Master	Lading	Damages, etc.
Unknown	-	-	-	-	Foundered at her anchor at the back of Portland and all perished.

(Sgnd) Drury (HMS *Alfred*).

WO/12/1512 Returns for 26th Light Dragoons:

Cornet Stukeley Burns,	joined 10 June	died 16 November 1795.
Serjeant Jesh. Clampson		ditto
Private Ebeneezer Watson		ditto

Lost on board the *Catharine* transport 16 November: Privates Jno Baker (?); Robt. Burden; Littleton Daws; John Guest; Thos Gibson; Edwd Lilley; Willm Musson; John Turner; Richd Tomlin; John Philips; Willm Princip; Jas Redman; Josh Speakman; Isac Jetham; Stephen Tasker.

PRO Cust 59/20: *Catherine* – Cromey, Master, bound to the West Indies and 28 horses and twenty-eight men. Lieut. Staines, Lieut Jenner, Cornet Burns, Mr Dodds, surgeon, and all the crew were drowned and Mrs Burns and a boy were only saved. NB: the ship went to pieces.

Sherborne and Yeovil Mercury, Mon. 30 November (*Weymouth, 24 November 1795*): 'Particulars of the Loss of the Ships and of those that have received Damage, on Portland Beach, and on this Coast on the 18 Instant, in a violent Gale of Wind at S.S.W.'

> The *Catherine* of *Montrose, a transport, Cromey, master, bound to the West Indies, with 28 horses &c. on board; the master, Lieutenants Jenner and Staines, Cornet Burns, Mr Dodd, surgeon, two women, 28 soldiers and the ship's crew were drowned; Mrs Burns and a boy are saved; the ship went to pieces – Lost on Portland Beach.*

Smith's Narrative:

> *The persons that perished, of the crew and passengers in this vessel, were: Twenty-two soldiers of the 26th Light Dragoons; Two soldiers' wives and twelve seamen. There were also the horses belonging to the soldiers on board. The officers were: Lt. Stains, of Keppel's West India Regt, [sic – Myers's, 2nd W.I.] Mr Dodd, of the Hospital Staff, Lieut. Jenner, (Col. Whitelocke's, 6th W.I.), Cornet Burns ... 'He was in his twenty-fourth year'. Saved: Mrs Burns and 'no other person ... but a Ship-boy, about fifteen ...'*

Lloyd's Register 1795: Ss (sheathed); A. Jollie; 235 (tons); SDE (single deck); MntrS (Montrose); 86 (year built); Drp (damages repaired); 92 (? year repaired); Gardner Riga-Ph (Riga-Portsmouth).
NB: Also *Catherine*, Ss; W. Steel; 324 (tons); Wtby (Whitby); 89 (year built); Potts; Lo(ndon)-Jamai(ca).

Lloyd's List (The Marine List) No.2770, Tues. 24 November 1795: The *Catharina* (Transport) of Montrose, is lost on Portland Beach. Only one Woman and a Boy saved.

Catherine Catherina, Cromey master 26 reg.

Catherine of Montrose, also spelt *Catherina*.
253 tons Cavalry transport. Owner George Browne. Master: Alex Jolly, Cromey. Date of Charter 6 Dec. 1793. Bound to W.I. 28 men and 28 horses 26th L Drag, 2 W.I. reg., 6 W.I. reg.

Catherine Lt Stephen Jenner; 6th W.I. regt, (Col. Whitelocke's regt), age 31; Lt Stains (2nd W.I. regt, Keppel's W.I. regt [*sic* – Myers']; Cornet Wm Stukeley Burns (26th Light Dragoons), aged 24; Mr Dodd, Surgeon, hospital staff.
Lost: 22 soldiers 26th L/D, 2 soldiers' wives, 12 seamen.
Saved: Mrs Burns, [a] Boy, 15 years old.

Thomas

R. & B. Larn, *Shipwreck Index of the British Isles*, Vol.I, Sec. 6:
Thomas; London-Oporto; Cargo: logwood (unspecified); built 1791 New Brunswick; Capt: Brown.

DDB/61/43 Shrapnell Narrative with letter to Mrs Wilson, Weymouth 21 December 1795:
[One of] *the ships which went to pieces opposite these Villages* [Chickerell, Langton and Fleet], *the Thomas, a Merchant Ship bound to Oporto, laden with logwood &c. from this wreck a young gentleman (passenger) whose name is Smith was miraculously saved long after every person had left it.* (p.48)

PRO Cust 59/20: *Thomas*, Thomas Brown, master, bound to Oporto, laden with bail [*sic*] goods, logwood, coppera [*sic* – probably *copperas*, another name for ferrous sulphate, for water purification and other uses] etc. etc.. The master, his son, 7 seamen, one man and three women passengers were drowned. The mate, four seamen and 1 passenger saved. NB: The ship went to pieces. No part of her cargo saved.

Sherborne and Yeovil Mercury, Mon. 23 November (*extract of a letter from Weymouth, 19 November*):
The ship Thomas *of London, burthen about 350 tons. Thomas Brown, master, for Oporto, laden with logwood, &c. Soon after she struck she went to pieces. The Captain, his son, a surgeon, seven seamen, a young man and three women passengers were drowned; a young man, a passenger whose name is Smyth and two seamen are saved. The ship went to pieces – Lost on Portland Beach.*

Sherborne and Yeovil Mercury, Mon. 30 November (*Weymouth, 24 November 1795*): 'Particulars of the Loss of the Ships and those that have received Damage, on Portland Beach and on this Coast, on the 18 Instant, in a violent Gale of Wind at S.S.W.'
The ship Thomas, *of London, burthen about 350 tons, Thomas Brown, master, bound to Oporto, partly laden with bale goods, logwood &c.&c; the Captain, his son, seven*

seamen, a young man and three women passengers were drowned; the mate, four seamen and a young lad whose name is Smyth, a passenger, are saved. The ship went to pieces – Lost on Portland Beach.

Smith's Narrative:

In the Thomas, *of London, a Merchant Ship bound to Oporto, the Master, Mr Brown, his Son and all the Crew except the Mate, three Seamen and one Passenger were lost: this Passenger was a young gentleman, about the age of fifteen, of the name of Smith, who was going to Lisbon. He too was probably preserved by remaining on board after all the rest had left the ship or been washed from it by the waves. It had then drifted high on the bank and he leaped from it to the ground.*

Lloyd's Register 1795: Ss (sheathed); T. Brown; 270 (tons); N. Bruns (New Brunswick); 91 (year built); T. Brown; Lo-Oporto.

Lloyd's List (The Marine List) No.2769, Fri. 20 November 1795: The Thomas, Brown, from London to Oporto is totally lost, on Portland Beach.

Thomas, Thos. Brown, Master, to Oporto.

Lost: Thomas Brown (master); his son; seven seamen; young man; three women passengers. Saved: The Mate; four seamen; lad named Smyth.

Appendix 3

Other Ships Lost and Stranded

Almost every one of the West India fleet has received damage as well as the men of war. The merchant ships are ordered to Spithead, so that their sailing again cannot be speedily expected.
The Times, Monday 23 November (*Portsmouth, 20 November*)
Sherborne and Yeovil Mercury 23 November (*extract of a letter from Portsmouth 20 November*)

Ships Lost

Commerce, 238 tons
WO/1/798 (Transport Office):

f 34 *Arrangement for proposed Services*, 4 September 1794. (Vessels) to receive at Chatham 700 Rank and File belonging to Regiments in the West Indies, thence to Netley Abbey. The *Commerce*, 238 tons, gone to Plymouth, there to receive the 96th Regt. of 597 Rank and File. Return to Portsmouth and thence to S. Domingo.
f 109 *List of Transports to receive Regiments*, 17 December 1794.
The *Commerce*, 230 tons (for women and baggage).

The Times; Sherborne and Yeovil Mercury (as above):
The *Commerce, Robinson*, with troops, one of said ships, is totally lost.

Lloyd's List, (The Marine List), No.2770, Tues. 24 Nov.: The *Commerce*, Robertson, (Transport) ... on shore at Portsmouth and much damaged. The People saved.

Troopship, Un-named
Sherborne and Yeovil Mercury, 23 November (*extract of a letter from Portsmouth, 20 November 1795*); *The Times*, Mon. 23 November 1795 (*Poole, 20 November*):
– it is said another Troop Ship is also totally lost on the Isle of Wight and only two persons saved.

Pitt
Sherborne and Yeovil Mercury, Mon. 30 November (*Weymouth, 24 November 1795*):
'Particulars of the Loss of the Ships and of those that have received Damage, on Portland Beach, and on this Coast, on the 18 instant, in a violent Gale of Wind at S.S.W.'
   The ship *Pitt*, of London, John Horn master, bound to the West Indies with stores and provisions; the crew are all saved and the ship sets a whale – On shore near Incomb, to the westward of St. Oldham's Head.

Lloyd's List (The Marine List) No.2769, Fri. 20 Nov.:
The *Pitt*, Horn, a Transport, is lost near St. Alban's Head. Crew saved.

Ships Stranded, Damaged, etc.

Britannia: Ordnance Transport.

WO/1/798 f 949 John Schank to War Office, 9 December 1795:
Britannia severely damaged by an East Indiaman.

WO/6/142   f 118 Huskisson to Crew, War Office 21 December 1795:
The *Britannia* ordnance transport to go under the protection of Madras to the West Indies.

Lloyd's List (The Marine List) No.2779, Tues. 24 November: The *Britannia*, Wood, (and the *Commerce*), (Transports), are on shore at Portsmouth and much damaged. The People saved.

Hannah: Ordnance Transport, 300 tons.

R. & B. Larn, Shipwreck Index of the British Isles, Vol.I, Sec. 6:
... carrying ordnance stores, was run foul of by the transport *Harmony*, which was in the same convoy, causing the *Hannah* to go on shore near Hills Harbour.

CO/318/18 *A Return of Transports Lost in West Bay and about Portland:*

Ships' Names	Masters' Names	No. of Horse/Foot	What Regiment
Hannah	A. Hickman	Loaded with Ordnance Stores.	

How many Sailors Saved	How many Soldiers Drowned	Officers Saved	Officers Names Drowned
All saved	And we have saved two lighterloads of Her Stores and have hopes of getting at them all.		

(Sgnd) Nathaniel Stuart, Weymouth, (?) November 1795.

ADM/1/1717 *A List of Vessels belonging to the Convoy under the Command of Rear Admiral Christian that are arrived in Portland Road with those that are stranded*:

Ship's Name	How employed	Agent	Master	Lading	Damages, etc.
Hannah	Ordnance stores	-	Hickman	Ordnance	Stranded in Weymouth Bay.

Crew saved.
(Sgnd) Thos. Drury (HMS *Alfred*).

WO/1/798   f 29 Christian, Patton and Searle to Dundas, Transport Office, 3 September 1794:
The *Hannah* a Cavalry Transport with horses on board, refitted and waiting for convoy to the Downs (from Great Yarmouth).
f 175 Lt Skipsey, Agent of Transports. Bought of John Wilkey, Tierces of moist sugar for the following ships: Hannah 5 0 24, Eolus (Attested Alex Whithead, Plymouth 1794.)
f 177 *Scheme for the distribution of sugar at the rate of half a pound each man per week for two months, being troops destined for foreign service under the direction of Capt. Geo. Rice, Principal Agent.*

Ship	Troops	(?) Sugar	Women	Children	(?) Sugar	Casks
Hannah	137	548	7	4	36	4

(January 1795)

WO/6/142 Dundas to Cornwallis, 20 November 1795: ... the *Hannah* transport, laden with Ordnance Stores for the Expedition to the West Indies, has been lost ...

WO/1/798   f 717 *Transports taking in Ordnance Stores at Woolwich:*
... *Hannah*, 323 tons (October 1795).

Sherborne and Yeovil Mercury, 23 November. (*Extract of a letter from Weymouth, 19 November 1795*):

> The ship Hannah, of London, Andrew Hickman Master, bound to the West Indies, with ordnance stores, the master and crew saved.

Sherborne and Yeovil Mercury, Mon. 30 November (*Weymouth, 24 November 1795*): 'Particulars of the Loss of the Ships and of those that have received Damage on Portland Beach and on this Coast on the 18 Instant in a violent Gale of Wind at S.S.W.'

> The ship Hannah, of London, burthen about 300 tons, Andrew Hickman, master, bound to Martinique with ordnance stores; the crew are all saved; the ship very much damaged. NB: This ship was run foul of by the Harmony transport.

Lloyd's List, (The Marine List), No.2679, Fri. 20 Nov.: The *Hannah*, Hickman, (Ordnance Transport) is on shore about four miles from Weymouth.

Harmony: Ordnance Transport

ADM/1/1717 *A List of Vessels belonging to the Convoy under the Command of Rear Admiral Christian that are arrived in Portland Road with those that are stranded*:

Ship's Name	How employed	Agent	Master	Lading	Damages, etc.
Harmony	Ordnance ship	-	Wilson	Ordnance	Bowsprit sprung

(Sgnd) Thos. Drury, (HMS *Alfred*)

WO/1/798   f 177 *Scheme for the distribution of sugar, etc*:

Ship	Troops	(?) Sugar	Women	Children	(?) Sugar	Casks
Harmony	146	584	7	2	32	4

(January 1795)

Sherborne and Yeovil Mercury, Mon. 30 November (*Weymouth, 24 November 1795*): 'Particulars of the Loss of the Ships and of those that have received Damage, on Portland Beach, and on this Coast, on the 18 Instant, in a violent Gale of Wind at S.S.W.'

... *Harmony* transport, of London, Alexander Wilson, Master, bound to the West Indies – on shore near Hills Harbour.

Firm: Ordnance Transport, 320 tons.

ADM/1/1717 *A List of Vessels belonging to the Convoy under the Command of Rear Admiral Christian that are arrived in Portland Road, with those that are stranded*:

Ship's name	How employed	Agent	Master	Lading	Damages, etc.
Firm	Ordnance ship	Stewart	Freestone	Ordnance	All her masts gone

(Sgnd) Thos. Drury, (HMS *Alfred*)

WO/1/798   f 177 *Scheme for the distribution of sugar, etc.*

Ship	Troops	(?) Sugar	Women	Children	(?) Sugar	Casks
Firm	105	420	11	-	44	3

(January 1795.)

WO/6/142 Dundas to Cornwallis, War Office, 20 November 1795:
>... the Firm *and* Sisters *Ordnance Transports intended for the* [West Indies] *are unable to proceed on account of the damage they have received ... the cargoes of the three vessels* [inc. Hannah] *are to be immediately replaced and shipped on board the* Madras *Man of War, now at Longreach, under orders to proceed to the Leeward Islands the moment its loading shall be completed.*

WO/1/798   f 34 *Arrangements for Proposed Services*, 4 September 1794:
Disposable Transports at Plymouth.
Firm, 320 tons.
f 717 *Transports taking in Ordnance Stores at Woolwich ...*
Firm, 320 tons (October 1795).

Sherborne and Yeovil Mercury, Mon. 30 November (*extract of a letter from Weymouth, 29 November 1795*): 'HMS *Alfred* and a frigate came into Portland Road, also the ship *Firm* of London, Dixon [*sic*] Master, bound to the West Indies, she is dismasted.'

Sherborne and Yeovil Mercury, Mon. 30 November (*Weymouth, 24 November 1795*): 'Particulars of the Loss of the Ships, and of those that have received Damage, on Portland Beach and on this Coast, on the 18 Instant, in a violent Gale of Wind at S.S.W.'
>   The ship *Firm*, of London, Joseph Theakston, Master, bound to Martinique with ordnance stores, dismasted. At anchor in Weymouth Bay.

Lloyd's List, (The Marine List), No.2769, Fri. 20 Nov.: The *Firm* (Transport), of London, is dismasted in Weymouth Roads.

Alexander: Ordnance Transport

'...Loaded with Field Pieces, Howitzers, Shot, Shells, and powder, is drove out of the Downes and has not since been heard of ...' (Sir Charles Saxton to Admiral Cornwallis, from G. Cornwallis-West, *The Life and Letters of Admiral Cornwallis*, p.305.)

Sisters: Ordnance Transport

'... that the *Sisters*, another Ordnance Storeship with nearly the same kind of Loading, was run foul of and is now in Margate Pier with her sides stove in ...' (Sir Charles Saxton to Admiral Cornwallis, from *The Lives and Letters of Admiral Cornwallis*, p.306)

WO/6/142 Dundas to Cornwallis, War Office, 20 November 1795:
>... the Firm *and* Sisters *Ordnance Transports intended for the* [West Indies] *are unable to proceed on account of the damage they have received ... the cargoes of the three vessels* [inc. Hannah] *are to be immediately replaced and shipped on board the* Madras *Man of War, now at Longreach, under orders to proceed to the Leeward Islands the moment its loading shall be completed.*

Hope of Bristol

ADM/1/1717 A List of Vessels belonging to the Convoy under the Command of Rear Admiral Christian that are arrived in Portland Road with those that are stranded:

Ship's name	How employed	Agent	Master	Lading	Damages, etc.
Hope	Transport	Orton	Retsen ?	197 troops of 88th	Main and Mizen Masts gone. Leaky

(Sgnd) Thos. Drury, (HMS *Alfred*).

Sherborne and Yeovil Mercury, 30 November (*Weymouth, 24 November 1795*): 'Particulars of the Loss of the Ships, and of those that have received Damage, on Portland Beach, and on this Coast, on the 18 Instant, in a violent Gale of Wind at S.S.W.'

> The Hope, *of Bristol (a transport), with troops on board for the West Indies, lost her main and mizen masts. At Anchor in Weymouth Bay.*

William Pitt

R. & B. Larn, Shipwreck Index of the British Isles, Vol.I, Sec. 6:
William Pitt Isle of Wight – West Indies; Port: London; Cargo: Provisions (and) Additional Cargo (stores); built 1776.

The Times, Mon. 23 November 1795 (*Poole, 20 November*):

> On Wednesday afternoon the William Pitt *transport, one of the outward-bound West India Fleet, was driven on shore near Encombe, in the Isle of Purbeck. A part of the ship's crew, and a few of the soldiers came on shore in the night, and the whole of the remaining part the next morning; providentially there were no lives lost, which is a little extraordinary, considering the situation of the place. One of the Hospital Mates had his thigh broken in attempting to get into the boat to come on shore; he was under the necessity of remaining in that state during the night and the greatest part of the next day until boats could take him from the ship, which they at last effected but with a great deal of difficulty.*

Lloyd's List (The Marine List) No.2770, Tues. 24 Nov.: The *William Pitt* (Transport) is on shore near Poole.

The *William Pitt*, driven ashore at Chapman's Pool, Isle of Purbeck. No lives lost.

Others, Un-Named

The Times, Fri. 20 November 1795 (*Portsmouth, 18 November*):
'Five sail of ships are on shore: two with troops, two with merchandize and one with horses.' (Probably including *Britannia.*)

Appendix 4

Ships Put in to Portland Roads

... the Admiral made ... the Rendezvous signal [for] *Torbay, but the violence of the wind not permitting us to carry the necessary sail to fetch that port, I gave directions to bear up for Portland, being the next Rendezvous to Leeward, in order to lead in such ships of the convoy as were in sight and had bore away.*

HMS Alcmene *anchored here soon after with several ships, names unknown, one of which is dismasted ... the others appear to be much damaged by loss of sails, etc.*
ADM/1/1717   HMS *Alfred* (Capt. Thomas Drury), in Portland Road, to Nepean at the Admiralty, 18 November 1795

ADM/51/1110   *A Journal of the Proceedings of HM Ship* Alcmene *Between the 25th January 1795 and the 31st January 1796 (Capt. Wm Brown):* 'Came in here and anchored HM Ship *Alfred* with eight sail of the Convoy.'

Sherborne and Yeovil Mercury, Mon. 23 November (extract from a letter from Weymouth, 20 November 1795):
   HM ship Alfred *and a frigate came into Portland Road; also the ship* Firm *of London, Dixon* [sic], *Master, bound to the West Indies; she is dismasted.* (see App. 3)
   There are several other ships in the Road, but cannot as yet learn their names.

Lloyd's List (The Marine List) No.2769, Fri. 20 Nov.: The *Alfred* Man of War, with several sail of ships, are safe in Weymouth and Portland Roads, after the Gale.

HMS *Alfred* (Capt. Thos. Drury).
Main topsail yard sprung (ADM/51/1178 ship's log Thurs. 19).

HMS *Alcmene* (Capt. William Brown).
Larboard bumpkin carried away (ADM/51/1110, log, 18 Nov.)

The ***Sally*** Infantry transport, with 130 troops of 29th Regt, undamaged. (ADM/1/1717, A List of Transports ... (Drury); Christian to Nepean, on board *Irresistible*, 25 November.)

The *Mary Ann* Infantry Transport. (ADM/1/317 Christian to Nepean, on board *Irresistible*, St Helens, 25 November 1795); (Lt-Col. Paget to the Earl of Uxbridge, extract from a letter dated 21 November 1795, Soldiers of Gloucestershire Museum Archive.)

The *Marquis of Worcester* Victualling Transport, Master Stephen Casey, undamaged. (ADM/1/1717, A List of Transports ... (Drury); ADM/1/317 Christian to Nepean, on board *Irresistible*, 25 November; ADM/D/39/23/09 Victualling Office to Nepean, 23 September 1795.)

The *Fanny* Victualling Transport, Francis Patterson, Master. (ADM/1/317 Christian to Nepean, 25 November; ADM/D/39/23/09 Victualling Office to Nepean, 23 September 1795.)

The *Enterprise* (ADM/1/317 Christian to Nepean, 25 November).

The *Juba* Hospital Ship, undamaged (ADM/1/1717, A List ... (Drury); ADM/1/317 Christian to Nepean, 25 November).

The *Patty* Cavalry Transport, several sails lost. (ADM/1/1717, A List ... (Drury); Christian to Nepean, 25 November).

The *General Cuyler* West Indiaman, undamaged. (ADM/1/1717, A List ... (Drury); ADM/1/317 Christian to Nepean, 25 November.)

The *Lady Jane* Transport, left at Portland, unfit to proceed. (ADM/1/317 Christian to Nepean, 25 November.)

Ships returned with Christian to St Helens, 21 November 1795

This morning Rear Admirals Christian and Pole returned to St Helens with as many of the fleet and convoy as could be collected, after the separation, in the very tremendous gale of Wednesday ...
Sherborne and Yeovil Mercury, 23 November (extract of a letter from Portsmouth, 20 November 1795)

This day arrived the Commerce de Marseilles, Prince George *and the other men of war which sailed for the West Indies. The greater part of the fleet are again at St Helens.*
The Times, Mon. 23 November (Portsmouth, 20 November)

(NB: the log of the *Prince George*, 21 November and Christian's letter to Admiralty, 21 November (both ADM/1/317) confirm that they anchored on the Saturday, the 21st.)

West India Ships:

Doncaster
Trelawney Planter
Leighton
Elizabeth Grant
Hope (Stevenson)
Brigetown
Sally (Johnston)
St Mary's Planter
Susannah
Astrea
Susannah (Shelton)
Welcome Messenger
Harriot
Francis and Harriot
William and Mary (carried 676 rank and file of the 17th to the West Indies in 1794 in a convoy with *Piedmont*. ADM/1/317 Vice Admiral Ben. Caldwell to Phillip Stevens, Admiralty, *Majestic*, off St Pierre, Martinique, 3 January 1795; WO/1/798 f25 *List of Transports at Spithead ready to proceed under Capt. Wm Hollanby*)

James (Navy victualler)

Mary E. Smith

Amelia

Draxhall

General Elliott (Ordnance ship)

Prince

Britannia (2)

Francis and Eliza

Eastridge

Britannia (1)

Belfast

Golden Grove (Master McLeod (?). NB: There were two *Golden Groves* in the convoy)

Argo

Success (invalid ship carrying the Hospital Corps WO/25/1146 Embarkation Returns)

Industry

Harbinger hospital ship (WO/25/1146 also WO/1/662 Hayes to ? Lewis, Southampton, 15 October 1795)

Bushy Park

Julius

East India Ships:

Raymond

Ganges

Britannia

Houghtons

Duke of Montrose

Dutton

Phoenix

King George (lost her mizen mast)

Middlesex (lost her bowsprit on 15 November 'by a ship getting foul of her')

Sullivan (ran foul of *Impregnable*).

Gen. Elliot 'mizen'

Contractor 'mizen'

Valentine 'mizen'

Sir Edward Hughes 'mizen'

Ponsborn 'mizen'

Rose 'mizen'

('mizen' = lost mizen masts ?)

(WO/1/798 Ships, (transports), sailed with Admiral Christian and put back to Portsmouth, 20 November 1795. (Sgnd) John Schank.)

(Believed Christian's whole squadron returned with him, with the exception of *Alfred* and *Alcmene*.)

The Ships of Christian's Fleet
(15 November 1795)

Christian's Naval Squadron

Prince George, Capt. James Bowen, ninety-eight guns[1].
Colossus, Rear Admiral Maurice Pole, Capt. Henry Jenkins, seventy-four guns[2].
Alcmene, Capt. William Brown, thirty-two guns.
La Prompte, Capt. Edward Leveson-Gower, twenty-eight guns.
Impregnable, Capt. John Thomas, ninety-eight guns.
Irresistible, Capt. George Murray, seventy-four guns.
Albacore, Capt. Edward Fellowes, sixteen guns.
Alfred, Capt. Thomas Drury, seventy-four guns.
Polyphemus, Capt. George Lumsdaine, sixty-four guns (ordered to store and victual at Cork).
Leda, Capt. Woodley, thirty-six guns (ordered to Cork to convoy a merchant fleet to the West Indies)[3].
Babet, Capt. William Lobb, twenty-two guns.
Lion, Capt. George Palmer, sixty-four guns (ordered to relieve *Trident*).
Trident, Capt. E. Osborne, sixty-four guns (to take charge of loading the transports).
Undaunted, Capt. Henry Roberts, thirty-eight guns (replaced *Lively*).
Requin armed brig, Lt William Champion (sailed 2 November with despatches to Laforey).
L'Eclair gunboat, Lt the Honourable Dunbar Douglas, eight guns, (unfit to proceed).
Crachefeu gunboat, Lt Lewis Mortlock.
Terror gunboat, Cdr David Hotchkiss, eight guns.
Vesuve, gunboat, Lt Halliday.
Etrusco storeship, Capt. Handon.
Commerce de Marseilles, Capt. Smith Childs, 120 guns (carried 900 rank and file of 57th Foot, under Gen. Campbell).

(ADM/1/317, note on letter from Christian to Nepean, *Prince George*, Spithead, 15 September and Christian to Nepean, *Prince George*, Spithead, 25 October 1795 (*Polyphemus* and *Vesuve*); ADM/2/129 Lords' Letters, Orders and Instructions, Spencer, Middleton and Gambier to Rear Admiral Maurice Pole, the Captains and Lieutenants of Christian's Fleet, dated 16 September 1795; ADM/2/941, Secretary's Letters to Commanders in Chief of Squadrons, Nepean to Christian, 23 October 1795 (*Polyphemus*), and Nepean to Christian, 26 October 1795 (*Vesuve*); CO/318/18 *A List of His Majesty's Ships, etc. at Spithead under the Command of Rear Admiral Christian, etc.*, dated 9 October 1795; *Commerce de Marseilles*: WO/1/84 War Office to

Abercromby, Horseguards, 28 September 1795 and folio 37, (undated) War Office to Abercromby; WO/25/1146 *Embarkation Returns – for Leeward Islands*; CO/318/18 Christian to Huskisson, Portsmouth, 2 October, Christian to Huskisson, on board *Prince George*, Spithead, 4 October 1795.)

The Transports: East and West Indiamen

Bellona, Ajax, Fowler, Harmony, Patty, Jane, William and Robert and *Lynx* carried the 26th Light Dragoons, embarked Southampton. *Fowler* cavalry transport, lost on Cornish coast 25 January 1796, all lives lost.

Ponsborn, Phoenix East Indiamen, carried the 3rd Regt of Foot, embarked Spithead 26 October.

Britannia, Ganges East Indiamen, carried the 19th Regt of Foot, embarked Spithead 3 Nov.

Raymond, Houghton East Indiamen, carried the 31st Regt of Foot, embarked Gosport 29 Oct.

Sullivan, Sir Edward Hughes East Indiamen, carried the 33rd Regt of Foot, embarked Gosport 2 November.

General Elliot, Duke of Montrose East Indiamen, carried the 8th Regt of Foot, embarked Gosport 3 November.

Basseterre, Belsey, Superb, Darlington, Guernsey Lilley and *Elizabeth* carried the 37th Regt of Foot, embarked Southampton 29 October.

Julian, Boddington, Marian, Trelawney, Eastridge carried the 44th Regt of Foot, embarked Southampton 26 October. *Boddington* also carried the 25th – one of the ten transports which reached Torbay in the first storm and arrived in the West Indies after the second. (*Dyott's Diary*, p.82 and 95)

Amelia, Francis, Eliza, Hope, Bridgetown and *Jonas* carried the 55th Regt of Foot, embarked Southampton 26 Oct.

Susannah, Forster, Mary Smith, Lively and *Ulysses* carried 38th Regt of Foot, embarked Southampton 26 Oct.

Stanley, Mary Spence, Mary Pickfield, Pritzler, Douglas carried 48th Regt of Foot, embarked Southampton 26 October. *Pritzler* 'foundered at sea, every soul perished' on the fleet's return to Southampton, second storm. (*The Times*, Mon. 1 February, *Southampton 29 January*)

Generous Planter, William and Mary, Polly, Mary Ford, Augustus Cesar carried 53rd Regt of Foot, embarked Southampton 27 Oct. *Augustus Cesar* also carried clothing for 1st West India Regt (Col. Whitelock's). (WO/4/337 Lewis to Transport Board 17 Sept 1795)

Brunswick, Bushy Park, Piedmont, Golden Grove (McLeod?) carried 63rd Regt of Foot, embarked Southampton 27 October. *Brunswick* allegedly saved nine men from the *Piedmont*. (H.C. Wylly, *History of the Manchester Regt*, p.120; WO/17/183). *Bushy Park* together with *Brunswick*, reputedly arrived in the West Indies after the second storm. (Wylly, p.121)

Prince, Brothers, Simon Taylor carried the 2nd Regt of Foot, embarked Southampton 4 November. *Simon Taylor* was one of the ten ships to reach Torbay in the storm. (ADM/1/3730 William Watt, Master, *Simon Taylor* Transport, Torbay, to Transport Board, 19 November 1795)

Mary Ann, Forster, Barham together with *Boddington*, carried the 25th Regt of Foot, embarked Southampton 25 October.

St Sebastian, Somerset, Sally carried the 29th Regt of Foot, embarked Southampton 18 October.

Jamaica, William Beckford, Hope carried the 88th Regt of Foot, embarked on the 3 November. *Hope* was stranded in Weymouth Bay.

Dutton, King George East Indiamen, carried the First Grenadiers, embarked Gosport 26 October.

Valentine, Contractor East Indiamen, carried Second Grenadiers, embarked Mother Bank 26 October.

Rose, Middlesex East Indiamen, carried 42nd Foot, or Highlanders, embarked Mother Bank 26 October.

Success, Venus carried invalids from the various Regiments and the Hospital Corps. Maj. John Charles Ker, Military Commandant of Hospitals in the Leeward Islands and his son Lt James Ker, 40th Foot were on board *Venus*. *Success* also took men from the *Pitt* transport (of the *Commerce de Marseilles* convoy) which sprang a leak. (CO/318/18 Christian to Huskisson, Portsmouth 7 October 1795)

Francis and Harriot, Calypso, Draxhall, Industry carried the 14th Regt of Foot. *Draxhall's* bowsprit was carried away by HMS *Vengeance* (74g) 5 November 1795. (*The Gentleman's Magazine*, Vol.XVI, Part II, p.963)

Alexander, Eagle, Rambler, Austrian, Elizabeth, St Mary's Planter carried the 27th Regt of Foot. *Elizabeth* was found unfit to proceed, troops transferred to *Impregnable*.

Sally, Lady Jane, Pitt, Lyde, Mary Anne, Mary and Elizabeth, carried the 28th Regt of Foot. *Lady Jane* was damaged 18 November, remained at Portland Roads.

The last three Regiments, total 2,600 men, together with the 57th Regt, 900 Rank and File on board the *Commerce de Marseilles*, embarked at Southampton under General Campbell on 29/30 September 1795. (CO/318/18 List of Transports to embark 2,600 men ... (sgnd) Schank, October 1795; CO/318/18 Christian to Huskisson, *Prince George*, Spithead, 4 October 1795; WO/1/84 Dundas to Abercromby, Horseguards 21 October 1795)

(WO/25/1146 Embarkation Returns – for the Leeward Islands.)

NB: This Embarkation Return is not complete. It does not, for example, include the *Catherine* cavalry transport which carried the 26th Light Dragoons (sank on the Chesil 18 November 1795) or some of the stranded and damaged transports. Several transports not included may have been added to the convoy at the last moment. Other transports (both troops and stores) known to have sailed are:

Commerce, Robinson, lost at Portsmouth, carried troops. (*Sherborne and Yeovil Mercury*, 23 November 1795)

Enterprise (troops), *General Cuyler* (troops). Put into Portland Roads with HMS *Alfred*. (ADM/1/1717 A List of Vessels .... (sgnd) Drury, HMS *Alfred*)

Traveller (troops), *Marquis of Carmarthen* (troops) (CO/318/18 *List of Transports, to embark 2,600 men* (Schank))

Auxiliaries

Hanna, (Ordnance) – stranded in Weymouth Bay, about four miles from Weymouth. (*Lloyd's List*, Fri. 20 November)

Harmony (Ordnance) – stranded in Weymouth Bay, near Hills Harbour. (*Sherborne and Yeovil Mercury*, Mon. 30 November 1795)

Firm (Ordnance), *Juba* (Hospital Ship). Put into Portland Roads with HMS *Alfred*. (ADM/1/1717 A List of Vessels ... (sgnd) Drury, HMS *Alfred*)

Golden Grove, Aeolus, Pitt, Adventure stores transports. *Golden Grove* sank on the Chesil 18 November 1795. *Aeolus* sank on the Chesil 18 November 1795. *Pitt* (Horn) sank near St Aldhelm's Head 18 November 1795 (*Sherborne and Yeovil Mercury*, 30 November; *Lloyd's List*, Fri. 20 November). *Adventure* (ADM/1/317 log of *Prince George*, 16 November.)

Britannia badly damaged by an East Indiaman, stranded at Portsmouth. (WO/1/798 f 949 Schank to War Office, 9 December 1795; Lloyd's List, Tues. 24 November)

Alexander 'loaded with Field Pieces, Howitzers, Shot, Shells and powder ... is drove out of the Downes and has not since been heard of ...' (*The Life and Letters of Admiral Cornwallis*, p.305)

Sisters (similarly loaded to the *Alexander*, 'run foul off [*sic*] and is now in Margate Pier with her sides stove in ...' (*The Life and Letters of Admiral Cornwallis*, p.306)

Mellish, Doncaster, John, Governor Wentworth Ordnance Transports. (WO/1/798 Heart to Transport Board, *Alexander*, in the Downs, 5 November 1795). *Governor Wentworth* was convoyed from Plymouth to Portsmouth with stores for the expedition – not known whether she sailed with Christian. (ADM/1/4166 Dundas to Admiralty, Horseguards, 2 October 1795)

Harbinger, William and John, Trio, Planter Hospital Ships. *Planter* arrived at Dover, damaged. (WO/1/798 Transport Office (George) to Huskisson, 23 November 1795)

Alice, Hope, Fanny, Mentor, Peggy, Commerce, Vine, Galatea, Marquis of Worcester [4] Victualling Ships. (ADM/D/39/23/09 Victualling Office to Nepean, 23 September, and ADM/2/612 f 1,2)

True Briton (ADM/51/1110 *A Journal of the Proceedings of HM Ship* Alcmene *25 January 1795 – 31 January 1796*)

Norfolk, Bredalbane, Juno (CO/318/18 Christian to Huskisson, *Prince George*, Spithead, on 4 November and 7 November 1795)

The exact total of ships in Christian's Fleet was not recorded. Estimates were given as around two hundred ships: 'Nearly two hundred sail,' wrote William Dillon, a mate on the *Prince George*. (Dillon, p.208) '[There were] many other ships under convoy beside the transports ...', wrote William Richardson, on board *La Prompte* (Richardson, p.124). Merchant ships sailing to the West Indies were included in the convoy for safe passage (including the *Thomas*, bound for Oporto, which sank on the Chesil 18 November 1795).

In his final letter to his friend Huskisson at the War Office before sailing on 15 November, Christian wrote: 'You have not been correctly informed respecting the Transports or the Tonnage. I therefore transmit you an accurate return.':

Recapitulation of Tonnage and Troops Embarked, etc.

	Tons	Men
16 East India Ships	12,827	6,320
17 Transports, having on board the		
1st Brigade (inc. *Commerce de Marseilles*)	5,529	2,437
West India Ships and Transports having		
on board the 3rd, 4th and 5th Brigades	15,586	8,994
Transports having Hospital Corps,		
Venereal Patients	1,426	601
Drafts, Recruits and		
Men of different Corps distributed		
since the General Embarkation		500
Total:	**35,368**	**18,742**
The *Elizabeth*, having part of the 27th on board,		
found unfit to proceed – deduct:	217	2
Total tonnage and men:	**35,151**	**18,740**

16 East India Ships
52 West India Ships
30 Transports
12 Cavalry Transports
12 Navy Victuallers
11 Ordnance Store Ships
(CO/318/18 (attached to) Christian to Huskisson, *Prince George* at St Helens, under Sail, 15 November 1795)

Notes

1.   The *Prince George* was present at the Battle of Cap St Vincent, under Admiral Jervis, two years later, in 1797. (J. Creswell, *British Admirals of the Eighteenth Century*, Allen and Unwin [n.d.])

2.   The *Colossus* also fought at the Battle of Cap St Vincent and at the Battle of the Nile under Nelson in 1798; she was wrecked returning from Italy off the Scilly Isles in 1799, carrying the collection of antique classical vases and statuary of Sir William Hamilton, Ambassador to Italy, and the body of Admiral Schuldham, which was later recovered and buried in Buckinghamshire. (R. Morris, HMS *Colossus*, Hutchinson, 1979; Naval Chronical Vol.1 (1799) p.86 (Monthly Register))

3.   The frigate *Leda*, ordered to convoy a merchant fleet from Cork to the West Indies, foundered near Madeira the following year while on the same duty. Only seven people on board were saved. (*Lloyd's List* (The Marine List) No.2798, 1 March 1796)

4.   The gallant little *Marquis of Worcester*, victualler, Thomas Scott master, survived the first and second storms, putting into Portland with Drury after the first, and into Kinsale, Ireland after the second, with her fore mast and bowsprit gone. (ADM/1/1717 *A List of Transports* ... (sgnd) Drury, HMS *Alfred*; CO/318/18 *Report of State and Condition of Transports belonging to Admiral Christian's Fleet that are put into different Ports in Ireland*. (Sgnd) Chichester Fortescue, Agent for Transports, Cork., Cove of Cork, 3 January 1795 (*sic* -1796))

In December 1797 on her return from St Vincents, laden with sugar, she sank on the Chesil, close to where the ill-fated transports of Christian's fleet had struck two years before, near the Fleet House. All lives were lost, save that of one seaman. She, too, went to pieces, and little of her cargo was saved. (*Lloyd's List* (The Marine List) No.2975, 19 December 1797; *Yeovil and Sherborne Mercury* 25 December 1797)

List of Men Missing (Presumed Drowned) from the *Piedmont*

The soldiers who lost their lives on the *Piedmont* transport came from just one regiment: the 63rd. They had all enlisted from one small town in the north-west of England – drawn by the glamour and personal magnetism of the young captain who recruited them, Ambrose William Barcroft, a local man from a landed family who had served in the War of American Independence, and bore the scars of battle. One hundred and twenty-six men from the regiment lost their lives that fateful day. This was the tragedy of the small town of Colne, in Lancashire.

The story was local history in that part of Lancashire, and, late in the 1960s, two members of the Lancashire Family History Society were working on transcribing the Parish Registers which covered the period of the disaster. They realised that a large number of entries for young men born in Colne who lost their lives on board the *Piedmont* would appear in the baptism registers there but not in those for burials. They sought, by means of the Muster Lists in the Public Record Office, to redress the balance by identifying the young men who were buried on the Chesil, or lost at sea.

From their work came two accounts of the storm: *The Loss of the Piedmont (The Colne Tragedy)* by Mrs G. Whittaker, in collaboration with Mr Wilfred Spencer (deceased) and *Capt. Barcroft and the Men of Colne Waterside* by Mr H. Foulds (deceased), based upon the work of the two aforementioned. (Avaliable at the Pendle Heritage Centre, Nelson, Lancs.) The author is indebted to the former two persons, and to them the following list of soldiers' names and approximate age is attributed:

Soldiers of the 63rd missing, presumed drowned from the *Piedmont*:

Robert Alexander, 43

William Anderton, 27

John Atkinson, 23

John Browne, 23

James Berry, 36

John Burrows, 31

John Barker, 41

Robert Browne, 26

Christopher Baldwin, 22

William Crabtree, 33

James Dickworth, 44

Thomas Foulds, 23

John Greene, 29

John Greenwood, 34

Aughton Greenwood, 27

William Halstead, 23

William Howarth, 24

John Hargreaves, 23

William Hartley, 22

James Hollywell, 38

John Hixon (Higson), 27

John King, 28

John Knowles, 35

William Lee, 38

John Molyneux (not in baptisms register)

William Oddy 32

William Robinson, 24

John Smith, 23

John Smith, 27

William Hair, 25

James Smith, 32

George Stansfield, 32

William Shaw, 21

William Tillotson, 22

William Tattersall, 26

William Thompson, 24

John Taylor, 22

William Taylor, 37

Henry Tomlinson, 19

John Pickles, 23

James Ridealgh, 24

John Robinson, 24

John Turner, 29

John Whitehead, 20

John Whitham, 44

John Wright, 29

John Walker, 23

Robert Wilson, 32

John Wilson, 27

James Wilson, 21

William Walton, 26

Richard Smith, 18

John Robinson, 36

Robert Smith, 23

Edward Smith, 29

James Smith, 25

John Sutclife, 25

James Shaw, 27

William Simpson, 21

Richard Tatersall, 26

James Turner, 34

James Thompson, 35

John Taylor, 26

Robert Thornton, 32

Richard Towers, 23

Matthew Ridealgh, 34

James Robinson, 26

John Robinson, 25

James Varley, 23

Richard Whitham, 28

James Whithead, 42

John Wright, 31

James Whitaker, 19

James Whitaker, 25 (survived)

John Wilson, 32

Matthew Wilson, 35

William Watson, 13

(Broken periods in Registers)

John Appleton, 17

John Dixon, 21

Henry Greenwood, 16

Blakey Nutter, 21

John Riley, 23

James Sutclife, 24

Thomas Whitaker, 35

Thomas Bailey, 22

James Dixon, 16

John Holden, 32

John Procter, 44

John Smith, 31

William Taylor, 37

Officers:

Ambrose Barcroft, 36

Alexander Greene, 20

John Smith, 31

John Scott, 38

George Wilkinson, 44

John Anderton, 42

John Patterson, 32

John Smith, 33

John Deardin, 20

John Mitchell, 18

Notes and References

Abbreviations Used
opp. = opposite
PRO = Public Record Office
ADM = Admiralty Papers
WO = War Office Papers
CO = Colonial Office Papers
Cust. = Customs Office Papers

Chapter 1

1. Foreword by Sean McGrail in S. Thirslund and C.L. Vebaek, *The Viking Compass* (Gullanders Bogtrylckeri AIS, 1992). (I am most grateful to Capt. Thirslund and Professor McGrail for their kind permission to reproduce this part of the Foreword.)
2. 'The Struggle for Empire 1713-1815' in *The Times Atlas of World History*, ed. G. Barraclough (Times Books Ltd, 1978), pp.194-195.
3. J. Brooke, *King George III* (Constable, 1972), p.184; M. Duffy, *Soldiers, Sugar and Seapower* (Clarendon Press, 1987), pp.160, 183, 196, 370; *Salisbury Journal*, 23 Nov. 1795; *The Times*, 14 Nov. 1795.
4. W. Page (ed.), *The Victoria History of the Counties of England*, Vol.II (Archibald Constable, 1908), p.223.
5. Michael Duffy, *Soldiers, Sugar and Seapower*, pp.5-16.
6. Dudley Pope, *Life in Nelson's Navy* (Unwin Hyman, 1987), p.1.
7. Ibid, p.6.
8. See Keith Dawson, 'The Industrial Revolution – The Take-off' in *History Makers*, Issue No.6 (1969), p.251.
9. Derek Jarrett, *Pitt* (Weidenfeld & Nicholson, 1974), p.144, 153, 216. See also Brooke, *King George III*, p.309. Keith Dawson, 'The Industrial Revolution – The Britain that Vanished' in *History Makers*, Issue No.5, 1969 p.230. (Many pre-1950s stamp albums make reference to Britain's Empire 'the British Dominions beyond the Seas'.)
10. Dawson, p.225.
11. See J. Hutchins, *History and Antiquities of the County of Dorset*, Vol.II, 1865.
12. Pope, *Life in Nelson's Navy*, pp.4-5.

Chapter 2

1. C.B. Firth, *From William III to Waterloo* (Ginn & Co. 1937), pp.41-43, 93, 94.
2. *The Times Atlas of World History*, pp.194, 195.
3. Brooke, *King George III*, p.165; W.H. Fitchett, *How England Saved Europe: The Story of the Great War* (Smith Elder, 1909).
4. PRO Reference Catalogue *The Guide, Part 1: History of Government – Home Affairs*.
5. Roger Buckley, *Slaves in Red Coats* (Yale University Press, 1979), pp.8-9.
6. Pope, *Life in Nelson's Navy*, p.14; *Oxford Illustrated History of the British Army* ed. David Chandler (OUP, 1995), p.133; Capt. R.H. Smythies, *Historical Records of the 40th Regiment of Foot* (A.H. Swiss, 1894), p.9.
7. Buckley, *Slaves in Red Coats*, p.9.
8. Jarrett, *Pitt*, pp.147, 153, 162.

9. Duffy, *Soldiers, Sugar and Seapower*, Intro., p.4. See also Dr J. Campbell, *Lives of the British Admirals* (John Stockdale, 1813), Vol.VI, pp.382-383, 387-388.
10. Buckley, *Slaves in Red Coats*, pp.9, 82-83.
11. Jarrett, *Pitt*, pp.125, 159, 163, 167; Brooke, *King George III*, pp.345, 363.
12. Jarrett, *Pitt*, pp.162-163; Duffy, *Soldiers, Sugar and Seapower*, Intro., p.4.
13. Brooke, *King George III*, p.160; Jarrett, *Pitt*, pp.144, 147, 163.
14. Duffy, *Soldiers, Sugar and Seapower*, p.30.
15. Ibid., pp.34-37.
16. Ibid., pp.42.
17. Pope, *Life in Nelson's Navy*, p.63.
18. Duffy, *Soldiers, Sugar and Seapower*, p.43.
19. Ibid., pp.56, 59-88.
20. Ibid., pp.91-95.
21. Ibid., Intro., p.6.
22. Ibid., pp.99-104.
23. Ibid., p.95.
24. Buckley, *Slaves in Red Coats*, p.10.
25. Duffy, *Soldiers, Sugar and Seapower*, p.116.
26. Duffy, *Soldiers, Sugar and Seapower*, pp.122-125; Smythies, *Historical Records of the 40th Regiment of Foot*, p.66; J.M. Brereton and A.C.S. Savory, *The History of the Duke of Wellington's Regiment 1702-1792* (1993), p.91.
27. Buckley, *Slaves in Red Coats*, p.18; Duffy, *Soldiers, Sugar and Seapower*, p.122.
28. Buckley, *Slaves in Red Coats*, pp.99-100.
29. Sir Neil Cantlie, *A History of the Army Medical Department* (Churchill Livingstone, 1974) Vol.I, pp.239-240, 244.
30. Buckley, *Slaves in Red Coats*, p.100.
31. Duffy, *Soldiers, Sugar and Seapower*, pp.130, 131.
32. Jarrett, *Pitt*, p.166.
33. Cantlie, *A History of the Army Medical Department*, p.240.
34. Duffy, *Soldiers, Sugar and Seapower*, p.127.
35. Ibid., p.45.
36. Ibid., pp.132-134, 137.
37. *Hampshire Chronicle*, Monday 9 Mar. 1795 (*from the* London Gazette, *Saturday 14 Feb. 1795*); ADM/1/317 Rear Admiral Charles Thompson to Vice Admiral Caldwell, on board *Vanguard*, 11 Dec. 1794; Duffy pp.134, 141.
38. ADM/1/317 Caldwell to Stephens, Admiralty, on board *Majestic*, off St Pierre, Martinique, 3 Jan. 1795, enclosing the accounts of Rear Admiral Charles Thompson and General Robert Prescott, on board *Vanguard*, off Guadeloupe, 11 Dec. 1795.
39. ADM/1/317 Caldwell to Stephens, on board *Majestic*, 3 Jan. 1795.
40. ADM/1/317 Caldwell to Stephens, on board *Majestic*, 30 Jan. 1795.
41. ADM/1/317 Caldwell to Stephens, on board *Majestic*, 3 Jan. 1795.
42. ADM/1/317 Robert Prescott to Caldwell, St Pierre, Martinique, 17 Dec. 1794.
43. ADM/1/317 Caldwell to Prescott, on board *Majestic*, off St Pierre, 18 Dec. 1794; ADM/1/317 Caldwell to Stephens, Admiralty, on board *Majestic*, 30 Jan. 1795; WO/1/83, Portland (?) to Vaughan, Horseguards, 18 Feb. 1795.
44. ADM/1/317 Caldwell to Stephens, *Majestic*, St Pierre, Martinique, 3 Jan. 1795.
45. ADM/1/317 Caldwell to Stevens, on board *Majestic*, off St Pierre, 11 Jan. 1795.
46. J. Campbell, *Lives of the British Admirals*, Vol.VII p.54; Cooper Willyams, *An Account of the Campaign in the West Indies 1794* (Bensley, 1796), p.149. (A monument to Robert Faulknor stands in St Paul's Cathedral, London – see *Naval Chronicle*, Vol 6 (1806), Frontispiece)
47. ADM/1/317 Caldwell to Stevens, on board *Majestic*, off St Pierre, 11 Jan. 1795.
48. ADM/1/317 Caldwell to Stevens, on board *Majestic*, off St Pierre, 15 Jan. 1795.
49. ADM/1/317 Letters Caldwell, Thompson and Vaughan 14 and 15 Jan. 1795.
50. WO/1/31 f99
51. WO/1/31 f145
52. Lancashire Record Office DDB/72/1485-1504 W.A. Barcroft to (?) B. Barcroft, Hervelt, 10 Nov. 1794.
53. Cantlie, *A History of the Army Medical Department*, p.218; Col. H.C. Wylly, *History of the Manchester*

Regiment (Forster Groom & Co., 1923), pp.110-113.

54. Col. B.R. Mullaly, *History of the South Lancashire Regiment* (The White Swan Press, [no date]), p.45; Smythies, *Historical Records of the 40th Regiment of Foot*, pp.68-70.

55. *Hampshire Chronicle*, Monday 9 Mar. 1795 (*from the* London Gazette, *28 Feb.*)

56. *Hampshire Chronicle*, Foreign News, 28 Mar. 1795.

57. Duffy, *Soldiers, Sugar and Seapower*, p.142.

58. ADM/1/317 Caldwell to Stevens, on board *Majestic*, off St Pierre, 2 Mar. 1795.

59. Duffy, *Soldiers, Sugar and Seapower*, pp.143, 146; Buckley, *Slaves in Red Coats*, p.17.

60. ADM/1/317 Caldwell to Stephens, on board *Majestic*, off St Pierre, 15 Mar. 1795.

61. ADM/1/317 Grovestein to Vaughan and Caldwell, Starbrock, Demerara, 4 May 1795.

62. ADM/1/317 Caldwell to Stevens, *Ocean* transport, 10 May 1795.

63. ADM/1/317 Sawyer to Caldwell, on board *Blanche*, Choiseul, St Lucia, 23 Apr. 1795.

64. Buckley, *Slaves in Red Coats*, p.12. Cantlie, *A History of the Army Medical Department*, p.238.

65. Buckley, *Slaves in Red Coats*, p.17; *The Times*, Friday 31 Jul. 1795.

66. *Lives of the British Admirals*, Vol.VII, p.67.

67. ADM/1/317 Laforey to Evan Nepean, on board *L'Aimable*, Fort Royal, Martinique, 23 Jun. 1795; *The Times*, Friday 31 Jul. (*Portsmouth, 27 Jul.*).

68. ADM/1/317 Laforey to Nepean, on board *L'Aimable*, Fort Royal, 23 Jun. 1795.

69. *Hampshire Chronicle*, Monday 25 May and 1 Jun. 1795.

70. Jarrett, *Pitt*, p.169.

71. *Hampshire Chronicle*, Monday 15 Jun. 1795

72. Pitt to Chatham, 3 August 1795 in A. Aspinall (ed.), *The Later Correspondence of George III* (Cambridge, 1967), p.368.

Chapter 3

1. Biographical notes taken from: The *Dictionary of National Biography*, Vol.IV, pp.278-279; The *Naval Chronicle*, Vol.XXI (1809), pp.177-184, 187; Lt. Cdr James Stewart, 'The Leeward Isles Command 1795-1796' *The Mariner's Mirror*, Vol.47); *Naval Biographical Dictionary, 1849*, p.190; Duffy, *Soldiers, Sugar and Seapower*, pp.166-168; CO/318/18 Christian to Huskisson, Portsmouth, 7 Oct. 1795, p.16; Christian to Huskisson, Portsmouth, 5 Nov. 1795, p.19; Christian to Huskisson, on board *Prince George*, St Helens, 13 Nov. 1795; William Richardson, *A Mariner of England: An Account of the Career of William Richardson* (John Murray, 1908), p.127; G. Cornwallis-West, *The Life and Letters of Admiral Cornwallis* (Robert Holden & Co., 1927), p.306; *The Times*, Thursday 13 Aug. 1795; A. Traherne, *Romantic Annals of a Naval Family*, Henry S. King, 1873 pp.17, 106.

2. Biographical notes taken from: The *Dictionary of National Biography*, Vol.I, pp.43-46; Duffy, *Soldiers, Sugar and Seapower*, pp.163-164; A. Aspinall (ed.), *The Later Correspondence of George III* (letter from the Duke of York to the king, Tournai, 13 Dec. 1793, p.133, Pitt to the king, Nov. 1794, p.274); J. Stewart 'The Leeward Isles Command, 1795-1796'; Cantlie, *A History of the Army Medical Department*, pp.241-242; Maj.-Gen. J.F. Maurice (ed.), *The Diary of Sir John Moore*, Vol.I (Edward Arnold, 1904), pp.208, 210.

3. Buckley, *Slaves in Red Coats*, pp.2,4,10; Cantlie, *A History of the Army Medical Department*, p.241.

4. Buckley, *Slaves in Red Coats*, p.11.

5. Ibid., pp.10-11, 14-15, 82-83.

6. Ibid., p.82. (I am most grateful to Yale University Press for permission to reproduce this extract.)

7. Quoted in Buckley, *Slaves in Red Coats*, p.91: Brig.-Gen. A. Campbell to Lord Cathcart, 19 Apr. 1795, quoted in H. Everard, *History of Thomas Farrington's Regiment, 1694-1891* (Littlebury, 1891), p.195.

8. WO/1/31 Vaughan to Portland, St Pierre, Martinique, 22 Dec. 1794.

9. Buckley, *Slaves in Red Coats*, pp.12, 13; WO/1/31 Vaughan to Portland 22 Dec. 1794.

10. Buckley, *Slaves in Red Coats*, pp.18, 24-25, 27, 38 (see also pp.140-141); WO/1/83 War Office to Vaughan, Horseguards, 19 Feb. 1795.

11. Buckley, *Slaves in Red Coats*, pp.38-39, 42; WO/1/83 War Office to Vaughan, No.14, Horseguards, 17 Apr. 1795.

12. ADM/1/317 Caldwell to Stephens, Admiralty, 15 Jan. 1795; Buckley, *Slaves in Red Coats*, p.17; Duffy, *Soldiers, Sugar and Seapower*, pp.142-143.

13. Buckley, *Slaves in Red Coats*, p.19; WO/1/83 War Office to Vaughan, no.14, Horseguards, 17 Apr. 1795.

14. *The Times*, Friday 31 Jul. 1795; *Hampshire Chronicle*, Monday 3 Aug. 1795; Buckley, *Slaves in Red Coats*, p.19; WO/4/338 Windham to Irving, 20 Nov. 1795.

15. Buckley, *Slaves in Red Coats*, pp.65, 73, 83-84.

16. *London Gazette*, 1795, pp.790, 691, 954, 1,041 and 838, respectively; WO/12/11239 Muster list, 1st West India Reg, 25 June-24 December 1795.

17. Brig. T.N. Grazebrook, *An Introduction to the Auxiliary Units of the Gloucester Regiments* (Soldiers of Gloucestershire Museum, 1960), p.9., Soldiers of Gloucestershire Musum Archive.

18. DDB 61/41-70/8 William Fisher Shrapnell, letters to the Barcroft family, Shrapnell to Mrs Wilson, Weymouth, 8 Dec. 1795, p.36.

19. WO/1/84 Return of the Army under the Command of Maj.-Gen. Sir Ralph Abercromby, 7 Nov. 1795; WO/25/1146 Embarkation Returns, Sept., Oct., Nov. 1795; Army List 1796.

20. *The Oxford Illustrated History of the British Army* (OUP, 1994), p.95; Buckley, *Slaves in Red Coats*, p.125.

21. E. Alfred Jones, *The Loyalists of Massachusetts* (St Catherine Press, 1930).

22. Charlotte Smith, *A Narrative of the Loss...*, (Sampson Low, 1796), p.29.

23. WO/25/1512 Muster Roll 26th Light Dragoons, 25 April-24 June 1795; Army List, 1796; *London Gazette*, 1795, p.598.

24. WO/58/167 ff.74, 75; WO/4/291 f.246; WO/4/338 f.49.

25. Cantlie, *A History of the Army Medical Department*, pp.223-225.

26. Obituaries, *Gentleman's Magazine*, Vol.65 Pt II, 1795, p.1,055.

27. WO/4/338 M. Lewis to Maj. Ker, 12 Sep. 1795; *London Gazette*, 1795, p.1,086.

28. *London Gazette*, 1795, p.18; according to general regulations and orders for the Army, the cost of an ensign's commission (the lowest commissioned rank) in a line regiment in 1776 was £400; The 'King's Regulations', (War Office, 1822); Buckley, *Slaves in Red Coats*, p.22.

29. Smythies, *Historical Records of the 40th Regiment of Foot*, p.70; *The Times*, Monday 27 July (*Portsmouth, 21 July*) and Friday 7 August 1795 (*Plymouth, 4 August*).

30. WO/25/1146 Monthly Return for the 40th Foot 'for the Leeward Islands', 11 July 1795.

31. *London Gazette*, 1795, p.970; WO/25/1146 Embarkation Return; C. Smith, *A Narrative of the Loss...*, p.15; DDB 61/43 W. Shrapnell, Narrative, undated, with letter to Mrs Wilson, Weymouth 21 Dec. 1795, pp.47-48.

32. C. Smith, *A Narrative of the Loss...*, p.35.

33. James Carr, *Annals and Stories of Colne* (John Heywood, 1878), pp.87-89. (I am extremely grateful to Mrs Fay Oldland of the Pendle Heritage Centre for providing me with this source.)

34. DDB/42/10 Certificate of Enlistment, 1 June 1794.

35. DDB/61/37 W.A. Barcroft to B. Barcroft, Hervelt, 4 Dec. 1794.

36. DDB/72/1485-1504 W.A. Barcroft to (?) B. Barcroft, Hervelt 10 Nov. 1794.

37. DDB/61/38 W.A. Barcroft to B. Barcroft, Portsmouth 21 Aug. 1795.

38. DDB/61/39 W.A. Barcroft to B. Barcroft, Spithead, 11 Nov. 1795.

39. Fay Oldland, *The Story of Foulridge* (Pendle Heritage Centre, 1990), p.11.

40. Jarrett, *Pitt*, pp.28, 30, 56, 67, 90, 98-99, 101, 105, 110; Brooke, *King George III*, p.254.

41. Duffy, *Soldiers, Sugar and Seapower*, p.41.

42. Jarrett, *Pitt*, p.167; Duffy, *Soldiers, Sugar and Seapower*, p.49.

43. Jarrett, *Pitt*, p.112.

44. Duffy, *Soldiers, Sugar and Seapower*, Intro., pp.4-22.

45. Ibid., p.41.

46. Jarrett, *Pitt*, pp.144, 205, 209.

47. Jarrett, *Pitt*, p.169; *The Gentleman's Magazine*, Vol.LXV, Pt. I, Jul.-Dec. 1795, p.519; *The Times*, Thursday 2 Jul. 1795 (*Salisbury 29 Jun.*); Brooke, *King George III*, p.364 refers.

48. Jarrett, *Pitt*, pp.169, 174; Brooke, *King George III*, p.364; S. Ayling, *Fox: The Life of Charles James Fox* (John Murray, 1991), p.192. (I am grateful to the publishers for permission to quote the later descriptions of Pitt and Fox.)

49. Jarrett, *Pitt*, p.170.

50. Ayling, *Fox*, pp.183, 185, 193.

51. Brooke, *King George III*, p.94; Ayling, *Fox: The Life of Charles James Fox*, pp.9, 18, 245.

52. Ayling, *Fox*, pp.36, 45-46, 87, 125, 139-140, 181, 191, 234, 246; Jarrett, *Pitt*, pp.50, 141; also see Brooke, *King George III*, p.228.

53. Ayling, *Fox*, p.191.

54. He had held office in previous governments: as a Junior Minister under Lord North (1770-1774),

and as Secretary of State under Rockingham (1782) and under Pitt (1783). On Pitt's death in 1806, he would hold office again for a few short months as Foreign Secretary and Leader of the House. Ayling, *Fox*, pp.109, 234, 245-247; Brooke, *King George III*, p.227.

55.   G.O. Trevelyan, *The Early History of Charles James Fox* (Thos. Nelson & Sons), p.505.

56.   Brooke, *King George III*, p.310.

57.   See A. Aspinall (ed.), *The Later Correspondence of George III*, Introduction. p.xiv; A.M. Broadley, *Royal Weymouth 1789-1805, The Court of King George III at the Seaside* (J.G. Commin, 1907), the letters of Frederick, Duke of York, to the king, Vol.III, p.94, Vol.IV, p.143; Brooke, *King George III*, p.364.

58.   A. Aspinall (ed.), *The Later Correspondence of George III*, Introduction p.xiv, the king to Dundas, Weymouth, 19 Aug. 1795, p.384.

59.   Brooke, *King George III*, pp.207, 215, 260, 263, 288, 289, 313, 314, 364.

60.   Ibid., pp.260, 288, 293, 363.

61.   A.M. Broadley, *Royal Weymouth 1789-1805*, Vol.I press cutting; Vol.II, p.147 illus.; Brooke, *King George III*, p.343.

62.   Broadley, *Royal Weymouth 1789-1805*, Vol.I, opp. p.231, pp.231, 233, 241, Vol.II, opp. p.190 Vol.IV, p.166.

63.   Broadley, *Royal Weymouth 1789-1805*, Vol.I, pp.124, 149, 171, 198, 199 and opp. p.278, Vol.II, opp. p.134, illus: Vol.IV, p.211; *Hampshire Chronicle*, Monday 2 Aug. 1795; *The Times*, Thursday 20 Aug. 1795 *(Weymouth, 17 August)*.

64.   Broadley, *Royal Weymouth 1789-1805*, Vol.I, p.207; *Western County Magazine*, Oct. 1789.

Chapter 4

1.   DDB/61/43 W.F. Shrapnell, Narrative, undated, with letter to Mrs Wilson, Weymouth, 21 Dec. 1795.

2.   C. Smith, *A Narrative of the Loss...*, pp.6–8.

3.   John Coode, 'Household Words', Apr. 1838, from John Kerridge, *Weymouth and Melcombe Regis Local Rakings (Manuscript)* Vol.I, 1866.

4.   *The Chesil Bank and Fleet Lagoon – A few Facts and Figures* (The Chesil Beach Centre, [no date]). (For details of the flora and fauna of the Chesil, many pamphlets and publications are available from the Chesil Bank and the Fleet Nature Reserve Centre.)

5.   *The Great Map of Dorsetshire* (Isaac Taylor, 1765), quoted by C. Smith in *A Narrative of the Loss...*, p.7.

6.   Les and Julie Kent, two of the people to whom this book is dedicated, 5 Sep. 2000.

7.   John Hutchins, *History and Antiquities of the County of Dorset*, Vol.II (John Bowyer Nichols, 1861).

8.   J. Coode, who read his pamphlet on the Chesil to a meeting of the Institution of Civil Engineers on 3 May 1853.

9.   From J. Kerridge, *Weymouth & Melcombe Regis and its Environs, including the Island of Portland: The Botany of the Chesil Bank*, by W.B. Barrett Esq., of this town.

10.   Letter from the king to the Duke of York, on board *Royal Sovereign*, 10 Sep. 1804, in Broadley, *Royal Weymouth 1789-1805*, Vol.IV, p.211.

11.   Extract of an article ([publisher unknown], 27 Feb. 1908), Soldiers of Gloucestershire Museum archive.

12.   The *Southern Times*, Saturday 3 Mar. 1866, *Wreck Reminiscences*; H. Costley-White, *Mary Cole, Countess of Berkeley* (Berkeley Castle, 1997), p.67; D.S. Daniell, *Cap of Honour* (White Lion Publishers, 1975), p.40.

13.   H. Costley-White, *Mary Cole, Countess of Berkeley*, pp.66, 73, 144.

14.   Broadley, *Royal Weymouth 1789-1805*, Vol.I, pp.1-2 (press cuttings), 123 and 244, Vol.II, p.138 and opp. p.145.

15.   Loraine Fletcher, *Charlotte Smith, A Critical Biography* (Palgrave, 1998), pp.191, 192, 196, 238, 247.

16.   Broadley, *Royal Weymouth 1789-1805*, Vol.III, p.94, (press cutting Weymouth, 23 Sep. 1795); *The Times*, Friday 11 Sep. 1795 *(Weymouth, 9 Sep.)*.

17   Brooke, *King George III*, p.348; The king to the Prince of Wales, Queen's House, 8 Apr. 1795, in A. Aspinall (ed.), *The Later Correspondence of George III*, pp.328, 329; Broadley, *Royal Weymouth 1789-1805*, Vol.I, press cutting, Weymouth, 20 Aug. NB: marked 1790 and 1808, opp. p.2.

18.   J. Brooke, *King George III*, p.295; also Broadley, *Royal Weymouth 1789-1805*, Vol.III, p.67 engraving; and from *The Public and Private Life of King George the Third* p.544; Broadley, Vol.II, opp. p.180.

19. *Gloucester Journal*, 7 Sep. 1795; *Hampshire Chronicle*, Monday 7 Sep. 1795.

20. Brig. T.N. Grazebrooke, *An Introduction to the Auxiliary Units of the Gloucester Regiments*, (Soldiers of Gloucestershire Museum), 1960, p.4.

21. The *Gloucester Journal*, 21 Dec. 1795, *Extract of a letter from Weymouth, 16 Dec.*

Chapter 5

1. Pitt to Chatham, 3 Aug. 1795, in A. Aspinall (ed.), *The Later Correspondence of George III*, p.368.

2. Cabinet Minute, 14 Aug. 1795, A. Aspinall (ed.), *The Later Correspondence of George III*, pp.380–381.

3. Earl of Moira to Maj.-Gen. John Doyle, Headquarters, Southampton *c.*17 Aug. 1795 *(Most Secret)*, in Aspinall, *Later Correspondence of George III* p.388.

4. Dundas to the Earl of Moira, Horseguards, 24 Aug. 1795, in A. Aspinall (ed.), *The Later Correspondence of George III*, p.391.

5. WO/1/798 Dimensions of troop transport *Progress*, Lt-Col. Adam Hay to Lt Skipsey, Transport Agent, Plymouth, on board *Adventure*, 10 Jan. 1795.

6. Cantlie, *A History of the Army Medical Department*, Vol.I, pp.241-242. (*Regulations for the use of His Majesty's Troops upon their arrival in the West Indies, 1795.*)

7. WO/4/338 Matthew Lewis (Secretary to William Windham, Joint Secretary of State for War) to William Huskisson (Secretary to Dundas), War Office, 8 Oct. 1795.

8. NEP/7 G. Jervis to Nepean, 11 Aug. 1795; ADM/1/317 Christian to (?) Nepean, on board *Prince George*, Spithead, 22 Sep. 1795; Duffy, *Soldiers, Sugar and Seapower*, p.182.

9. CO/318/18 Christian to (?) Huskisson, 9 Aug. 1795.

10. Cantlie, *A History of the Army Medical Department*, pp.242-243.

11. WO/1/662 Maj.-Gen. Crozbie [*sic*] to Lewis, 8 Oct. 1794.

12. Buckley, *Slaves in Red Coats*, p.11.

13. Pope, *Life in Nelson's Navy*, pp.96-97; Brooke, *King George III*, p.179.

14. R.E. & T.N. Dupuy, *The Collins Encyclopaedia of Military History* (Collins, 1993), p.743.

15. WO/1/798 Capt. Home Popham, Transport Agent on the Continent, to Huskisson, Stade, 25 Aug. 1795; WO/6/142 Dundas to Cornwallis, Master General of the Ordnance, Horseguards, 23 Jul. 1795.

16. Robert Gardiner, *The Line of Battle: The Sailing Warship 1650-1840* (Conway Maritime Press, 1992) p.110.

17. Pope, *Life in Nelson's Navy*, pp.120, 122.

18. *London Gazette*, 17 Dec. 1794; Revd J. Silvester Davies, *History of Southampton* (Hampshire Books,1909), p.505; Pope, *Life in Nelson's Navy*, pp.104-106.

19. WO/6/142 Dundas to Cornwallis, Horseguards, 12 Jun. 1795.

20. WO/74/338 Hodson & Hayter to Lewis, War Office, 6 Oct. 1795.

21. WO/4/338 Lewis to Messrs Pearce, War Office, 20 Oct. 1795.

22. WO/4/338 Windham to Thos. Fauquier, Esq., War Office, 11 (?) Oct. 1795.

23. WO/6/142 Dundas to Cornwallis, Horseguards, 9 Aug. 1795; WO/4/338 Lewis to Milford, 7 Oct. and Whitehead to War Office, 24 Oct. 1795; WO/1/798 Dundas to Transport Board, Horseguards, 20 Sep. 1795.

24. See WO/6/142 Dundas to Cornwallis, Horseguards 19 Jul. 1795; WO/1/662 Maj.-Gen. Crosbie to Lewis, War Office, 8 Oct. 1794. WO/6/142 Dundas to Cornwallis, Horseguards 29 Sep. 1795; for reference see WO/6/156 f.91 Dundas to Transport Dept.

25. Pope, *Life in Nelson's Navy*, p.59; Cantlie, *A History of the Army Medical Department*, p.243; ADM/1/317 Christian to Nepean, Admiralty, *Prince George*, Spithead, 24 Oct. 1795. See also WO/1/798 f.175, 177; WO/6/156, ff100, 104.

26. House of Commons Journals, Vol.LI, 29 Oct. 1795 – 19 May 1796, pp.73, 77.

27. WO/4/338 Lewis to Messrs Cox and Greenwood, Agents of Corps, 19 Oct. 1795.

28. WO/4/338 Lewis to Cox and Greenwood, War Office, 21 Oct. 1795.

29. M.E. Condon, 'Freight Rates and the British Transport Service during the War against Revolutionary France', *Maritime History* (May 1977) pp.26-33.

30. WO/1/798 f.25.

31. DDB/70/8 Letter dated 27 Nov. 1795, accompanying Copy Will of Capt. A.W. Barcroft.

32. *Hampshire Chronicle*, Monday 31 Aug. 1795; WO/1/798 f.669, *List of East and West India Ships, Common Transports to carry 16,276 troops ...* (sgnd) John Schank, dated Portsmouth, 15 Oct. 1795, f673 John Schank – *Observations ... Oct.* 1795.

33. *Hampshire Chronicle*, Monday 21 Sep. 1795.
34. Steel's Navy List, Mar. 1797; ADM/1/317 Christian to Capt. Smith Child, *Commerce de Marseilles*, '[You are] to receive on board nine hundred Rank and File together with the usual proportion of Officers, baggage, two Howitzers, Eight six-pound guns, their Carriages, Side Guns, Ammunition ...' (Copy order, enclosed with letter dated 24 Sep. 1795, Christian to Nepean); Sir W.H. Dillon, *A Narrative of my Professional Adventures, 1790-1839* (Naval Records Society, 1953), p.110); *Hampshire Chronicle*, Monday 31 Aug. 1795.
35. ADM/1/317 Christian to Nepean, *Prince George*, Spithead, 15 Sep. 1795.
36. ADM/2/129, Lords Letters, Orders and Instructions; ADM/1/317 Christian to Nepean, *Prince George*, Spithead, 25 Oct. 1795; ADM/2/941 f.429 Nepean to Christian, 23 Oct.; ADM/1/317 Christian to Nepean, *Prince George*, Spithead, 2 Nov. 1795; ADM/7/67 f.87, 31 Oct. 1795; ADM/1/317 Note on Christian's letter to Nepean, 15 Sep. 1795.
37. ADM/1/317 Christian to Nepean, *Prince George*, Spithead, 18 Oct. 1795; ADM/2/941 f.411, Note to Christian, 19 Oct. 1795; ADM/7/67 f.62, Monday 19 Oct. 1795; ADM/2/129, Lords letters ...; ADM/1/317 Christian to Nepean, *Prince George*, Spithead, 3 Nov. 1795; ADM/2/941 f.389, 408, 473; ADM/1/317 Note on Christian's letter to Nepean, 25 Oct. 1795; ADM/2/129 f.267, 26 Oct. 1795; ADM/2/941 f.437 Nepean to Christian, 26 Oct. 1795; ADM/2/129 f.355, (?) 16 Nov.; ADM/2/129, Lords Letters, Orders and Instructions – Hugh Cloberry Christian Esq., Rear Admiral of the Blue, f.113 Admiralty to Captains of ships of Christian's Fleet; CO/318/18 *A List of His Majesty's Ships at Spithead under the Command of Rear Admiral Christian*, 9 Oct. 1795.
38. *Hampshire Chronicle*, Monday 17 Aug, Monday 7 Sept 1795; *The Times*, Wed 5 Aug 1795 (*Southhampton Aug 1st*); *Hampshire Chronicale* Sat 26 Sept 1795; *The Times* sat 26 Sept 1795; *Hampshire Chronicle* sat 3 Oct 1795 (*Home News*); *Gentleman's Magazine* Vol LXV p.787 (*from the London Gazette*); WO/1/84 *Return of the Army under the Command of Maj.-Gen. Sir Ralph Abercromby*, 7 Nov. 1795.
39. CO/318/18 Christian to (?) Huskisson, *Prince George*, Spithead, 4 Oct. 1795.
40. WO/1/84 Dundas to Abercromby, Horseguards, 28 Sep. 1795; WO/1/798 f.669 *List of Transports*, John Schank; WO/25/1146 *Embarkation* List; C/318/18 List of *Transports to ... Embark 2,600 Men at Southampton*.
41. CO/318/18 Christian to Huskisson, Portsmouth, 7 Oct. 1795.
42. ADM/1/317 Christian to Nepean, Southampton, 22 Oct. 1795.
43. CO/318/18 Christian to Huskisson, Portsmouth, 25 Sep. and 26 Oct. 1795.
44. ADM/1/317 Christian to Nepean, *Prince George*, Spithead, 24 Oct. 1795, and letter to Portsmouth Victualling Office, Cooper to Bowen.
45. ADM/7/67 P77, 26 Oct. 1795; ADM/2/129 Admiralty to Commissioners for Victualling, 26 Oct. 1795.
46. ADM/1/317 Lobb to Christian, *La Babet*, Spithead, 9 Oct. 1795; ADM/2/941 Nepean to Christian, 10 Oct. 1795.
47. CO/318/18 Christian to Huskisson, Portsmouth, 25 Sep. and Portsmouth, 23 Oct. 1795.
48. ADM/1/317 Christian to Nepean, *Prince George*, Spithead, 6 Sep. and Portsmouth, 8 Oct. 1795; *Hampshire Chronicle*, Saturday 3 Oct. 1795.
49. CO/318/18 Christian to Huskisson, *Prince George*, Spithead, 9 Oct., 11 Oct. and 20 Oct. 1795.
50. CO/318/18 Christian to Huskisson, Isle of Wight, 18 Sep. 1795; CO/318/18 Christian to (?) Huskisson, *Prince George*, Spithead, 4 Oct. 1795.
51. Duffy, *Soldiers, Sugar and Seapower*, pp.173, 174, 176; *Hampshire Chronicle*, sat 24 Oct. 1795; Cantlie, *A History of the Army Medical Department*, p.240.
52. Duffy, *Soldiers, Sugar and Seapower*, p.188.
53. WO/6/142 Dundas to Cornwallis, Horseguards, 28 Sep. 1795; WO/6/156 Dundas to Commissioners for Transports, Horseguards, 17 Sep. 1795; CO/318/18 Christian to Huskisson, Portsmouth, 23 Oct. 1795.
54. ADM/1/317 Christian to Nepean, *Prince George*, Spithead, 8 Oct. 1795.
55. ADM/2/941 Nepean to Christian, 9 Oct. 1795.
56. Duffy, *Soldiers, Sugar and Seapower*, pp.183, 189.
57. Pope, *Life in Nelson's Navy*, p.145; Duffy, *Soldiers, Sugar and Seapower*, p.183; ADM/2/129, f.289 (Sick and Wounded Board).
58. *Hampshire Chronicle*, Monday 21 Sep. 1795; *The Times*, Saturday 29 Aug. 1795.
59. ADM/1/4166 f210, Huskisson to Nepean, Horseguards, 21 Oct, 1795; ADM/1/317 Christian to Nepean, *Prince George*, Spithead, 21 and 25 Oct. 1795.

60. WO/1/798 John Schank – *Observations*, Portsmouth, Oct. 1795.
61. ADM/1/317 Christian to Nepean, *Prince George*, Spithead, 27 Oct. 1795.
62. ADM/1/317 Christian to Nepean, *Prince George*, Spithead, 5 Oct. 1795.
63. WO/1/798 Patton to Huskisson, War Office, 1 Nov. 1795.
64. WO/1/798 Popham to Huskisson, Stade, 4 Nov. 1795.
65. CO/318/18 Christian to Huskisson, Portsmouth, 1 Nov. 1795, Christian to Huskisson, Portsmouth, 8 Nov. 1795; WO/1/84 Huskisson to Abercromby, Horseguards, 9 Nov. 1795.
66. Christian sent several letters to the War Office and the Admiralty expressing his anxiety over the delayed transports: 'It is with much concern and surprise the transports having on board the 3, 4 and 5 Brigades have not yet come from Southampton. I have sent to Southampton to be informed of the reason of the delay,' (ADM/1/317 Christian to Nepean, *Prince George*, Spithead, 4 Nov. 1795) and: 'I know not which cause can possibly have detained the transports at Southampton as yet not one of them have reached this Anchorage. My orders and opinion and everything I cou'd urge to Schank was to cause them to quit Southampton as the troops embarked' (CO/318/18 Christian to Huskisson, *Prince George*, Spithead, 4 Nov. 1795). On 11 November to Nepean: 'The variety of arrangements (many of them I think of trifling moment) which the transports have assigned as the cause of their detention has given occasion for excuses that the Transport Department should not have permitted' (ADM/1/317 Christian to Nepean, *Prince George*, 11 Nov. 1795). On 8 November, his exasperation boiled over in a letter to the War Office: 'My dear Huskisson, I am concerned to say in most decisive terms that you must immediately cause Schank to be withdrawn. I write ... without any wish to injure in the smallest degree the individual but in truth you must at once recall him' (CO/318/18 Christian to Huskisson, Portsmouth, 8 Nov. 1795). Christian is reputed to have had 'an unfortunate and untimely dispute' with Schank 'which ... went to very indiscreet lengths ... on the part of the Admiral, Who Collar'd Schank and then parted with a Challenge from [him] which they say the Adml Accepted and promised to fulfil at his return from the Expedition.' (Sir Charles Saxton to Admiral Cornwallis, Nov. 1795, from G. Cornwallis-West, *The Life and Letters of Admiral Cornwallis*, p.306; Duffy, *Soldiers, Sugar and Seapower*, p.201).

    Admiral Sir Charles Saxton, was the Navy Board Commissioner at Portsmouth and the man who fell out with Christian over the payment of troops on board the *Commerce de Marseilles* at St Helens, Isle of Wight. Saxton had insisted that it was contrary to established rule to pay ships at St Helens and refused to do so. In view of the great draught of this huge ship, Christian deemed it inadvisable to move her across several hazardous shallows to Spithead and appealed to Nepean, Secretary to the Admiralty, to ask that, in this instance, the troops should be paid at St Helens. (ADM/1/317 Christian to Nepean, *Prince George*, Spithead, 20 Oct. 1795). This Nepean did. The Admiralty overrode Saxton's refusal and ordered the Navy Board to send payment to St Helens. (ADM/2/612 Nepean to Navy Board, 21 Oct. 1795; ADM/2/941 Nepean to Christian, 21 Oct. 1795). This probably created animosity in Sir Charles towards Christian to the extent that this unfavourable report and other harsh remarks about Christian were made after the tragedy of the storm.
67. Dr John MacNamara Hayes, appointed to select soldiers fit enough for the expedition and oversee the medical supplies and hospital ships, made liberal use of exclamation marks and underlined words in his letters, which probably indicated something of his temperament: 'Dear Sir!' he wrote to the War Office on 15 October, 'I waited on Sir Ralph Abercromby ... he told me that he had settled everything with Admiral Christian respecting the hospital ships and that I should not on any account break in on his stores or medicines... and that he would not alter his present number of hospital ships...' Hayes had intended to supply the Cork contingent with some of the Portsmouth ships and medicines, in compliance, he claimed, with the War Office's request (WO/1/662 John MacNamara Hayes to (?) Lewis, Southampton, 15 Oct. 1795). Abercromby intended his four hospital ships *Harbinger*, *William and John*, *Trio* and *Planter* for the Portsmouth contingent and it was one of these, *Harbinger*, which MacNamara Hayes intended to send to Cork. By this time, the Cork contingent had fallen so far behind in preparations that Abercromby expressed doubt that they would be ready to depart in time (as indeed proved to be the case) and pointed out that it would be better to complete the ships for Portsmouth. Abercromby wrote in far more restrained tones than Hayes to Lewis: 'We have had many disagreeable interruptions in the arrangement of the hospital ships – after repeated promises only two ... are sent hither and today I understand these two are to proceed to Cork ... We have not medicines and stores sufficient to send to Cork ... I see a great deal of confusion in this new arrangement without any

point gained for the general good (WO/1/662 Extract of letter from Sir Ralph Abercromby to Mr Lewis, Southampton, 15 Oct. 1795). The four ships remained, to depart with the Portsmouth contingent.

68. In making up numbers for the expedition, Dundas had calculated that 3,000 of the Guards should be used, 'to give a fair chance of prosecuting the war with vigor [*sic*], or of bringing it to an honorable [*sic*] conclusion' (Cabinet Minute, 14 Aug. 1795, A. Aspinall (ed.), *The Later Correspondence of George III*, p.381). The king protested by letter on 16 August, saying that the Guards were wanted at home, for the 'interior quiet of the Kingdom'. He subsequently suggested to his son, the Duke of York, that troops from the Scotch Brigade be sent instead. Dundas replied that he had allocated the Scotch Brigade for taking the Cape of Good Hope from the Dutch, a vital staging post on the route to India, before it fell to the French. (Dundas to the king, Wimbledon, 18 Aug. 1795, in A. Aspinall (ed.), *The Later Correspondence of George III*, pp.381-382). At this, the king's exasperation with Dundas' territorial ambitions boiled over. In an uncharacteristically strongly worded letter, he told Dundas that his reply 'in no manner removes my objections to sending any of the Foot Guards to the West Indies ... I cannot say that I think the reasons suggested in the least an excuse for preventing the sending of the Scotch Brigade to the West Indies... The truth is we attempt too many objects at the same time, and we forget for them that we must keep some force at home' (The king to Dundas, Weymouth, 3.58 p.m., 19 Aug. 1795, (Ann Arbor MSS) in A. Aspinall (ed.), *The Later Correspondence of George III*, p.384). It was then proposed to recall the troops under General Doyle from the coast of Brittany (see p.46). (*Hampshire Chronicle*, Saturday 24 Oct. 1795). In the event, 1,216 rank and file of the 1st and 2nd Grenadiers joined the expedition, together with 231 from the 26th Light Dragoons, and 656 from the English and Irish Artillery (WO/1/84 *Return of the Army under the Command of Maj.-Gen. Sir Ralph Abercromby*, 7 Nov. 1795; WO/25/1146 (Embarkation List) for *Lee'd Islands*).

69. WO/1/84 Dundas to Abercromby, Horseguards, 3 Nov. 1795.

70. ADM/1/317 Laforey to Nepean, *Majestic* (?), Martinique (?) 11 and 12 Sep. 1795.

71. ADM/1/317 Laforey to Nepean, on board *Majestic*, 1 Oct. 1795.

72. ADM/1/317 Laforey to Nepean, on board *Majestic*, 8 Oct. 1795.

73. ADM/1/317 Christian to Nepean, *Prince George*, Spithead, 3 Nov. 1795.

74. CO/318/18 Christian to Huskisson, Portsmouth, 2 Nov. 1795.

75. ADM/1/317 Christian to Nepean, *Prince George*, Spithead, 4 Nov. 1795; CO/318/18 Christian to Huskisson, Portsmouth, 5 Nov. 1795.

76. Duffy, *Soldiers, Sugar and Seapower*, p.201.

77. ADM/1/317 Christian to Nepean, *Prince George*, Spithead, 6 Nov. 1795.

78. ADM/1/317 Christian to Nepean, *Prince George*, Spithead, 9 Nov. 1795.

79. ADM/1/317 Christian to Nepean, *Prince George*, Spithead, 10 Nov. 1795.

80. WO/1/798 Schank to Huskisson, Portsmouth, 11 Nov. 1795.

81. ADM/1/317 Christian to Nepean, *Prince George*, St Helens, 11 Nov. 1795.

82. Ibid.

83. ADM/1/317 Christian to Nepean, *Prince George*, St Helens, 14 Nov. 1795.

84. ADM/1/317 Christian to Nepean, *Prince George* off Dunnose, 16 Nov. (wrongly dated?) 1795. (Until 1805, the nautical day on board ship began officially at noon and was twelve hours in advance of the calendar day.)

85. CO/318/18 Christian to Huskisson, *Prince George*, Spithead, 9 and 10 Nov. 1795.

86. CO/318/18 Christian to Huskisson, *Prince George*, St Helens under sail, 8.00 a.m., 15 Nov. 1795.

87. ADM/1/317 Christian to Nepean, *Prince George*, off Dunnose, dated 16 Nov. (?) 1795.

88. CO/318/18 Christian to Huskisson, *Prince George* at Sea, St Helens, under sail, 8.00 a.m., 15 Nov. 1795.

89. ADM/1/317 Note overleaf on Christian's letter to Nepean, *Prince George*, Spithead, 10 Oct. 1795; ADM/2/129 f.153, 154 Admiralty to Christian, 1 Oct. 1795; ADM/2/129 p.162, 2 Oct. 1795; Duffy, *Soldiers, Sugar and Seapower*, p.197; Sir W.H. Dillon, *A Narrative of my Professional Adventures, 1790-1839*, p.208; ADM/1/317 Christian to Nepean, *Prince George*, Spithead, 21 Nov. 1795.

90. ADM/51/1119 *Journal of the Proceedings of HM Ship* Prince George – Capt. James Bowen, 14 Sep. – 23 Nov. 1795.

91. ADM/1/317 Christian to Nepean, *Prince George*, off Dunnose, 16 Nov. (?) 1795; *The Times*, Tuesday 17 Nov. 1795 (*Portsmouth 15 Nov.*).

92. Dr George Pinckard, *Notes on the West Indies* (Longman, 1806) Vol.I, pp.102-104; Duffy, *Soldiers,*

Sugar and Seapower, p.203.

93. C. Smith, *A Narrative of the Loss...*, p.3.
94. ADM/1/317 Log of *Prince George*, 8-9 hours Sunday 15 Nov. 1795.
95. CO/318/18 *A Return of Transports Lost in West Bay and about Portland*, (sgnd) Nathaniel (?) Smith, Weymouth (?), Nov. 1795.
96. *London Gazette*, annual for 1795, Tues Sept. 8 – Sat Sept. 12 p.931, Tues Oct. 20 – Sat Oct. 24 p.1,086.
97. DDB/70/8 Letter dated 27 Nov. 1795, accompanying Copy Will of Capt A.W. Barcroft.
98. All taken from DDB/61/43 Shrapnell Narrative, undated, with letter to Mrs Wilson, Weymouth, 21 Dec. 1795; ADM 108/148 Ships' Ledgers; ADM/198/158 Freight Ledgers; *Sherborne and Yeovil Mercury*, Monday 23 Nov. 1795; Cust. 59/29; C. Smith, *A Narrative of the Loss...*; WO/1/84 Army Return, 7 Nov. 1795; *Lloyd's List* (The Marine List), Friday 20 Nov., Nos 2769 and 2770; *Lloyd's Register* 1794 and 1795; ADM/1/1717; WO/12/1512 *Returns for 26th Light Dragoons*; WO/6/168. See Appendices 1 and 2, pp.106-120.
99. The buoys were markers for the shallows, and other hazards, between Spithead and the Channel, among them the buoy of the *Edgar*, the wreck of a ship accidentally burned at Spithead in 1711; the buoy of the Nab, a rock; the buoy of the Warner (sands); the buoy of Kelley's, etc.
100. ADM/51, Captains' logs; ADM/1/317 Christian to Huskisson, *Prince George*, off Dunnose, dated 16 Nov. (?) 1795.
101. ADM/1/317 *Prince George's* log, Monday 16 Nov.
102. ADM/1/317 Christian to Admiralty, *Prince George* at sea, dated (erroneously) 18 Nov. 1795.
103. ADM/1/317 ship's log, Monday 16 Nov.
104. CO/318/18 Christian to Huskisson, Portsmouth 21 Oct., *Prince George* at St Helens under sail, 8.00 a.m., 15 Nov.
105. Dillon, *A Narrative of my Professional Adventures, 1790-1839*, pp.204, 207.
106. *Salisbury Journal*, 23 Nov. 1795; *The Times*, Saturday 14 Nov. 1795.
107. CO/318/18 Christian to Huskisson, *Prince George* at sea, 15 Nov. 1795. *Recapitulation of Tonnage and Troops Embarked...*; W.H. Dillon, *A Narrative of my Professional Adventures, 1790-1839*, p.208; See Appendix 6.
108. Duffy, *Soldiers, Sugar and Seapower*, pp.160, 183, 196, 370.

Chapter 6

1. John Hutchins, *The History and Antiquities of the County of Dorset*, Vol.II (John Bowyer Nicols, 1861), pp.808-832.
2. ADM/1/317 Christian to Admiralty, 18 Nov. 1795, and ship's log, Monday 16 Nov.
3. ADM/51/1118 *Journal of the Proceedings of HM Ship* Colossus (*Henry Jenkins, Esq., Capt., 30 Sep. 1795 – 12 Feb. 1796, 16 Nov.*).
4. ADM/1/317, Christian to Admiralty 18 Nov. and ship's log 16 Nov.
5. ADM/1/317 ship's log 16 Nov.; ADM/1/317 Christian to Admiralty, 18 Nov.
6. ADM/1/317 ship's log, 16 Nov.
7. C. Smith, *A Narrative of the Loss...*, p.30.
8. Ibid., pp.4-5. (A hoy – a small merchant ship, hired to carry troops and seamen to their ship. See *The line of Battle – Support Craft*, p.110.)
9. ADM/1/317, ship's log, 17 Nov.
10. ADM/1/317 Christian to Admiralty, 18 Nov.
11. ADM/1/317 ship's log 17 Nov.
12. ADM/1/317 ship's log 17 Nov. and ADM/1/317 Christian to Admiralty, 18 Nov.
13. ADM/51/1110 *A Journal of the Proceedings of HM Ship* Alcmene (*Capt. Wm Brown) 25 Jan. 1795 – 31 Jan. 1796, 17 Nov.*
14. ADM/1/317 Christian to Admiralty, 18 Nov.; Ship's log 17 Nov.
15. ADM/1/317 ship's log 18 Nov.
16. ADM/1/317 ship's log 17 Nov.
17. ADM/1/317 Christian to Admiralty, 18 Nov.
18. ADM/51/4407 *Journal of the Proceedings on Board HM Sloop* Albacore, *Capt. Geo. Parker,* 17 Nov.
19. ADM/1/317 Christian to Admiralty, 18 Nov.; Ship's log, 18 Nov.; Christian to Brown, *Prince George*, 17 Nov.
20. ADM/1/317 Christian to Admiralty, 18 Nov.; Ship's log, 18 Nov.

21. C. Smith, *A Narrative of the Loss...*, pp.17–18.
22. ADM/1/1717 Drury to Admiralty, HMS *Alfred* 18 Nov. 1795; ADM/1/317 Christian to Nepean, on board *Irresistible*, 25 Nov. 1795.
23. ADM/51/1110 ship's log, *Alcmene*, 18 Nov.
24. ADM/1/317 Christian to Admiralty, 18 Nov.
25. C. Smith, *A Narrative of the Loss...*, p.8.
26. Diary of John Andrews, Modbury, Devon. National Meteorological Archive, the Met Office.
27. ADM/1/317 Christian to Huskisson, *Prince George* off Dunnose, 16 Nov.; WO/1/798 Schank to Huskisson, 17 Nov. 1795.
28. ADM/1/317 Christian to Admiralty, 18 Nov.
29. ADM/1/317 ship's log, 18 Nov.; C. Smith, *A Narrative of the Loss...*, p.6.
30. ADM/1/317 Christian letter 18 Nov., ship's log, 18 Nov.
31. *The Times*, Saturday 21 Nov. 1795 (*Portsmouth 19 Nov.*).
32. ADM/1/317 ship's log, Wednesday 18 Nov., 7–9 hrs.
33. ADM/1/317 ship's log Wednesday 18 Nov.
34. ADM/51/4407 log of *Albacore*, 18 Nov.
35. ADM/51/1118 log of *La Prompte*, 18 Nov.
36. ADM/51/1110, log of *Alcmene*, 18 Nov.
37. ADM/1/317, ship's log, Wednesday 18 Nov.
38. C. Smith, *A Narrative of the Loss...*, p.6; DDB/61/43 Shrapnell Narrative, with letter to Mrs Wilson, Weymouth, 21 Dec. 1795.
39. ADM/51/1178 log of HMS *Alfred* 18 Nov.
40. ADM/1/1717 Drury to Admiralty, HMS *Alfred*, 18 Nov.
41. Wreck Act, 2 Geo. II, cap 19. (*The Victoria History of the Counties of England*, Vol.II Dorset, Constable 1908, p.223).
42. DDB/61/43 Shrapnell Narrative with letter to Mrs Wilson, Weymouth, 21 Dec., (p.42); C. Smith, *A Narrative of the Loss...*, p.10.
43. C. Smith, *A Narrative of the Loss...*, p.9; DDB/61/43 Shrapnell Narrative with letter to Mrs Wilson, Weymouth, 21 Dec., pp.41–42.
44. C. Smith, *A Narrative of the Loss...*, pp.9–10.
45. C. Smith, *A Narrative of the Loss...*, pp.9–11; DDB/61/43 Shrapnell Narrative with letter to Mrs Wilson, 21 Dec., pp.41–42; *The Sherborne and Yeovil Mercury*, Mon. 28 Dec. 1795 (*Sherborne, Dec. 21*). *Copy of a letter from the Mate and others saved out of the ship* Aeolus*, which was unfortunately cast away in the late Gale of Wind.* NB: The authenticity of this letter is doubtful.
46. DDB/61/43 Shrapnell Narrative with letter to Mrs Wilson, Weymouth 21 Dec. 1795, pp.41–42.
47. ADM/1/1717 List of Vessels ... Stranded (sgnd) T. Drury.
48. C. Smith, *A Narrative of the Loss...*, p.18.
49. *Hampshire Chronicle*, Saturday 28 Nov. 1795.
50. C. Smith, *A Narrative of the Loss...*, pp.18–26.
51. Shrapnell to Dr Edward Jenner, Weymouth, 26 Nov. 1795, from J. Baron, *The Life of Dr Edward Jenner*, (Henry Colburn, 1827) Vol.I, p.114.
52. DDB/61/43 Shrapnell Narrative with letter to Mrs Wilson, 21 Dec., p.49.
53. C. Smith, *A Narrative of the Loss...*, p.28.
54. C. Smith, *A Narrative of the Loss...*, pp.12, 14–15; *Hampshire Chronicle*, Saturday 28 Nov. 1795.
55. C. Smith, *A Narrative of the Loss...*, pp.15–17; DDB/61/43 Shrapnell Narrative with letter to Mrs Wilson, 21 Dec. 1795, pp.47–48.
56. Cust. 59/29.
57. C. Smith, *A Narrative of the Loss...*, p.32.
58. Cust 59/20; DDB/61/43 Shrapnell Narrative with letter to Mrs Wilson, 21 Dec. 1795, pp.48–49.
59. C. Smith, *A Narrative of the Loss...*, pp.31–32.
60. DDB/61/43 Shrapnell Narrative with letter to Mrs Wilson, 21 Dec. 1795, pp.48–49; Steel's Navy List, Mar. 1797, *Revenue Cutters with their Commanders and Stations*.
61. C. Smith, *A Narrative of the Loss...*, p.14; *Hampshire Chronicle*, Sat 28 Nov. 1795.
62. DDB/63/41 Shrapnell Narrative with letter to Mrs Wilson, Weymouth, 21 Dec. 1795, pp.42–43, 49.
63. ADM/1/1717 Drury to Admiralty, HMS *Alfred*, 18 Nov. 1795; ADM/51/1110 log of *Alcmene*, 18 Nov.
64. ADM/1/1717 Drury to Admiralty, HMS *Alfred*, 18 Nov. 1795; ADM/51/1110 log of *Alcmene*, 18 Nov.

65. ADM/1/317 Christian to Admiralty, 18 Nov.; Ship's log, Wednesday 18 Nov., noon.

66. *The Times*, Friday 20 Nov. 1795 (*Portsmouth 18 Nov.*).

67. Dillon, *A Narrative of my Professional Adventures, 1790-1839*, p.210; See *The Line of Battle: Ships Fittings*, pp.137, 177.

68. ADM/1/317 Christian to Admiralty, dated 18 Nov.; Ship's log, 18 Nov.; ADM/51/1119 Captain's log, *Prince George*, 18 Nov.; W.H. Dillon, *A Narrative of my Professional Adventures, 1790-1839*, p.210.

69. ADM/1/317 ship's log, 18 Nov.; ADM/1/317 Christian to Admiralty, 18 Nov.

70. ADM/1/317 ship's log, 19 Nov.; see also Dillon, *A Narrative of my Professional Adventures, 1790-1839*, p.210.

71. ADM/1/317 Christian to Admiralty, 18 Nov.; Ship's log, 19 Nov.

72. ADM/1/317 Christian to Admiralty, 18 Nov.

73. ADM/1/317 ship's log, 19 Nov.

74. ADM/51/1118 *Journal of the Proceedings of HM Ship La Prompte* (*Capt. Edward Leveson Gower*) 19 Nov.; W. Richardson, *A Mariner of England*, p.124.

75. For good measure, and to complete this awful day, an earthquake was felt in central and western England:

    ... about five minutes past eleven, a shock of an earthquake was very sensibly felt by the inhabitants of Leicester, Worcester, Birmingham, Witney, Gloucester... and Bristol... At Dursley... people leaped from their beds in surprise and apprehension – the evening serene, the mercury in the barometer had sunk rapidly down... At Nottingham... several stacks of chimneys were thrown down... The shock was felt at Manchester, Stafford, Litchfield, Derby, Sheffield, Doncaster, Stamford and Newcastle. Its direction appears to have been from north-west to south-east and the shock was felt in a line of wide extent from Yorkshire to Bristol.

    (*Sherborne and Yeovil Mercury*, Monday 30 Nov. 1795) The earthquake was also noted in the diary of John Andrews of Modbury (see p.56).

Chapter 7

1. ADM/1/3730 William Watt, master of the *Simon Taylor* transport to the Transport Board, Torbay, 19 Nov. 1795; The *Gentleman's Magazine*, Vol.LXV Part II, p.963 (from the *London Gazette*).

2. *The Times*, Friday 20 Nov. 1795 (*Dover, Nov. 18*) and Sat. May 21 1795 (*Portsmouth Nov. 19*).

3. *Lloyd's List* (The Marine List) No.2697, Friday 20 Nov. 1795; *Sherborne and Yeovil Mercury*, 30 Nov. (from the *London Gazette*, 28 Nov. 1795); *Lloyd's List* (The Marine List) No.2770, Tuesday 24 Nov. 1795.

4. *The Times*, Friday 20 Nov. 1795 (*Portsmouth, 18 Nov.*).

5. *Sherborne and Yeovil Mercury*, Monday 23 Nov. 1795.

6. ADM/51/1178 Captain's log, *Alfred* 19 Nov.; ADM/1/317 Drury to Admiralty, on board *Alfred*, 18 Nov. 1795.

7. Lt-Col. Paget to the Earl of Uxbridge, 21 Nov. 1795. (Soldiers of Gloucestershire Museum archive).

8. ADM/1/317 ship's log, Thursday 19 Nov.

9. ADM/1/317 Christian to Admiralty, *Prince George*, Spithead, 21 Nov. 1795.

10. ADM/1/317 Christian to Admiralty, 18 Nov.

11. ADM/1/317 ship's log, 19 Nov.

12. ADM/1/317 *Ships in Sight on the morning of 18* [sic] *November.* (Sgnd) Henry Elcock, Signal Lieutenant.

13. ADM/1/317 Christian to Admiralty, 18 Nov.

14. WO/1/798 Schank to Huskisson, Portsmouth, 18 Nov. 1795.

15. ADM/1/317 Christian to Admiralty 18 Nov., ship's log, 19 Nov.

16. DDB/61/43 Shrapnell Narrative with letter to Mrs Wilson, Weymouth, 21 Dec. 1795, p.43.

17. C. Smith, *A Narrative of the Loss...*, p.33.

18. Shrapnell Narrative, p.44; C. Smith, *A Narrative of the Loss...*, p.33.

19. C. Smith, *A Narrative of the Loss...*, p.33.

20. Shrapnell Narrative, p.44.

21. C. Smith, *A Narrative of the Loss...*, p.27.

22. Shrapnell Narrative, p.45.

23. DDB/61/43 Shrapnell Narrative, p.44; C. Smith, *A Narrative of the Loss...*, p.33.

24. C. Smith, *A Narrative of the Loss...*, p.34; *Gentleman's Magazine*, Vol.LXV Part II, p.963.
25. DDB/61/43 Shrapnell to Mrs Wilson, Weymouth, 21 Dec. 1795, p.38.
26. C. Smith, *A Narrative of the Loss...*, p.35.
27. Shrapnell Narrative, p.45.
28. Ibid., p.46.
29. Ibid., p.46; Shrapnell to Dr Edward Jenner, Weymouth, 22 Nov. 1795, J. Baron, *The Life of Dr Edward Jenner*, p.111.
30. ADM/1/317 ship's log, Friday 20 Nov.
31. ADM/1/317 Christian to Admiralty, 18 Nov.
32. ADM/51/1118 *Journal of the Proceedings of HM Ship* Colossus (*Henry Jenkins, Esq., Capt.*) *between 30 Sep. 1795 and 12 Feb. 1796.*
33. ADM/1/317 Christian to Admiralty, 18 Nov.
34. ADM/1/317 ship's log Friday 20 Nov. (3.00-7.00 p.m. Thurs.).
35. ADM/1/317 Christian to Admiralty, 18 Nov.
36. ADM/1/317 ship's log, Friday 20 Nov.
37. ADM/1/317 Christian to Admiralty, *Prince George* at anchor, Dunnose six miles, 20 Nov. 1795; ship's log, Saturday 21 Nov.
38. ADM/1/317 Christian to Admiralty, *Prince George*, Spithead, 21 Nov.; Ship's log, Saturday 21 Nov. and Sunday 22 Nov.
39. Shrapnell Narrative, p.46.
40. C. Smith, *A Narrative of the Loss...*, p.35.
41. Shrapnell Narrative, pp.37-45.
42. DDB/61/43 Shrapnell to Mrs Wilson, Weymouth, 21 Dec. 1795, pp.37, 39.
43. Shrapnell to Dr Edward Jenner, Weymouth, 22 Nov. 1795, J. Baron, *The Life of Dr Edward Jenner*, p.111; Shrapnell Narrative, 46; C. Smith, *A Narrative of the Loss...*, pp.36, 37.
44. Shrapnell to Dr Jenner, Weymouth, 26 Nov. 1795, J. Baron, *The Life of Dr Edward Jenner*, p.112.
45. Wellcome Library for the History and Understanding of Medicine, MS 5232/1, Revd Henry Jenner to Edward Jenner, Burbage, Wilts, 7 Dec. 1795.
46. Shrapnell to Dr Jenner, Weymouth, 22 Nov. 1795, J. Baron, *The Life of Dr Edward Jenner*, p.111; Shrapnell Narrative, p.46.
47. C. Smith, *A Narrative of the Loss...*, p.37; Shrapnell Narrative, p.46.
48. DDB/61/43 Shrapnell to Mrs Wilson, Weymouth, 21 Dec. 1795, pp.37-38.
49. Shrapnell to Dr Jenner, Weymouth, 26 Nov. 1795, J. Baron, *The Life of Dr Edward Jenner*, p.112.
50. C. Smith, *A Narrative of the Loss...*, p.37.
51. Ibid., p.38.
52. DDB/61/42 Payne to (?) Mrs Wilson, Weymouth, 9 Dec. 1795.
53. *Sherborne and Yeovil Mercury*, 30 Nov. 1795.
54. DDB/61/41 Shrapnell to Mrs Wilson, Weymouth, 8 Dec. 1795, p.35; C. Smith, *A Narrative of the Loss...*, p.36.
55. Shrapnell Narrative, pp.51-52.
56. DDB/61/47 Shrapnell to Mrs Wilson, Weymouth, 10 Feb. 1796, p.66.
57. DDB/61/47 Shrapnell to Mrs Wilson, Weymouth, 10 Feb. 1796 (p.66); Shrapnell Narrative, p.48.
58. DDB/61/43 Shrapnell to Mrs Wilson, Weymouth, 21 Dec. 1795, p.38; DDB/61/48 Shrapnell to (?) Mrs Wilson, Weymouth, 25 Mar. 1796, p.73.
59. DDB/61/47 Shrapnell to Mrs Wilson, Weymouth, 10 Feb. 1796, pp.65-66.
60. ADM/51/1110, Log of HMS *Alcmene*, 19 Nov.; ADM/1/1717 A List of Vessels ... (Drury); W. Richardson, *A Mariner of England*, p.124.
61. ADM/1/317 Christian to Admiralty, *Prince George*, Spithead, 21 Nov. 1795.
62. *Steel's Navy List* Mar. 1797; *Hampshire Chronicle*, Saturday 28 Nov. 1795; Richardson, *A Mariner of England*, p.125; Dillon, *A Narrative of my Professional Adventures* pp.110, 209.
63. Dundas to the king, Portsmouth, 23 Nov. 1795, in A. Aspinall (ed.), *The Later Correspondence of George III*, p.429; Duffy, *Soldiers, Sugar and Seapower*, pp.204-205.
64. ADM/1/4166/003 Dundas to Abercromby, *Most Secret*, 23 Nov. 1795; ADM/2/1349 Admiralty Secret Instructions and Letters, Nepean to George Bowen, HM ship *Canada* at Cork, 23 Nov. 1795; CO/318/18 *The proprietors and merchants concerned in our West India Colonies* to Dundas, London, 21 Nov., and his reply, dated Portsmouth, 27 Nov. 1795.
65. ADM/1/317 Christian to Nepean, on board *Irresistible*, St Helens, 23 Nov. 1795.

66. ADM/1/317 Christian to Admiralty, on board *Irresistible*, St Helens, 24, 25 and 26 Nov. 1795.
67. ADM/1/4166/N17, Dundas to Admiralty, 17 Nov.
68. ADM/2/1349, Admiralty Secret Instructions and Letters, Nepean to Christian, 27 Nov. 1795.
69. *Naval Chronicle*, 181-182; *Naval Biography*, 267; ADM/1/317 Christian to Nepean, on board *Glory*, Spithead, 30 Nov. 1795.
70. ADM/1/317 Christian to Nepean, on board *Glory*, St Helens, 4 Dec. 1795.
71. ADM/1/317 Christian to Nepean, on board *Glory*, off Sandown Bay [Isle of Wight], 9 Dec. 1795.
72. WO/1/798 f.913, *Scheme of Embarkation of 7,000 Infantry at Cork*, Nov. 1795; WO/25/1146 Embarkation Returns, Cork; *Sherborne and Yeovil Mercury*, 12 Dec. 1795; Duffy, *Soldiers, Sugar and Seapower*, p.181.
73. W. Richardson, *A Mariner of England*, p.125.
74. ADM/1/317 *A Return of Ships of War, Transports observed in company*, 26 Dec. 1795; CO/318/18 f.234; Duffy, *Soldiers, Sugar and Seapower*, p.206.

Chapter 8

1. DDB/61/44 Ann Burns to John Crouch, Boston, 2 Jan. 1796, copied by Shrapnell in his letter to Mrs Wilson, Weymouth, 10 Jan. 1795 (*sic*-1796), p.57.
2. DDB/61/45 and 46, Shrapnell to Mrs Wilson, Weymouth, 24 Jan. 1796 and Shrapnell to Miss Wilson, Weymouth 7 Feb. 1796, pp.59, 62.
3. DDB/61/43 Shrapnell to Mrs Wilson, Weymouth, 21 Dec. 1795, p.39.
4. DDB/61/44 Shrapnell to Mrs Wilson, Weymouth, 10 Jan. 1796, pp.54-55.
5. *Oxford Illustrated History of the British Army*, p.95; WO/1/62 War Office to Whyte, 22 Sep., N.A.S. GD 225/33/21 Stewart to Hay, 16 Oct. 1795; Duffy, *Soldiers, Sugar and Seapower*, p.188; WO/1/84 *Return of the Army under the Command of Maj.-Gen. Sir Ralph Abercromby, K.B.*, 7 Nov. 1795; WO/25/1146 *Embarkation Return For West Indies under R.A. Abercromby*.
6. DDB/61/43 Shrapnell Narrative, p.52.
7. C. Smith, *A Narrative of the Loss...*, pp.22, 24, 30.
8. DDB/61/44 Ann Burns to John Crouch, Boston, 2 Jan. 1796, copied by Shrapnell in his letter to Mrs Wilson, Weymouth, 10 Jan. 1796, p.57.
9. DDB/61/44 Shrapnell to Mrs Wilson, Weymouth, 10 Jan. 1796, pp.55, 58.
10. DDB/61/44 Shrapnell to Mrs Wilson, Weymouth 10 Jan. 1796, p.53.
11. DDB/61/48 Shrapnell to (?) Mrs Wilson, Weymouth, 25 Mar. 1796, p.72.
12. DDB/61/44 Shrapnell to Mrs Wilson, Weymouth, 10 Jan. 1796, p.53.
13. Spies working for Britain were paid out of a 'Secret Service account' (J. Brooke, *King George III*, pp.209-210).
14. See: Broadley, *Royal Weymouth 1789-1805*, Vol.III, p.100; *Sherborne and Yeovil Mercury*, 28 Nov. 1795.
15. DDB/61/48 Shrapnell to (?) Mrs Wilson, Weymouth, 25 Mar. 1796, p.72.
16. DDB/61/47 Shrapnell to Mrs Wilson, Weymouth, 10 Feb. 1796, p.64.
17. DDB/61/46 Shrapnell to Miss Wilson, Weymouth, 7 Feb. 1796, p.62.
18. DDB/61/45 Shrapnell to Mrs Wilson, Weymouth, 24 Jan. 1796, p.59.
19. DDB/61/46 Shrapnell to Miss Wilson, Weymouth, 7 Feb. 1796, p.62.
20. DDB/61/47 Shrapnell to Mrs Wilson, Weymouth, 10 Feb. 1796, p.64.
21. ADM/1/317 Christian to Nepean, *Glory* at Sea, Lat. 48 deg. 35 min. No., Long. 9 deg. 50 W., 14 Dec. 1795.
22. W. Richardson, *A Mariner of England*, pp.125-126.
23. ADM/1/317, Christian to Nepean, *Glory* at Sea, 16 Dec. 1795.
24. ADM/1/317 Christian to Nepean, *Glory* at Sea, 24 and 26 Dec. 1795.
25. ADM/50/78 Log of HMS *Glory*, 18 Jan. 1796, CO/318/18, *List of the Ships of Rear Admiral Christian's Convoy, arrived 31 Jan. 1796*.
26. E. Brenton, *The Naval History of Great Britain* (C. Rice, 1823), Vol.II, p.42.
27. *The Times*, 29 Jan. and 12 Feb. 1796.
28. *Naval Chronicle*, Vol.19, 1808, p.41.
29. *The Times*, 29 Jan. and 12 Feb. 1796.
30. A.T. Mahan, *A History of the British Navy*, (Sampson, Low, Marston & Co., 1904) p.453.
31. *Naval Chronicle*, Vol.19 (1808), p.41.

32.   A.T. Mahan, *A History of the British Navy*, p.453.

33.   Ibid., p.452.

34.   Ibid., p.453; *Naval Chronicle*, Vol.19 (1808), p.41.

35.   *Naval Chronicle*, Vol.19, pp.41-42.

36.   *Naval Chronicle*, Vol.8 (1802), p.172; T. Grocott, *Shipwrecks of the Revolutionary and Napoleonic Eras* (Chatham Publishing, 1997), pp.30-31; *The Times*, 29 Jan and 12 Feb 1796.

37.   A. Duncan, *Mariner's Chronicle* (James Cundee, 1811), Vol.4, p.383.

38.   W. Richardson, *A Mariner of England*, p.127.

39.   *The Times*, Monday 1 Feb. 1796 (*Ships News, Portsmouth, Jan. 29*). For a list of the ships which made it back to St. Helens with Christian, see this report.

40.   *The Times*, Monday 1 Feb.; ADM/50/78 Log of HMS *Glory*, Friday 29 Jan. 1796; W. Richardson, *A Mariner of England*, p.127.

41.   W.H. Dillon, *A Narrative of my Professional Adventures, 1790-1839*, p.217.

42.   W. Dyott, *Dyott's Diary*, R.W. Jeffrey, (ed.), (Constable, 1907), Vol.I, p.83; *Naval Chronicle*, p.182; *Naval Biography* p.267.

43.   Duffy, *Soldiers, Sugar and Seapower*, p.153; J. Peddie, *The Hatcher Review*, Vol.4 No.34, Autumn 1992, pp.24-25; *The Senator, or Clarendon's Parliamentary Chronicle*, Vol.XV, London 1796, pp.1487-1501, 1546-1569; the *Annual Register* 1796, pp.67-68; *House of Commons Journal*, Vol.LI (Oct. 1795 – May 1796), pp.633-634; *Cobbett's Parliamentary History*, Vol.32 (1795-1797), pp.1118-1124.

44.   DDB/61/46 Shrapnell to Miss Wilson, Weymouth, 7 Feb. 1796, p.62.

45.   *The Times*, Saturday 30 Jan. 1796 (*Marazion, Cornwall, 26 Jan.*); T. Grocott, *Shipwrecks of the Revolutionary and Napoleonic Eras*, pp.29-30, 411; *Lloyds List* (The Marine List) No.2789, Friday 29 Jan. 1796.

Chapter 9

1.   DDB/61/46 Shrapnell to Miss Wilson, Weymouth, 7 Feb. 1796, p.61.

2.   DDB/61/48 Shrapnell to Mrs Wilson, Weymouth, 23 Mar. 1796, p.72.

3.   DDB/61/52 Shrapnell to Mrs Wilson, Weymouth, 30 Mar. 1796, p.82.

4.   DDB/61/48 Shrapnell to Mrs Wilson, Weymouth, 23 Mar. 1796, p.72.

5.   DDB/61/45 Shrapnell to Mrs Wilson, Weymouth, 24 Jan. 1796, pp.59-60.

6.   DDB/61/52 Shrapnell to Mrs Wilson, Weymouth, 30 Mar. 1796, p.80.

7.   DDB/61/47 Shrapnell to Mrs Wilson, Weymouth, 10 Feb. 1796, pp.64, 65.

8.   DDB/61/45 Shrapnell to Mrs Wilson, Weymouth, 24 Jan. 1796, p.60.

9.   DDB/61/47 Shrapnell to Mrs Wilson, Weymouth, 10 Feb. 1796, p.65.

10.   DDB/61/48 Shrapnell to Mrs Wilson, Weymouth, 23 Mar. 1796, pp.70-72.

11.   DDB/61/51 Shrapnell to (presumed) Mrs Wilson, Weymouth, 28 Mar. 1796, pp.76-78; C. Smith, *A Narrative of the Loss...*, p.26.

12.   DDB/61/48 Shrapnell to Mrs Wilson, Weymouth, 23 Mar. 1796, p.73.

13.   DDB/61/52 Shrapnell to Mrs Wilson, Weymouth, 30 Mar. 1796, pp.80-81.

14.   DDB/Box 187/Bdle 25, Shrapnell to Mrs Wilson, Weymouth, 1 Jun. 1796.

15.   DDB/61/47 Shrapnell to Mrs Wilson, Weymouth, 10 Feb. 1796, p.66.

16.   DDB/61/40 Lt-Col. J. Leveson Gower, on board *Brunswick*, Spithead, 27 Nov. 1795.

17.   DDB/61/53 Shrapnell to Miss Elizabeth Barcroft, Weymouth, 12 Apr. 1796, p.83.

18.   Wellcome library for the History and Understanding of Medecine MS 5232/5 Shrapnell to Jenner, Weymouth, 9 May 1796 refers.

19.   DDB/61/49 Shrapnell to Miss Elizabeth Barcroft, Weymouth, 23 Mar. 1796, p.68.

20.   DDB/61/52 Shrapnell to Mrs Wilson, Weymouth, 30 Mar. 1796, p.82.

21.   DDB/61/45 Shrapnell to Mrs Wilson, Weymouth, 24 Jan. 1796.

22.   W.H. Dillon, *A Narrative of my Professional Adventures, 1790-1839*, p.217.

23.   Earl Spencer to the king, Admiralty, 30 Jan. 1796, in A. Aspinall (ed.), *The Later Correspondence of George III*, pp.456-457.

24.   Earl Spencer to the king, Admiralty, 30 Jan. 1796 in A. Aspinall (ed.), *The Later Correspondence of George III*, p.457.

25.   W.H. Dillon, *A Narrative of my Professional Adventures*, Vol.I, p.15 and mentioned again in Vol.II.

26.   DDB/61/43 Shrapnell Narrative, p.40.

27.   C. Smith, *A Narrative of the Loss...*, p.6.

28.   ADM/1/317 Christian to Admiralty, *Prince George* at sea, 18 Nov. 1795.

29. Ibid; and ship's log, 17 Nov. 1795.

30. Duffy, *Soldiers, Sugar and Seapower*, p.215; Lt-Cdr J. Stewart, *The Leeward Isles Command 1795-1796*, *Mariner's Mirror*, Vol.47, (1961); *Clarendon's Parliamentary Chronicle*, Vol.XV, (1796), p.1,490.

31. William Pitt to the king, Downing Street, 14 (15) Feb. 1796, in A. Aspinall (ed.), *The Later Correspondence of George III*, p.459; *Naval Biography*, p.267; *Naval Chronicle*, Vol.XX (1809), p182.

32. The king's reply, Windsor 15 Feb, 5.57 p.m, in A. Aspinall (ed.), *The Later Correspondence of George III*. p.459.

33. Duffy, *Soldiers, Sugar and Seapower*, p.215; *Naval Chronical* Vol .XXI (1809), p.182; *Naval Biography*, p.267.

34. Duffy, *Soldiers, Sugar and Seapower*, p.223; *Naval Chronicle* Vol.XXI (1809), p.182; Capt. I. Schomberg, *Naval Chronology (1780-1796)* (Egerton, 1802), p.440; James' *Naval History*, p.368.

35. Campbell, *Lives of the British Admirals*, Vol.VII, p.68. (Note: p.69 of Campbell's *Lives of the British Admirals* Vol.VII includes an interesting account of the order of Laforey's funeral.)

36. Duffy, *Soldiers, Sugar and Seapower*, p.217.

37. *Naval Biography*, pp.268-269; J.F. Maurice, *The Diary of Sir John Moore*, Vol.I, pp.219-220; *Dictionary of National Biography*, Vol.XIII, p.814.

38. Duffy, *Soldiers, Sugar and Seapower*, pp.221, 236-240; *Naval Chronicle*, Vol. XXI (1809), pp.182-188.

39. Duffy, *Soldiers, Sugar and Seapower*, pp.298-311.

40. Buckley, *Slaves in Red Coats*, pp.58, 92-94.

41. Duffy, *Soldiers, Sugar and Seapower*, pp.194-195, 311-313, 331-333, 334, 375.

42. *Dictionary of National Biography*, Vol.I, 43-46; *Naval Chronicle*, Vol.21 (1809), p.188; *Naval Chronology* 1780-1796, p.443; Duffy p.240.

43. *Naval Chronology*, p.429.

44. Duffy, *Soldiers, Sugar and Seapower*, pp.267-291; J.F. Maurice, *The Diary of Sir John Moore*, Vol.I, pp.247-253.

45. *Dictionary of National Biography*, Vol.I, pp.43-46.

46. Gloucester Records Office, Jeayes' Catalogue.

47. Wellcome Library for the History and Understanding of Medicine. MSS Catalogue 5230-5235; Richard B. Fisher, *Edward Jenner* (Andre Deutsch, 1991), pp.263, 290.

48. Berkely Church parish records, 1817.

49. DDB/61/52 Shrapnell to Mrs Wilson, Weymouth, 30 Mar. 1796; DDB/61/53 Shrapnell to Miss Elizabeth Barcroft, Weymouth, 12 Apr. 1796, pp.79, 80, 83.

50. Lancashire Record Office, The Parker Muniments.

51. *The European Magazine and London Review*, Nov. 1806.

52. *Naval Biography*, p.279; J. Brereton and A. Savory, *The History of the Duke of Wellington's Regiment 1702-1992* (1993), p.97.

53. *Naval Biography*, p.279; *Naval Chronicle*, Vol.I (1799) p.263 (*obit.*).

54. *Naval Chronicle* Vol.I (1799) p.176 (*obit.*); *Naval Chronicle*, Vol.XXI (1809), p.188.

55. Sir Ralph Abercromby, Headquarters, St Lucia, 31 May 1796, *Naval Chronicle*, Vol.21 (1809), p.187.

56. *Naval Biography*, p.270

57. J.F. Maurice, *The Diary of Sir John Moore*, pp.195, 236, Letter to Sir Ralph Abercromby, 2 Sep. 1796, pp.237-240; WO/1/662 Medical Staff to Sir John Vaughan, 23 Mar. 1795 refers; Buckley, *Slaves in Red Coats*, pp.34, 89-90, 100-105, 118.

58. Buckley, *Slaves in Red Coats*, pp.84, 89-90; Moore to Abercromby, 2 Sep. 1796, in J.F. Maurice, *The Diary of Sir John Moore*, p.240.

59. *The Light Infantry, A Brief History* (The Light Infantry, 1994), p.2.

60. Buckley, *Slaves in Red Coats*, pp.84-85, 92-93.

61. J.F. Maurice, *The Diary of Sir John Moore*, Vol.II, pp.294-295, 371, 396; *Dictionary of National Biography*, Vol.XIII, p.818.

62. Brereton and Savory, *The Duke of Wellington's Regiment*, p.90.

63. J. Wilson, *Wellington's Marriage* (Weidenfeld & Nicolson, 1987), pp.21-22.

64. WO/25/1146, *Embarkation Return (33rd Foot-Absent Officers)*.

65. J. Brereton and A. Savory, *The History of the Duke of Wellington's Regiment*, pp.96, 101, 102, 103; *Dictionary of National Biography*, Vol.XX, pp.1082-3.

Bibliography

Manuscript Sources

Public Record Office (PRO)

Admiralty Papers

ADM/1/317 In-letters, Commanders-in-Chief, Leewards Station
ADM/1/1717 Records of Admiralty, naval Forces, RM and Coastguard, 1795
ADM/1/3730 Transport Board, 1794-1795
ADM/1/4166 Directions, Admiralty and Min. Defence Secretaries of State, 1689-1839
ADM/2/129 Lords' letters, Orders and Instructions, 1795
ADM/2/277 Lords' personal letters, 1795, 1796
ADM/2/612 Secretary's letters to Public Officers and Flag Officers, 1795
ADM/2/941 Secretary's letters to Flag Officers, Home Squadrons, 1795
ADM/2/1018 Secretary's letters to Flag Officers, Portsmouth, 1795
ADM/2/1349 Admiralty Secret Instructions and Letters, 1795
ADM/3/133 Admiralty Board, rough minutes, 1795
ADM/7/67 Correspondence, disposition of convoys, 1795
ADM/49/127 Transports, 1774-1794
ADM/50/78 Admirals' Journals, 1779-1801
ADM/51/1110 Journal of Proceedings of HMS *Alcmene*
ADM/51/1115 Journal of Proceedings of HMS *Prince George*
ADM/51/1118 Journal of Proceedings of HMS *La Prompte*; Journal of Proceedings of HMS *Colossus*
ADM/51/1119 Captain's log, HMS *Prince George*
ADM/51/1178 Journal of Proceedings of HMS *Alfred*
ADM/51/4407 Journal of Proceedings of HM Sloop *Albacore*
ADM/108/148 Transport Board, Ships' Ledgers, 1793-1799
ADM/198/158 Transport Board, Freight ledgers, 1795-1799

War Office Papers

WO/1/31 Correspondence, in-letters, Secretary at War, 1795
WO/1/61 Correspondence, in-letters, Secretary at War, 1795
WO/1/62 Correspondence, in-letters, Secretary at War, 1795
WO/1/82 War Office despatches, West Indian islands, 1793-1797
WO/1/83 War Office in-letters, Commanders-in-Chief, Windward and Leeward Islands, 1794-1795
WO/1/84 War Office in-letters, Commanders-in-Chief, Windward and Leeward Islands, June-Nov. 1795
WO/1/85 War Office in-letters, Commanders-in-Chief, Windward and Leeward Islands, Nov. 1795-Nov. 1796
WO/1/161 War Office in-letters, Commanders-in-Chief, Windward and Leeward Islands, West Indies, South America, 1806
WO/1/171 War Department, in-letters, Europe
WO/1/662 In-letters, Secretary at War, 1794-1795
WO/1/688 In-letters, Secretary at War, Admiralty, July-Dec. 1795

WO/1/780 In-letters, Ordnance Office, 1795
WO/1/798 In-letters, Transport Office, 1794–1795
WO/3/13 War Office, general out-letters, Jan.-June 1795
WO/3/14 War Office, general out-letters, June 1795-Dec. 1795
WO/4/291 Out-letters, Secretary at War, Continent, Feb. 1793-July 1794
WO/4/337 Out-letters, Secretary at War, West Indies, 1793-1795
WO/4/338 Out-letters, Secretary at War, West Indies, 1795-1797
WO/4/401 Secretary at War letters to Medical Dept., July-Dec. 1805
WO/6/142 Secretary of State out-letters to Ordnance Board, 1794–1808
WO/6/147 Secretary of State out-letters to Admiralty, 1794-1797
WO/6/156 Secretary of State out-letters to Commissioners of Transport, 1794-1809
WO/6/168 Secretary of State out-letters to Treasury, 1794-1797
WO/12/1512 Muster returns for 26th Light Dragoons
WO/12/5319 Muster roll, 40th Regiment
WO/12/7243 Muster lists, 63rd Regiment
WO/12/11239 Muster lists, 1st West India (WI) Regiment, 1795
WO/12/11449 Muster lists, 3rd (or Prince of Wales') WI Regiment, 1795
WO/12/11542 Pay lists and muster book for 6th WI Regiment
WO/17/183 Monthly returns, 63rd Foot Regiment, 1763-1812
WO/25/1145 Embarkation returns, 1748-1797
WO/25/1146 Embarkation returns, 1783-1798
WO/25/3502 Embarkation and disembarkation returns, Foot battalions, officers, NCOs, R.A. 1789-1869.
WO/25/644 Regimental description and succession books (2nd WI Regiment)
WO/58/167 Commissariat Dept. out-letters, Treasuary, 1793-1797

Home Office Papers
HO/51/147 War Office Correpondence, 1792-1795
HO/51/150 War Office Correpondence, 1795-1815

Colonial Office Papers
CO/318/18 Correspondence, Secretary of State, West Indies, 1795-1796

Customs Office Papers
Cust.59/20 Outport records, Weymouth, 10 March 1794-13 Nov. 1796

National Archives, Scotland (N.A.S.)
GD 225/33/31 The Leith Hall Muniments: Stewart to Hay, Camp, Southampton, 16 October 1795

Preston Record Office
DDB 61/4 –70/8 The Parker Muniments: Letters by Capt. A.W. Barcroft, 63rd Regiment, and Lt William Shrapnell, Surgeon, South Gloucestershire Militia. (*I am extremely grateful to the Depositor, Mrs Parker of Browsholme Hall, Lancashire, for her kind permission to publish extracts and illustrations from the Parker Muniments.*)

Wellcome Library for the History and Understanding of Medicine, London
MS 5229(2) Correspondence of Dr Edward Jenner (to William and Anne Davies)
MS 5230–5235 (Shrapnell)

The Met. Office, National Meteorological Archive
The Diary of John Andrews, Modbury, Devon, November 1795
(*I am grateful to the National Meteorological Archive for permission to reproduce from this diary.*)

Printed Sources

Periodicals

The British Library, London
House of Commons Journal, Vol.51 (1795–1796)
The Senator or Clarendon's Parliamentary Chronicle, Vol.15 (1796)
Annual Register (1795–1796)
Cobbett's Parliamentary History, Vol.32 (1795–1797)
The Times (1795–1796)
The Gentleman's Magazine, Vol.65 (1795)
Chronicles of the Sea, Vol.1, No.48 (20 October 1838)
The Western County Magazine (1789)

The Guildhall Library, London
Lloyd's Register (1795)
Lloyd's List (The Marine List) (1795)

Winchester Library, Hampshire
Hampshire Chronicle (1795–1796)

The Portsmouth Royal Naval Museum Library, Hampshire
London Gazette (1795–1796)

Yeovil Library, Somerset
Sherborne and Yeovil Mercury (1795–1796)

Weymouth Library, Dorset
Southern Times (1866)
Rhodes, William, 'A Night of Horror on the Chesil Beach', *Dorset Evening Echo*, 6 October 1962

Other Periodicals
History Makers magazine (1969–1970)
The Salisbury Journal (1795)
The Gloucester Journal (1794–1795)
The European Magazine (1806)

Pamphlets, Papers and Articles

Barrett, W.B., 'Notes on the Flora of The Chesil Bank and The Fleet', Proceedings of the Dorset Natural History and Archaeological Society, Vol.26 (1905)
The Chesil Bank and Fleet Lagoon – A Few Facts and Figures (The Chesil Beach Centre, [no date])
Stewart, Lt Cdr James, 'The Leeward Isles Command 1795–1796', *Mariner's Mirror*, Vol.47 (1961)
Condon, M.E., 'Freight Rates and the British Transport Service during the War against Revolutionary France', *Maritime History* (May, 1977)
Peddie, J., 'A Melancholy Example of the Uncertainty of Human Affairs', *The Hatcher Review*, Vol.4, No.34 (Autumn 1992)
Grazebrook, Brig. T.N., *An Introduction to the Auxilliary Units of the Gloucester Regiment* (December 1960). From the Soldiers of Gloucestershire Museum Archive, Gloucester

Books

Aspinall, A. (ed.), *The Later Correspondence of George III*, Vol.2 (Cambridge University Press, 1967)

Ayling, Stanley, *Fox: The Life of Charles James Fox* (John Murray, 1991)

Baron, John, *The Life of Dr Edward Jenner*, Vols 1 and 2 (Henry Colburn, 1827 and 1838)

Brereton, E., *The Naval History of Great Britain,* Vol.2 (C. Rice, 1823)

Brenton, J.M., and Savory, A.C.S., *The History of the Duke of Wellington's Regiment* (published by the Regiment, 1993)

Broadley, A.M., *Royal Weymouth 1789–1805, The Court of King George at the Seaside*, 4 Vols (J.G. Commin: Exeter, 1907)

Brooke, John, *King George III* (Constable, 1973)

Buckley, Roger, *Slaves in Red Coats: The British West India Regiments, 1795-1815* (Yale University Press, 1979)

Campbell, Dr John, *Lives of the British Admirals*, Vol.7 (John Stockdale: London, 1813)

Cantlie, Lt-Gen. Sir Neil, *A History of the Army Medical Department* (Churchill Livingstone: London, 1974)

Carr, James, *Annals and Stories of Colne and Neighbourhood* (John Heywood, 1898)

Cornwallis-West, G. (ed.), *The Life and Letters of Admiral Cornwallis* (Robert Holden & Co.: London, 1927)

Costley-White, Hope, *Mary Cole – Countess of Berkeley* (Berkeley Castle, 1997)

Cresswell, J., *British Admirals of the Eighteenth Century* (Allen & Unwin, 1972)

Daniell, David, *Cap of Honour – The Story of the Gloucester Regiment* (White Lion Publishers: London, 1975)

Dalyell, John Graham, *Shipwrecks and Disasters at Sea*, Vol.3 ([publisher unknown], 1812)

Dictionary of National Biography, Vols 1, 4, 13 and 20

Dillon, Sir William Henry, *A Narrative of My Professional Adventures, 1790-1839*, ed. by Lewis, Michael A. (Naval Records Society, 1953)

Duncan, Archibald, *Mariner's Chronicle*, Vol.4 (James Cundee, 1811)

Duffy, Michael*, Soldiers, Sugar and Seapower: The British Expeditions to the West Indies and the War Against Revolutionary France* (Clarendon Press, 1987)

Dupuy, R.E. and Dupuy, T.N., *The Collins Encyclopedia of Military History* (Collins, 1993)

Dyott, William, *Dyott's Diary*, Vols 1 and 2 (Constable, 1907)

Everard, H., *A History of Thomas Farrington's Regiment, 1694-1891* (Littlebury, 1891)

Farr, Graham, *Wreck and Rescue on the Dorset Coast: The Story of the Dorset Lifeboats* (Bradford Barton, 1911)

Firth, C., *From William III to Waterloo* (Ginn & Co., 1937)

Fisher, Richard B., *Edward Jenner 1749–1823* (Andre Deutsch, 1991)

Fisk, Dorothy, *Dr Jenner of Berkeley* (Heinemann, 1959)

Fletcher, Loraine, *Charlotte Smith – A Critical Biography* (Palgrave, 1998)

Fortescue, Sir John, *Six British Soldiers* (Williams & Norgate, 1928)

Gardiner, Robert, *The Line of Battle: The Sailing Warship, 1650-1840* (Conway Maritime Press, 1992)

Glossary of Marine Navigation (American Practical Navigator series), Vol.2, (Defence Mapping Agency, 1981)

Grocott, Terence, *Shipwrecks of the Revolutionary and Napoleonic Eras* (Chatham Publishing, 1997)

Hutchins, J., *The History and Antiquities of the County of Dorset*, Vol.II (John Bowyer Nichols, 1861)

Jarrett, Derek, *Pitt the Younger* (Weidenfeld & Nicholson, 1974)

Jones, Alfred E., *The Loyalists of Massachusetts: Their Memorials, Petitions & Claims* (St Catherine Press, 1930)

Kerridge, John, *Weymouth & Melcombe Regis – Local Rakings*, Vol.1, (Manuscript) 1866.

Larn, R. and Larn, B., *Shipwreck Index of the British Isles* (Lloyd's Register of Shipping, [date unknown])

Lavery, Brian, *Nelson's Navy: The Ships, Men and Organisation 1793-1815* (Conway Maritime Press, 1989)

Light Infantry, The, *A Brief History,* Peninsula Barracks (The Light Infantry, 1994)

Log Book, The – or Nautical Miscellany (Robins, undated)

Mackesy, Piers, *British Victory in Egypt, 1801: The End of Napoleon's Conquest* (Routledge, 1995)

Mahan, Alfred T., *History of the British Navy* (Sampson Low, Marston & Co., 1904)

Maurice, Maj.-Gen. Sir J.F. (ed.), *The Diary of Sir John Moore*, Vols 1 and 2 (Edward Arnold, 1904)

Morris, Roland, *HMS* Colossus (Hutchinson, 1979)

Morris, Stuart, *Portland – An Illustrated History* (Dovecote Press, 1985)

Mullaly, Col. B.R., *The South Lancashire Regiment* (White Swan Press, undated)

Naval Biographical Dictionary (Hayward & Son: Polstead, 1849)

Naval Chronicle, The, Vol.I (1799), Vol.VIII (1802), Vol.XVI (1806), Vol.XIX (1808) and Vol.XXI (1809)

Navy List, The, Steel (May 1794)

Oldland, Fay, *The Story of Foulridge* (Pendle Heritage Centre, 1990)

Pinckard, Dr George, *Notes on the West Indies,* Vol.1 (Longman, 1806)

Pope, Dudley, *Life in Nelson's Navy* (Unwin Hyman Ltd., 1987)

'Q' (ed.), *The Story of the Sea* (Cassell & Co., 1896)

Ralphe, J., *The Naval Biography of Great Britain,* Vol.2 (Whitmore and Fenn, 1828)

Richardson, William, edited by Childers, S., ed., *A Mariner of England: An Account of the Career of William Richardson … [1780 to 1819] … as told by himself* (John Murray, 1908)

Schomberg, Capt. Isaac, *Naval Chronology (1780–1796)* (Egerton, 1802)

Silvester-Davies, Revd John, *A History of Southampton* (Hampshire Books, 1909)

Smith, Charlotte, *A Narrative of the Loss of the Catherine, Venus and Piedmont Transports, and the Thomas, Golden Grove and Aeolus Merchant Ships, near Weymouth, on Wednesday the 18th November last, drawn up from Information taken on the Spot and published for the Benefit of an unfortunate Survivor … and her Infant Child* (Sampson Low, 1796)

Smythies, Capt. R.H., *Historical Records of the 40th Regiment* (A.H. Swiss: Devonport, 1894)

Temple-Patton, A., *A History of Southampton* (Southampton University Press: Southampon, 1966)

The Times Atlas of World History, edited by Barraclough, G. (Times Books, 1986)

The Oxford Illustrated History of the British Army, edited by Chandler, D. (Oxford University Press, 1994)

Thirslund, Capt. Soren, and Vebaek, C., *The Viking Compass* (self-published, 1992)

Trevelyan, Sir G.O., *The Early History of Charles James Fox* (T. Nelson and Sons, undated)

Page, W. (ed.), *The Victoria History of the Counties of England,* Vol.2: Dorset (Archibald Constable, 1908)

Whittaker, Gladys, *The Loss of the Piedmont (The Colne Tragedy)* (Lancashire Family History Society, 1974)

Wilson, Joan, *Soldier's Wife: Wellington's Marriage* (Weidenfeld & Nicolson, 1987)

Willyams, Rev. Cooper, *An Account of the Campaign in the West Indies in the Year 1794* (Bensley, 1796)

Wylly, Col. H.C., *History of the Manchester Regiment,* Vol.1 (Forster Groom & Co., 1923)

Index